Humphry Repton in Hertfordshire

Humphry Repton in Hertfordshire

Documents and landscapes

Edited by Susan Flood and Tom Williamson

Hertfordshire Publications
an imprint of
UNIVERSITY OF HERTFORDSHIRE

First published in Great Britain in 2018 by
Hertfordshire Publications
an imprint of
University of Hertfordshire Press
College Lane
Hatfield
Hertfordshire
AL10 9AB

British Library Cataloguing in Publication Data
A catalogue record for this book is available from the British Library

ISBN 978-1-909291-98-0

Design by Arthouse Publishing Solutions Ltd
Printed in Great Britain by Hobbs the Printers Ltd

Contents

Illustrations

Abbreviations

BL   British Library
HALS Hertfordshire Archives and Local Studies
JSM   John Soane Museum
LMA   London Metropolitan Archives
NRO   Norfolk Record Office
OSD   Ordnance Survey Drawings
TNA   The National Archives
VCH   Victoria County History

Acknowledgements

MANY PEOPLE HAVE HELPED WITH this book, providing information, encouragement, access to sites and archives or financial support. We would like to thank, in particular, Debbie Brady, Ben Cowell, Stephen Daniels, Heather Falvey, Matt Hill, Liz Lake, Andrew MacNair, Johnny Phibbs, Charles and Bridgid Quest-Ritson, Anida Rayfield, Anne Rowe, Sarah Rutherford, Anne Shellim and Sarah Spooner. The staff at Hertfordshire Archives and Local Studies and the John Soane and Watford Museums have been unfailingly helpful throughout the long period of research.

Figures have been reproduced with permission as follows:
  The British Library Board: Nos 35, 36 and 108
  Getty Research Institute, Los Angeles: Nos 12–30
  Gorhambury Estates Company Ltd: Nos 44–51
  Haileybury Society: No. 32
  Hertfordshire Archives and Local Studies: Nos 9, 33, 38, 40, 41, 43, 51, 53–67, 69–80, 83, 84, 96, 117–19, 121–3, 125, 127, 133, 134 and 136
  John Soane Museum: Nos 98–107
  Royds family, West Sussex: Nos 85–95
  Watford Museum: Nos 113–15

Above all, we would like to thank the following organisations and individuals for their generous financial support, without which production of this book would not have been possible:
  The Gretna Trust
  The Hertfordshire Gardens Trust
  Joan Stuart-Smith
  George Mitcheson
  Mary Campbell

Preface

HUMPHRY REPTON DIED ON 24 March 1818. The Hertfordshire Gardens Trust decided to commemorate the bicentenary of this event by producing a volume which did not simply describe the various parks and gardens in the county with which Repton was involved but also presented the principal evidence for his activities. The first section of this volume provides a brief overview of Repton's work in Hertfordshire and is followed by transcriptions of the complete texts of all seven known Red Books that he prepared for places in Hertfordshire, together with reproductions of their illustrations. These are accompanied by brief discussions of the character of the places in question, the nature of Repton's proposals and the extent to which they were implemented. This section also presents a transcription of the correspondence and other documents relating to Repton's important work for the East India Company at Haileybury. The final part of the book briefly discusses those places for which no Red Book (or similar documentation) has survived, presents the key evidence for associating them with Repton and, again, briefly discusses their history and the probable nature of Repton's activities there.

Studying the work of individual designers within a relatively limited local area, such as a county, can bring real benefits to the garden historian, for it allows us to see with some clarity how the individuals concerned responded to the challenges and possibilities of a particular range of environments. The way that Repton's 'improvements' were related to the character of Hertfordshire in the decades either side of 1800 – in terms of its social structure as much as its physical landscape – can throw important new light on his style more generally and on the notions and beliefs that underpinned it.

The research was undertaken by members of the Hertfordshire Gardens Trust Research Group at Hertfordshire Archives and Local Studies (HALS), at the National Archives at Kew, in private archives and elsewhere. The following individuals were responsible for researching the named sites and – where relevant – transcribing the Red Books or similar documents:

Kate Banister: Bedwell Park

Roger Beament[†] and Liz Carlin: Lamer House

Kate Harwood: Wall Hall

Diana Kingham: Little Court, Buntingford

Alison Moller and Tosh Moller: Wyddial Hall

Toby Parker: Haileybury

Sally Pearson and Alan Fletcher: New Barnes and Organ Hall

Anida Rayfield and Tom Williamson: Hilfield House, Aldenham

Alison Robinson: Brookmans Park

Anne Rowe: Digswell House, Tewin Water and Panshanger

Anne Shellim and Liz Carlin: Offley Place

John Sloan: Cashiobury Park and The Grove

Monica Stenning: Woodhill

Mick Thompson: Ashridge House

David Willis: Marchmont House

Editorial conventions

The transcribed texts have been faithfully copied from the original, although some modern punctuation has been inserted to aid the reader. The majority of abbreviations have been silently extended. The use of the symbols < and > denotes material interlined by the original writer.

Repton in Hertfordshire: an introduction

AFTER 'CAPABILITY' BROWN, HUMPHRY REPTON is probably the best known of English landscape designers, or 'landscape gardeners', to use the term which he himself employed (Figure 1). His professional career began in 1788, five years after Brown's death, and ended in 1816 with his last work, Sheringham Hall in Norfolk.[1] He died two years later. His fame – in marked contrast to that of Brown – arose as much from his writings as from his actual works, for he was the author of several published texts, including: *Sketches and Hints on Landscape Gardening* (1794), *Observations on the Theory and Practice of Landscape Gardening* (1803), *An Inquiry into the Changes in Taste in Landscape Gardening* (1806) and *Fragments on the Theory and Practice of Landscape Gardening* (1816). His prominent critics, the 'Picturesque' writers Richard Payne Knight and Uvedale Price, declared that Repton slavishly continued Brown's style: his work was, Price suggested, 'designed and executed exactly under Mr Brown's receipt'.[2] But at the outset of his career Repton in fact claimed a wider set of influences, describing in a letter sent to prospective clients how he had visited the landscapes not only of Brown but also those of his predecessor, William Kent, and of his contemporary, Nathaniel Richmond – an individual who had initially worked with Brown (mainly at Moor Park in Hertfordshire) before launching out, in 1759, on his own, and who designed more than 30 landscapes, including Hitchin Priory and Lamer in Hertfordshire.[3] Repton may also have studied the works

1 Portrait of Humphry Repton by John Downman, *c*.1790.

2   Repton's trade card, which appears as a frontispiece in most of his Red Books.

and crossed by serpentine drives. But Brown and Repton differed from each other in a number of important ways. Brown received vast sums from clients because he usually provided not only a design but a whole team of men – contractors and labourers – to implement it.[5] Repton, in contrast, usually produced only the design itself (Figure 2). The line of a drive or the shape of a clump might be staked out on the ground, but he did not normally employ hydraulic engineers, plantsmen or labourers, although occasionally, as at Haileybury, he provided direct supervision for a contractor – in this case the prominent London nurseryman Thomas Barr. Repton's clients essentially bought ideas and advice, usually presented in the form of a 'Red Book', so called because it was often bound in red Moroccan leather. Each comprised a text that analysed the current appearance of the landscape and recommended improvements, and watercolour illustrations, many of which had a flap which could be lifted to provide an impression of a particular scene before and after proposed changes. Many Red Books – including those for Panshanger, Tewin and Ashridge – include one image in which Repton himself is shown, with sketch book in hand. All the Hertfordshire Red Books – with the exception of Ashridge – have a text that was dictated by Repton but actually written by another individual, probably a family member. The watercolour illustrations, in contrast, are all by Repton himself, assisted – in the case of Ashridge and Panshanger – by his son, John Adey Repton.[6] The Red Books were an excellent commercial device, although not universally applauded. William Mason famously remarked how Repton:

Alters places on Paper and makes them so picturesque that fine folks think that all the oaks etc he draws will grow exactly

of other contemporary landscape gardeners of note. A payment for a visit to Brocket Park in Hertfordshire, a landscape created by the important designer Richard Woods, is among the earliest entries in Repton's first and only surviving account book, which runs from 1788 until 1790.[4]

Repton's designs, and especially his earlier ones, were indeed broadly similar to those of Brown and his contemporaries. They mainly comprised 'naturalistic' parkland, devoid of avenues, straight lines and geometric planting, ornamented with clumps and belts in the shape and fashion in which he delineated them, so they employ him at great price; so much the better on both sides, for they might lay out their money worse, and he has a numerous family of children to bring up.[7]

The Red Books were thus in most, although not all, cases the 'product' that clients purchased, and -- as Rogger and others have argued – works of art in their own right.[8] Combined with Repton's published works, the Red Books – and the Hertfordshire ones perhaps especially – provide clear insights not only into what Repton did but also into why he did it – in sharp contrast to the situation with Brown, who wrote very little, so that we are obliged to speculate on the aesthetic, philosophical and ideological notions underpinning his style. Although there were broad similarities in their style, there were also important differences between the kinds of landscape produced by the two men. While Brown (contrary to what is sometimes suggested) often created elaborate pleasure grounds and even flower gardens in the vicinity of mansions, if largely to one side of the main façade, Repton from the start paid much more attention to such immediate grounds, often dealing exclusively with this aspect of the landscape. Shrubberies, flower beds and flowers trailed on trelliswork fixed to the walls of the house were favourite devices throughout his career. In the wider parkland, moreover, Brown generally worked on a grand scale, altering landforms, smoothing the ground surface, creating lakes and making extensive plantations. Repton's touch was usually lighter: a clump here and a few trees there – and seldom extended to earth-moving or lake-making. If an unpleasant object intruded into the view from the mansion, Brown might hide it

with massed planting; Repton, in contrast, would be more likely to plant judiciously on a smaller scale, and closer to the house. Panshanger, one of the most important of Repton's Hertfordshire commissions, is rather unusual in this respect, as here he did work on a grand scale, creating the wonderful lake that still survives and overseeing massed planting. But, for the most part, if Brown was a cosmetic surgeon, Repton was a make-up artist.

These and other differences in the landscapes created by the two men were to an extent connected with the types of client for whom they mainly worked. Brown was, for the most part, employed by the greatest in the land, owners of vast estates. Repton also worked for such men, especially in the early years of his career.[9] But when he did so his activities were often directed towards one part of the landscape, usually the pleasure grounds and gardens. The majority of his clients were lesser landowners – local knights and squires – with smaller parks; or were men who, though wealthy, owned no significant estate at all, but only a 'villa' with diminutive grounds. As he described in 1816:

> It seldom falls to the lot of the improver to be called upon for his opinion on places of great extent … while in the neighbourhood of every city or manufacturing town, new places as villas are daily springing up, and these, with a few acres, require all the conveniences, comforts and appendages, of larger and more sumptuous, if not more expensive place[s]. And … these have of late had the greatest claim to my attention.[10]

Repton explained that for places such as these a subtle approach was required. It was not by 'adding field to field, or by taking away hedges, or by removing roads to a distance' that the surroundings of a villa were to be improved. Instead, it was by exploiting 'every circumstance of interest or beauty within our reach, and by hiding such objects as cannot be viewed with pleasure'.[11]

Repton's emphasis on gardens, rather than on open parkland, was thus related in part to the limited extent of the properties attached to many of the villa residences at which he was employed. A structured garden could look impressive even if it occupied only a relatively small area of ground, but a small park was little different from a grass field. Repton's designs, and especially those for the smaller residences at which he worked, have a homely, practical feel: they were eminently suitable for an elegant and affluent, but not necessarily extravagant, life in the countryside. Their domestic practicality stood in contrast to the more self-consciously artistic, evocative and dramatic styles advocated by his great Picturesque critics, Richard Payne Knight and Uvedale Price, with their emphasis on roughness, drama, detail and emotion. But we might also note in passing that, while Repton's Red Books frequently show flowers planted informally in his pleasure grounds, against the walls of mansions or in special Hardenberg baskets – a new fashion, imported from Germany – it is often very difficult to say what varieties or even species these are supposed to represent. Repton was no plantsman: he was a designer of landscapes, not a gardener.

In his later commissions Repton began to lay out more elaborate and complex gardens and pleasure grounds designed in an increasingly formal and geometric style – as at Woburn in Bedfordshire and, in particular, at Ashridge on the Hertfordshire/ Buckinghamshire border. Moreover, whereas Brown's parks had been separated from the mown lawn beside the mansion only by a sunken fence or 'ha-ha' – so that the parkland turf appeared to continue uninterrupted to its walls – Repton in his later commissions often placed a terrace beneath the main façade. These tendencies were to develop and intensify in the nineteenth century under designers such as William Sawrey Gilpin and William Andrews Nesfield and may in part have been influenced by changes in architectural fashion. In the early and middle decades of the eighteenth century elite residences had normally been built in a broadly classical style – first Palladian and then Neoclassical – and were set off to perfection by the simple sweeping open parklands produced by Brown and his contemporaries. Indeed, in many ways Brown's rather minimalist style mirrored the concerns of the Neoclassical architects, with their emphasis on planes, simplicity and distinct, continuous outlines rather than complex, fussy forms.[12] But in the later years of the century classical buildings began to be accompanied by ones designed in more diverse styles, drawing in particular on medieval gothic and Elizabethan models, for which a more structured setting seemed appropriate, especially one that alluded to indigenous antiquity with, for example, the revival of the formal *parterres* that had characterised elite gardens before the rise of the 'natural' style in the first half of the eighteenth century.

From the start of his career Repton was understandably keen on developing ways in which the owners of comparatively modest estates could display to the full their status and the extent of their property. At Livermere in Suffolk in 1790, for example, he suggested that all the fences in the village should be painted the same colour to demonstrate unity of ownership; elsewhere he proposed that the coat of arms of the landowner should be displayed on milestones, or the parish church ornamented in a similar way to the country house – all moves intended to establish, in clear visual terms, the dominance of a locality by a particular family, something he described as 'appropriation'.[13] In a similar way, Repton's parkland belts were often less continuous than Brown's had been, allowing views out into the surrounding countryside and thus ensuring that the landscape of the estate was read as an undivided whole, a single property. 'Appropriation' had other aspects too – it included, for example, the establishment of seats, shelters, urns and the like in the grounds of a mansion, 'appropriating' it to the use of the residents: or, in Rogger's words, 'the property must bear throughout indicators commensurate with its role in the everyday life of the family living on it'.[14] Appropriation was also closely connected with another concept much discussed by Repton – that of 'Character'. Repton, a social conservative, was concerned that the grounds attached to a residence should be of the appropriate extent (or apparent extent), and of the appropriate degree of elaboration. Great palaces required vast parks and extensive pleasure grounds; small villas did not, but these in turn needed to appear quite different from 'mere farm-houses'.

One interesting aspect of Repton's career is the way in which elements of his style remained unchanged while at the same time the manner in which he explained them, in published texts or Red Books, underwent a significant development.[15] In the later stages of his career establishing a connection between parks and pleasure grounds, on the one hand, and the wider countryside, on the other, was given a different or at least an additional justification. Repton became convinced that the rise of new wealth and accelerating rural poverty, resulting in part from the Napoleonic Wars, were a threat to

social stability, and advocated a return to the paternalistic sentiments that he associated with the old-established landed families. Signs of a landowner's dominance in a locality, such as heraldic symbols placed on milestones or cottages, were now also intended to express his sympathetic involvement in the life of the community. No longer should the mansion stand solitary and isolated within its private park: the labourer's cottage, if made 'a subordinate part of the general scenery … so far from disfiguring it, add[s] to the dignity that wealth can derive from the exercise of benevolence'.[16]

There are, in all, six places in Hertfordshire for which a Red Book, or a similar collection of written proposals, has survived: Ashridge House, New Barnes, Panshanger, Tewin Water, Wall Hall and Woodhill. A Red Book for Lamer House survived until recently and cannot now be traced, but exists as a photocopy. In addition, while the Red Book for Wyddial Hall is likewise lost, parts of it are quoted in other Repton texts, most notably in the Red Book for Stoke Park in Buckinghamshire. Lamer and Wyddial both date from the early years of Repton's career and thus also appear as entries in his only surviving account book, which runs, as already noted, from 1788 until the end of 1790; and this source also includes payments for another Hertfordshire site, Little Court in Buntingford.[17] A further three Hertfordshire commissions can be identified on the basis of references made in one of his published works or in his *Memoirs* – an account of his life that remained unpublished until the twentieth century:[18] these are Brookmans Park, Organ Hall and Cashiobury Park. And an additional three, Bedwell Park, Haileybury and Hilfield, are known from other documentary evidence, such as letters written to or by Repton. We can be confident that Repton advised at all these 15 places, although how many of his proposals were acted upon is (as we shall see) a different matter.

There are, in addition to these secure attributions, three sites that we have credited to Repton on the grounds that they appear among the illustrations that he prepared for *The Polite Repository, or Pocket Companion*, a diary-cum-almanack that was published annually between 1790 and 1811 by William Peacock. For a short period – between 1793 and 1795 – this publication included a text expressly stating that the country seats illustrated were ones that had been 'improved' under Repton's direction, although even in these years it appears that some of the places pictured do not in fact fall into this category.[19] It is less certain whether most of the illustrations produced outside this narrow period also represent places where Repton had worked, but – in the case of Hertfordshire – many clearly were, for Ashridge, Bedwell, Cashiobury, Organ Hall, Tewin Water, Wall Hall, Woodhill and Wyddial are all included. The three additional sites that appear *only* as *Polite Repository* illustrations and for which no other hard evidence for a connection with Repton has yet been discovered are Marchmont House in Hemel Hempstead, Offley Place and The Grove near Watford. Lastly, we briefly discuss the possibility that he worked at Digswell, for this mansion was owned by a member of the Cowper family, for whom Repton also worked at nearby Panshanger and Tewin Water, and its grounds boasted a number of distinctive Reptonian features.

To summarise: there are six places in Hertfordshire for which a Red Book survives, one where it is lost but a copy remains and one – Wyddial – where we know one was produced because Repton himself quotes from it. In addition, there are a further 10 places where Repton very probably worked and another (Digswell)

where he may have done. We do not know what proportion of these additional sites were originally provided with a Red Book. Repton certainly produced one for Brookmans Park and (very probably) for Organ Hall, for their existence is stated or implied in his published writings, while the amount of money paid to him, or time spent by him, at Hilfield, Little Court and Bedwell strongly implies that their owners, too, were supplied with them. It thus seems likely that Repton prepared a Red Book for a clear majority of the places where he worked in Hertfordshire, and this is probably true of the country more generally. There is certainly little in the Hertfordshire evidence to support Rogger's suggestion that, in the middle years of his career especially, Repton often provided advice only verbally or by letter, without producing a Red Book.[20]

In terms of their status and character, Repton's 18 or 19 Hertfordshire commissions can be divided into three broad groups, although these tend to blur and merge, and the distinctions between them are to some extent arbitrary. The first comprises residences associated with major estates, most notably Cashiobury, Ashridge and Panshanger. At Ashridge certainly and at Cashiobury very probably his activities were directed mainly towards the pleasure grounds around the mansion: both houses were being rebuilt at around the same time as great gothic edifices to designs by James Wyatt and Jeffry Wyatt. At Panshanger, likewise rebuilt in gothic style (although not to the design originally proposed by Repton in the Red Book), his advice embraced the parkland around the house, which (as noted) was laid out on a grand, Brownian scale. The second group consists of residences that lay at the heart of rather smaller landed estates, such as Offley, Wyddial, Bedwell, Lamer and Tewin Water, together (arguably) with the Grove near

Watford and Digswell. The most interesting of his commissions, however, fall into a third category. These were the residences of wealthy merchants and financiers, rather than long-established landowners, and their presence reflected Hertfordshire's proximity to London. Some remained relatively small residences – 'villas' that lacked any real estate, their associated land amounting to less than 250 acres (c. 100 hectares) each in the case of Marchmont House, Organ Hall, New Barnes and Woodhill. Others began in this way, but grew to larger estates as their owners gradually purchased neighbouring farms, as at Wall Hall or Hilfield in Aldenham.[21] Such places originated as small farms or minor manors. But the county was so firmly in the grip of the London land market that many of the older-established, larger estates on which Repton worked, such as Bedwell Park or Brookmans Park, had also been acquired by the newly rich. Conversely, great aristocrats might purchase or erect Hertfordshire villas as convenient second homes close to London – such as Marchmont House near Hemel Hempstead, which originally served as a base for the prominent politician the third earl of Marchmont before passing to the client for whom Repton worked.[22]

Indeed, Repton's activities in Hertfordshire – and the development of the eighteenth- and nineteenth-century landscape of the county more generally – can only be fully understood in terms of its closeness to London. This had long ensured a high rate of turnover of landed property, as men who made their money in the metropolis sought a rural retreat within easy travelling distance of their place of work or a retirement residence close to contacts and associates. Already, in 1766, well over 60 per cent of the country seats with named proprietors that

appear on Dury and Andrews' map of Hertfordshire had been acquired by their families in the period since the Restoration of 1660 – new recruits to the landowning class from the worlds of trade, government service and finance. Indeed, over a quarter of the named proprietors had purchased the property themselves, or their spouse had done so.[23] Four decades later Arthur Young memorably described how 'Property in Hertfordshire is much divided: the vicinity of the capital; the goodness of the air and the roads; and the beauty of the country' had led 'great numbers of wealthy persons to purchase land for villas'.[24] Not surprisingly, parks – and especially the smaller examples – were, by the early nineteenth century, particularly densely clustered in the southern half of the county, close to London (Figure 3). Such was the scale of this incipient suburbanisation that, as Sarah Spooner has emphasised, clusters of three or more contiguous but diminutive parks might develop, their owners to an extent co-ordinating their schemes of landscape design.[25] As Kate Harwood has shown, individuals associated with the East India Company and the South Seas Company were particularly numerous in this exodus during the eighteenth century. George Thellusson, Repton's client at Wall Hall, was director of the East India Company from 1796 to 1809, while Haileybury, one of Repton's few institutional commissions, was built as a college for the training of the Company's administrators.[26]

Repton was often uneasy about working for the newly wealthy: he was unquestionably more at home advising long-established landed families. In the eighteenth century acceptance of the upwardly mobile into polite society was conditional on them displaying 'taste' – an understanding of established etiquette and

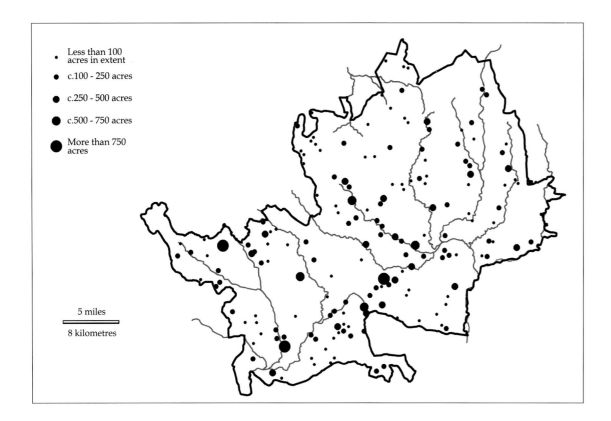

Less than 100
acres in extent

c.100 - 250 acres

c.250 - 500 acres

c.500 - 750 acres

More than 750
acres

5 miles

8 kilometres

3 The distribution of landscape parks in Hertfordshire, as shown on Andrew Bryant's county map of 1822.

an appreciation of current fashions in art, literature and music. To Repton, 'the rule of taste must operate not only in the production of beauty, i.e., governing the work of the landscape gardener, but also in the recipients of such work, who must experience the garden with alert senses and discernment'.[27] There are slight hints in some of the Red Books, most notably that for New Barnes, that Repton was not entirely convinced that his client (in this case the banker Matthew Towgood) fully understood the principles of 'taste' as applied to landscape design and as expressed in Repton's proposals for his property.

In simple numerical terms, Hertfordshire comes fifth in the county rankings of probable Repton commissions, after Essex with 37, Norfolk with 22, Surrey with 21 and Suffolk with 20, and just ahead of Kent with 17 and Middlesex with 15.[28] Superficially, this would seem to place a particular importance on the counties in which Repton was born (Suffolk); lived for most of his early life and was eventually buried (Norfolk); and in which he resided (at Hare Street, Essex) during his time as a practising designer. But when the differing *size* of the various counties is taken into account, this rank order is radically changed. Hertfordshire, one of the smallest English counties, then comes second, with around one Repton commission for each 91 square kilometres of land, well behind Middlesex, with one for every 49 square kilometres, but just ahead of Surrey, with one for every 93 square kilometres, and Essex, with one for every 107. Norfolk, in contrast, a large county, has only one Repton site for each 240 square kilometres, and Suffolk one for every 191 square kilometres.

The high totals in Middlesex, Hertfordshire, Surrey and Essex clearly reflect the close packing of Repton's commissions in the hinterland of London. This concentration broadly reflects the overall distribution of parks within the country by the start of the nineteenth century, with concentrations in the industrialising areas of the west Midlands and parts of the north but, in particular, in the environs of London. Indeed, within Hertfordshire it is noticeable that more than twice as many of Repton's commissions lie to the south of a line drawn from Tring in the west to Sawbridgeworth in the east than to the north; and this north–south contrast is even greater when we consider the different kinds of residence at which Repton worked. Commissions involving large estates and medium-sized 'gentry' properties were scattered fairly evenly across the county, but those concerning smaller residences and 'villas' were mainly located in the south (Figure 4).

The Hertfordshire Red Books, combined as we shall see with other evidence, throw important new light on Repton and his works. The Red Books have always been something of a problem to garden historians. At a number of places in England the proposals they contain appear to have been only partially carried out, or alternative designs executed, in spite of Repton's fame; elsewhere they appear to account for only a small proportion of the improvements made during the period in question. Panshanger is particularly important in this respect because the Red Book deals mainly with the architecture and siting of, and views from, the new house, together with suggestions about a new lake; but the estate accounts and correspondence leave no doubt that Repton was actively involved in many other aspects of the new landscape, especially the details of the planting. A Red Book, in short, may sometimes document only one part of Repton's activities at a particular place, and this raises interesting questions about some of his other Hertfordshire commissions. At Wall Hall, for example, the Red Book is almost entirely restricted to a consideration of the approach drives and to buildings and features to be erected along them, but many aspects of the park and pleasure grounds recorded a decade or so later seem very much in Repton's style.

But it is for what they can tell us more broadly about Repton's ideas about landscape design – about the principles underlying his work – that the Hertfordshire Red Books are especially important, for the particular characteristics of the county brought out key aspects of his style very clearly. Repton

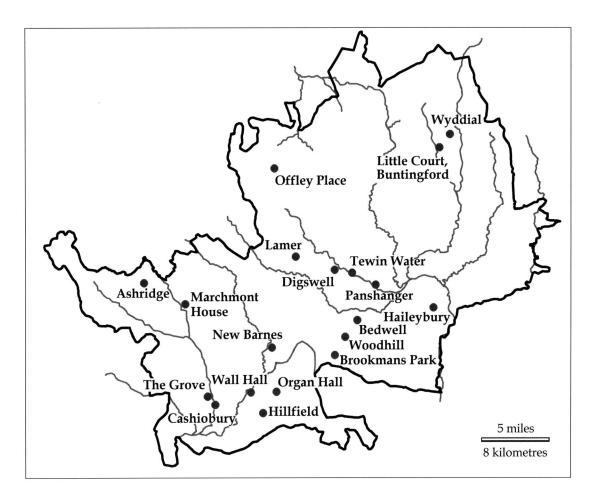

made considerable use of 'borrowed views', glimpses of the surrounding countryside: both to enhance the experience of the rather constricted grounds of villas and, at larger properties, to forge a clear visual link between a house and the wider estate to which it was attached. This in turn ensured that, on a number of occasions, he reflected on the character of the local landscape. Hertfordshire was, for the most part, an old-enclosed county, its

4   Repton's Hertfordshire commissions. Note the marked concentration in the southern half of the county, towards London.

numerous woods and hedges providing useful raw materials for the park-maker.[29] Repton thus described how, in the case of New Barnes, although there was little actual woodland 'belonging to this Estate, yet the richness of the hedgerow Timber, and the abundance of Woods in the neighbourhood, make up this deficiency, and only require to be shown by opening views towards them'. But the topography of the county – the wide, relatively level interfluves between major valleys, especially in the west of the county – caused problems. As Repton noted in the Red Book for Wall Hall of 1803:

> There are few Counties in England which possess more natural beauties than Hartfordshire, yet there is none in which these beauties require to be more brought into notice by the assistance of Art, since however contradictory it may appear, almost every part of Hartfordshire altho' uneven, appears flat; and the wooded, appears naked. This seeming paradox I shall thus explain – The whole County like the environs of Wall hall, is intersected by valleys, but there are few hills, because the summits of the eminences are broad and flat, or what is called table land; and therefore unless the Spectator be placed near the brow which slopes into the valley, he will only look across a plain, and as these flat surfaces are generally arable land and less wooded than the sides of the vallies, both the richness of cloathing and the inequality of the ground will be in a great measure lost … .

The same problem was faced at Lamer in 1792, where Repton described how

the summit of that hill on which Lamer is situated, is so broad in front of the house; that in many respects it must be treated as if the situation were flat; because the distant views seen from the lower apartments, tho' in some directions extensive and very interesting in themselves, are seen over too great an expanse of uninteresting Lawn.

At Panshanger in 1800 these same topographical challenges were critical in deciding the position of the new house:

> The chief Beauty of the Estate consists in the Valley, or rather the two hanging banks which form the Valley, because the Summits of the Hills on each side are flat, or what is called <u>Table Land</u>; and unless the House were to stand very near the Edge of the slope, it would command no View of the Valley: this is the Case with respect to the present Mansion at Cole Green.

But Repton, here as elsewhere, also wrestled with the issue of precisely how views of the surrounding countryside – whether owned by the client or otherwise – should be integrated into the experience of the more overtly 'designed' landscape, of park and pleasure ground. The parkland around a great mansion was different in its essential 'character', he believed, from the wider estate farmland. The former was a landscape of leisure comprising open expanses of turf; the latter was a productive tract of land (and most visibly so when under arable cultivation) and was subdivided into fields by hedges. The two should not, therefore, lie contiguous in the view, nor should they be separated by the sharp line of a fence or a hedge. Instead, the working countryside should be distantly glimpsed, preferably above – or through a gap in – a perimeter belt of trees. Such a boundary would have another advantage, as Repton explained in the Red Book for Wyddial:

> If the park be divided from the farm only by a hedge, we know the breadth of the hedge and its proximity is as offensive as if a pale made the line of separation, but if instead of a pale or hedge as a boundary, we substitute a wood of sufficient depth to act as a skreen, the imagination gives still greater extent to that wood than it really has, and when we see a distant arable country over the tops of this mass of trees, it becomes so much softened by the aerial perspective that instead of offending, it is a pleasing appendage to the Landscape, because it is subordinate.

'Character' was, as I have noted, a key element in Repton's design philosophy. It was a complicated concept, but essentially involved a belief that the surroundings of a mansion should, in both style and extent, be appropriate to its status, function and appearance. As he expressed it in the Red Book for Woodhill in 1803:

> Every rational improvement of a place must depend on its Character, and the Character must depend on its uses. If a Nobleman lets a palace to a Farmer, it will cease to be a palace; and if a Gentleman visibly lives in the midst of barns and dung yards, his house will no longer be a mansion but a farm house. A Villa, a Shooting box and every Rural retreat

of elegance require the removal or the concealment of all that is dirty and offensive.

At Panshanger, more simply, he emphasised how 'that which may be adviseable in the Neighbourhood of a Cottage, will be totally inconsistent with the Environs of a Palace: and in Landscape Gardening as in every other Art, there must be a Consistency and Unity of character preserved, or the whole will be made up of discordant parts'. At New Barnes – a place which had until recently been a 'mere farm-house', but was now the 'the residence of a gentleman' – he similarly argued that 'If profit were only to be considered, the lawn in front of the House must continue to be sown with Corn, and the flower garden at the back with potatoes and cabbages; but the Character of the Mansion being distinct from that of the Farm, the ground should partake of the same Character.'

All this was perhaps a particular issue in a county such as Hertfordshire, where – alongside large landed estates and smaller gentry properties – there were numerous 'villas' without significant estates attached. There was a strong need to distinguish these places from neighbouring farms; many, indeed, had been but recently upgraded from working farms. At Woodhill, for example, Repton worried that the stables had all too clearly been converted from an earlier barn. As we have just seen in his discussion of perimeter belts at Wyddial, Repton was adept at the art of visual illusion or suggestion – of subtly manipulating the landscape to make the best of a place, and to make a little go a long way. At Woodhill he thus advised placing a covered seat in the paddock to the south-west of the house in order to 'change its Character from a common green field to the Lawn of a Gentleman's Place'. The diminutive estate here was bisected by a public road but, rather than re-routing this away from the house and its grounds, Repton suggested that both sides of the road should be provided with identical fencing, so as to make it clear that 'the road passes thro' the premises', with the mansion at its centre. At a great mansion, in contrast, such an arrangement could not be tolerated, and at both *Tewin Water* and *Panshanger* he advised the diversion of public roads to a distance – something relatively easy to achieve in legal terms using a magistrates' Road Order, but an expensive undertaking nevertheless.

> Altho' the late possessor of Tewin water might think a public road no less appropriate than cheerful immediately in front of the house; or a foot path with all its attendant inconveniences, cutting up the lawn in another direction, and after crossing the water, passing close under the windows, leaving the house on a kind of peninsula surrounded by carts, waggons, gypsies, poachers, &c. &c. who feel they have a right of intrusion; yet when the place with all its beauties and all its defects, shall pass under the correcting hand of good taste, the views from the house will be changed with the views of its possessor.

In establishing the 'character' of a house as the residence of a gentleman, Repton placed a particular emphasis on entrances and approaches, following the adage (employed in a number of his writings) that 'first impressions last longest'. In the Red Book for Lamer, as at many other places, he cautioned against having the drive to the mansion leave the public road at right angles, because such an arrangement 'robs the entrance of importance'.

Instead it should begin at a bend in the road and if possible in such a manner that travellers on the former were obliged to veer off at an angle, while those heading for the house went straight on: 'the high road may appear to branch from the approach rather than the approach from the high road'. Having entered the park, the drive should then proceed in a fairly direct manner to the mansion. This was one of the ways in which Repton's style differed subtly from that of Brown, for the latter had often introduced rather long, circuitous drives that presented a series of glimpses of the mansion, set in its manicured parkland. The difference may, in part, reflect the fact that in the rather smaller landscapes with which Repton was often concerned there was simply insufficient space for a meandering approach, which might (as he explained at Lamer) have the unfortunate effect of revealing the limited extent of the grounds. This said, the route was also chosen so that it displayed the owner's grounds to best advantage: it should 'shew the natural beauties of the situation' and 'give importance to a place' (Wall Hall Red Book); it should show 'the extent of the place' (New Barnes Red Book). Above all, the approach should display the mansion itself to best advantage, and this was not to be achieved (as so often in the designs of Brown) by beginning with a series of distant glimpses. Instead, the house should be revealed suddenly, in a single 'burst', and – as he explains in his discussion in the Red Book for Lamer – not 'at so great a distance as to make it appear less than it really is'.

Repton was not simply concerned to match the 'character' of the grounds to that of the house. The converse was also important: he saw the design of the two as inextricably connected. In the Red Book for Panshanger he thus asserted that 'I am convinced from experience that some knowledge of Architecture is inseparable from the art I profess.' By this time (1800) Repton was beginning to work closely with his son, John Adey, who had just finished his period of employment with the architect John Nash, and he appears to have assisted his father in the design for the new gothic house that was a prominent feature of the Red Book for Panshanger. In fact, from early in his career Repton had felt obliged to offer some advice on architecture, although it was often restricted to external appearances, treating the house as part of the landscape, as it were – as at Lamer. But as time went on he also made suggestions about the layout of the rooms from which the park and pleasure grounds would be viewed, and sometimes – as at Witton in north Norfolk – more general proposals for improving a residence.[30]

The connections between architecture, landscape design and the concept of 'character' in Repton's work is perhaps nowhere clearer than at Ashridge. Here his design for the grounds – drawn up with the assistance of John Adey – included a complex series of separate gardens that contained numerous references to the place's medieval past, most bizarrely in the case of the 'Monk's Garden', which was designed to resemble a monastic burial ground. The grounds thus served to complement the vast new gothic house designed by James and Jeffry Wyatt, and as a unit reflected the specific history of an ancient spot in a romantic and isolated location on the crest of the Chilterns and on the county boundary with Buckinghamshire – the latter circumstance explicitly commemorated in another feature of the garden, the 'County Stone'. The 'character' of the grounds thus embraced the status of the mansion, as the centre of an extensive estate;

its architectural style, as rebuilt as a vast gothic edifice; the early history of the place, as a medieval monastery and royal residence; and its landscape setting, in the high, wooded Chilterns.

At Ashridge Repton worked with an assured hand; elsewhere, 'character' presented challenges rather than possibilities, as, in particular, at Haileybury. This was purpose-built as a college for the East India Company. It was not a private mansion but an institution, a type of building that neither Repton nor his contemporaries had much experience of designing grounds for. Repton was later to prepare a design for a new workhouse at Crayford in Kent (in 1812) for his son Edward, the parish curate, but it was never erected; nor were his proposals for altering the appearance and surroundings of another workhouse, at Sheringham in 1812, ever carried out.[31] Before working at Haileybury in 1808 Repton had been commissioned to improve the grounds of Magdalen College, Oxford, but his proposals were only very partially implemented and a designed setting of some kind was already in existence beside the college. Haileybury, a college erected on a virgin site, was a challenge indeed.

In some ways Repton treated the place, perhaps unsurprisingly, like a country house. A new entrance, in the form of an avenue leading in from the turnpike road from the west, had already been decided by the Committee of College before he was commissioned, as had the plan to expand the college grounds to the south, following the diversion of the public road – Hailey Lane – southwards. But much else was decided by Repton. In particular, as was often the case with his later designs for country houses, Repton placed the college on a great terrace which formed the foreground to a fine view to the south, with a diminutive park forming the middle ground and with a backdrop provided by the woods towards Hoddesdon and the still unenclosed open fields in the Lea valley in the far distance. But what is striking, in contrast to his country-house landscapes, was the way in which the grounds at Haileybury were subdivided. What was anyway a small landscape was broken down into smaller, self-sufficient fragments: small gardens enjoyed not only by the Master but by the individual Fellows – the latter lying beside their private residences – and all surrounded by high fences. Such an arrangement was a direct reflection of both the social hierarchies operating within the college and the requirement for both private spaces (gardens) and a shared setting for the building as a whole (the parkland and entrance area). All this fitted in well with Repton's more general ideas about the way that design should reflect usage – a landscape should be appropriate to its purpose, and to the character of the building with which it was associated. What is superficially more surprising is the way in which a substantial wooden fence appears to have run along most of the southern and much of the western boundaries of the property: an unusual feature from a designer who usually advised blurring the boundaries between the park and the wider countryside, so that there was no hard barrier between them. But here again Repton's design reflected appropriate social realities and 'character'. There was here no 'connection' between a mansion and its estate to be affirmed, no property in the view to be 'appropriated' or displayed, and the members of the college were largely unrelated, both socially and economically, to the community occupying the wider agricultural landscape. To hide the bounds of the property would, perhaps, have seemed both inappropriate and unnecessary. The fence, moreover, was sufficiently low as to not inhibit the main view out from the terrace, southwards towards the Lea valley, nor to hide the view towards the college, standing proudly in its grounds, from the turnpike road. Repton's design for Haileybury thus displayed a measure of overall coherence above and beyond its superficially rather fragmented character. Repton was, nevertheless, perhaps struggling to adapt an aesthetic developed for private residences to a very different institutional context.

Identifying both the individual features and elements of Repton's style and the manner in which, in practice, he worked through the concept of 'character' on the ground can help us to speculate on the nature of his contribution at those places where no Red Book or similar documentation has survived, but where we can be sure, or reasonably sure, that he worked. The somewhat fragmentary evidence for Cashiobury, for example, suggests a long involvement with the grounds. Their chief feature as described by observers in the 1820s and 1830s was a complex sequence of 'themed' gardens. This seems so similar to what Repton designed at Ashridge that it is hard to believe that he was not also the prime mover in this case as well – not least because both Ashridge and Cashiobury were large mansions standing at the centres of great estates that were rebuilt at the start of the nineteenth century in flamboyant gothic form by the Wyatts. In the case of Marchmont House in Hemel Hempstead, to take another case, the main entrance left the public road at a slight bend and in a curve, rather than at right angles, much as Repton proposed at Lamer. Other examples are explored in the case studies that follow. It must be emphasised, however, that such a procedure makes an important and perhaps erroneous assumption: that these kinds of stylistic touches and attitudes were specific to Repton, rather than being more widely shared. Repton may have been a real innovator, rather than the most prolific and articulate spokesman for more broadly shared fashions; but, even if he was, the success of his many publications must have ensured that his practices and attitudes were soon widely assimilated, making identification of his work on stylistic grounds alone rather problematic.

Eschewing unnecessary pomp and grandeur, Repton's rather practical and domestic approach to landscape design, and his development of principles more suitable than those of Brown for laying out the grounds of comparatively small properties, make his creations seem particularly appropriate for Hertfordshire. This is not simply because, for the reasons explained, the county was, in the eighteenth and nineteenth centuries, well populated by a plethora of small and medium-sized properties, but also because of the more general character of its countryside: small-scale and intimate. To Charles Lamb, Hertfordshire was 'homely'; to E.M. Forster, it was 'England meditative'.[32] This makes it a particular pity that so little of Repton's work in the county, as we shall see, survives on the ground today. In part this reflects the fact that, by its very nature, much that he proposed was ephemeral: relatively minor changes to parkland planting; the establishment of shrubberies and flower beds in gardens and pleasure grounds; the addition of essentially impermanent structures such as fences and trellises. Such features were easily swept away as fashions changed and changed again in the course of the nineteenth and twentieth centuries – more easily than the more substantial planting, ground-levelling and lake creation undertaken by his predecessor Brown. But, in addition, like other landscapes from the eighteenth and nineteenth centuries, those created by Repton have been vulnerable to later patterns of social and economic change, as well as to developments more specific to the history of the county. The eighteenth-century villas at which he worked represented the first wave of Hertfordshire's suburbanisation, the full tide of which has now swept over much of the south and centre of the county. Some of the houses at which he was employed have been demolished and their immediate grounds built over, such as Organ Hall or Cashiobury. Others have been converted to institutional use or divided into flats or apartments, usually leading to a steady degradation of their grounds. A surprisingly high proportion of the parks where Repton worked have become golf courses, including much of Cashiobury, Bedwell, Brookmans Park, The Grove, Lamer, New Barnes and Wall Hall. Repton's most extensive work in the county has suffered a more dramatic fate: Panshanger House was demolished in 1954 and a large proportion of its park now comprises gravel pits. Nevertheless, in a surprising number of cases quite extensive fragments of his work remain. Even at Panshanger Repton's lake survives largely intact, as it does at nearby Tewin Water; at New Barnes, his perimeter belt still forms the bounds of the golf course; at Haileybury, his diminutive 'water' and some planting survive in the college grounds. Probably the best place we can obtain an impression of Repton's work is at Ashridge, where the gardens designed by him, albeit in part reinterpreted by Jeffry Wyatt, are being extensively restored. All such remains need to be treasured and preserved into the future. They are not only of critical importance for understanding the history of English landscape design – perhaps more importantly, they are a crucial part of the long and immensely interesting history of this increasingly crowded county.

Notes

1   The best general accounts of Repton's art and career are: G. Carter, P. Goode and K. Laurie (eds), *Humphry Repton, Landscape Gardener* (Norwich, 1983); S. Daniels, *Humphry Repton: landscape gardening and the geography of Georgian England* (London, 1999); D. Stroud, *Humphry Repton* (London, 1962); L. Mayer, *Humphry Repton* (Princes Risborough, 2014).

2   R. Payne Knight, *The Landscape: a didactic poem in three books, addressed to Uvedale Price* (London, 1795), p. 99.

3   D. Brown and T. Williamson, *Lancelot Brown and the Capability Men: landscape revolution in eighteenth-century England* (London, 2016), pp. 142–5.

4   NRO: MS10.

5   Brown and Williamson, *Capability Men*, pp. 135–8.

6   A. Rogger, *Landscapes of Taste: the art of Humphry Repton's Red Books* (London, 2007), pp. 199–210.

7   William Mason to William Gilpin, 26 December 1794: Bodleian Library Ms Eng. Misc d.571.f.224.

8   Rogger, *Landscapes of Taste*.

9   Rogger, *Landscapes of Taste*, p. 15.

10 H. Repton, *Fragments on the Theory and Practice of Landscape Gardening* (London, 1816), p. 69.

11 *Ibid.*

12 Brown and Williamson, *Capability Men*, pp. 172–88.

13 P. Goode, 'The Picturesque controversy', in Carter *et al.* (eds), *Humphry Repton*, p. 34.

14 Rogger, *Landscapes of Taste*, p. 133.

15 S. Daniels, 'The political landscape', in Carter *et al.* (eds), *Humphry Repton*, pp. 110–21.

16 H. Repton, *Observations on the Theory and Practice of Landscape Gardening* (London, 1803), p. 119.

17 NRO: MS10.

18 A. Gore and G. Carter (eds), *Humphry Repton's Memoirs* (London, 2005).

19 N. Temple, 'Humphry Repton, illustrator, and William Peacock's "Polite Repository" 1790–1811', *Garden History*, 16/2 (1988), pp. 161–73.

20 Rogger, *Landscapes of Taste*, pp. 18–20.

21 Aldenham is probably unique as the only parish in England to have contained *three* places where Repton was employed. Wall Hall is included because, although the house actually stood in the adjacent parish of St Stephen, St Albans, much of the park lay within Aldenham; the other sites were Hilfield and Organ Hall.

22 S. Spooner, *Regions and Designed Landscapes in Georgian England* (London, 2015), p. 57.

23 A. MacNair, A. Rowe and T. Williamson, *Dury and Andrews' Map of Hertfordshire: Society and landscape in the eighteenth century* (Oxford, 2015), pp. 142–3.

24 A. Young, *General View of the Agriculture of Hertfordshire* (London, 1804), p. 18.

25 Spooner, *Regions and Designed Landscapes*, pp. 61–9.

26 K. Harwood, 'Some Hertfordshire Nabobs', in A. Rowe (ed.), *Hertfordshire Garden History: A miscellany* (Hatfield, 2007), pp. 49–77.

27 Rogger, *Landscapes of Taste*, p. 189.

28 Daniels, *Humphry Repton*, pp. 255–70. Daniels compiled this gazetteer with the assistance of John Phibbs. The calculations outlined omit Digswell as a possible but not proven commission.

29   O. Rackham, 'Pre-existing trees and woods in country-house parks', *Landscapes*, 5/2 (2004), pp. 1–15; T. Williamson, 'The character of Hertfordshire's parks and gardens', in Rowe (ed.), *Hertfordshire Garden History*, pp. 1–24.

30   University of Florida: SB471. R427, Red Book for Witton Hall, Norfolk, 1801.

31   Daniels, *Humphry Repton*, pp. 57–8, 97–8.

32   C. Lamb, *Elia and the Last Essays of Elia* (London, 1903), p. 89; E.M. Forster, *Howard's End* (London, 1910), p. 226.

Part I: The Major Sites

The eight sites described in Part I are the most important of Repton's commissions in Hertfordshire: not in terms of the extent of his work or its survival but by dint of the quality and quantity of the surviving evidence. They are arranged in alphabetical order, rather than chronologically, partly for ease of reference but also because in some cases the precise duration of Repton's activities at a particular place are unclear. All except Haileybury have Red Books that exist either in their original form or, in the case of Lamer, as a photographic copy. Haileybury has no Red Book, but extensive correspondence and other important documents survive that cast important light on Repton's working practices.

5   Ashridge House, rebuilt as a vast gothic mansion between 1803 and 1820 to designs by James and Jeffry Wyatt.

Ashridge House, Little Gaddesden[1]

SP 994122[2]

ASHRIDGE HOUSE AND ITS PARK occupy a magnificent position on the crest of the Chiltern Hills in the far north-west of the county; at the time, the boundary between Hertfordshire and Buckinghamshire ran through the pleasure grounds. Humphry Repton was commissioned by the seventh earl of Bridgewater in 1812 to draw up proposals for new gardens. These were to occupy the area to the south of his new house, initially designed by James Wyatt but, following his death in September 1813, completed and extended by his son Benjamin and nephew Jeffry Wyatt, later Sir Jeffry Wyatville, as a vast gothic extravaganza (Figure 5). Repton's *Report Concerning The Gardens of Ashridge* was submitted in March 1813: it is not, in fact, technically a 'Red Book', for it was presented as an unbound folio. As well as a hand-written text and watercolour illustrations, the folio includes a pencil sketch, probably by Repton, of an alcove with fountain, a working drawing of the pleasure ground and handwritten notes to accompany this.

Repton's proposals for Ashridge are very detailed and are of considerable significance because of their innovative nature. Combining open lawns with smaller gardens – both formal and informal in character – in the environs of the mansion, they mark a decisive shift in garden style and the beginning of a return of structure and order to the immediate vicinity of major houses that was to continue and intensify in the course of the nineteenth century. The proposals thus developed ideas that Repton had already advanced in his designs for the Pavilion at Brighton (1805) and at Woburn Abbey (1804–10), and which he was to further elaborate at Endsleigh in Devon (1814) for the sixth duke of Bedford. Ashridge also features in Repton's last book, *Fragments on the Theory and Practice of Landscape Gardening* of 1816, a publication that brought together descriptions of many of his later works. Repton in fact asked to borrow the proposals for Ashridge in order to refresh his memory of what he had suggested there but was told they had been mislaid. His account is thus written from memory, and includes an important assessment of his achievement:

> The novelty of this attempt to collect a number of gardens, differing from each other, may, perhaps excite the critics' censure; but I will hope there is no more absurdity in collecting gardens of different styles, dates, characters and dimensions in the same inclosure, than in placing the works of a Raphael and a Teniers in the same cabinet, or books sacred and profane in the same library.[3]

The account in *Fragments* also includes a number of illustrations that differ in significant details from those contained in Repton's original design proposals. In addition, Repton prepared a

6 An engraving of the
previous house at Ashridge,
designed by Henry Holland
in the 1760s, appeared in
Peacock's Polite Repository
for 1809, suggesting that
Repton may have had an
earlier involvement with the
place before the erection
of the new mansion.

Repton's own words, 'suited his declining powers'. It was a work that would become his 'youngest favourite'.

Repton's client had inherited Ashridge from his cousin Francis Egerton, third duke of Bridgewater, in 1803, along with a huge income. The earl immediately set about expanding the estate, enclosing land and improving the management of the property, which extended over nearly 2,300 acres (*c.* 930 hectares). Ashridge had originated as a monastic community, the College of Bonhommes, and became a royal residence in 1539 following the Dissolution of the Monasteries. The gothic style of the grand new mansion designed by the Wyatts consciously evoked this royal and monastic past: although described as 'Elizabethan Gothic' by Repton, it was more medieval in character and featured prominent statuary representing ecclesiastical and royal figures. Repton also attempted, in his design for the grounds, to create a connection with this romantic past as well as gardens which fitted in well with the style of the mansion. Some areas of the gardens thus have a decidedly antiquarian feel that in part reflects the influence of John Adey, who became a respected antiquary and published extensively on early architecture. But not all of Repton's design was intended to reflect the medieval past. As Stephen Daniels has noted: 'Within the compass of the plans for Ashridge are described deeper and wider historical and geographical worlds, both ancient and modern, retrospective and prospective, traditional and experimental.'[4]

The gardens thus demonstrate, in particular, Repton's awareness of the need to accommodate new styles and new forms of planting. In the early years of the nineteenth century the sheer scale of the influx of new plant species from abroad meant that

handwritten note to accompany working drawings of the 'Modern Pleasure Ground', the text of which we transcribe below, accompanied by illustrations that we also reproduce.

By the time Repton was commissioned by the earl he was not in good health. The ongoing effects of a carriage accident a few years earlier, combined with a probable heart problem, meant that he may well have been in a wheelchair when he made his three visits to Ashridge between March and June 1813, accompanied by his son John Adey Repton, who worked closely with his father from *c.*1800 after training as an architect with William Wilkins senior and John Nash – both of whom worked closely with Repton himself, the former at the start of his career, the latter in the mid–late 1790s. The area he was asked to advise on covered only *c.*15 acres and, although occupying the summit of a hill, was almost level, making access easy and ensuring that the commission, in it was difficult to include them all in a single garden. A range of separate spaces was required, to provide clear definition and coherent planting themes. At Ashridge Repton's proposals thus included an arboretum for exotic trees, a garden dedicated to magnolias and American plants (introduced on a large scale from the middle of the eighteenth century, and avidly collected and displayed by the wealthy), and a grotto and garden for rock plants.

Repton was given an almost free hand within the area of the commission. The whole site had been cleared of earlier buildings and features and, with the exception of avenues of lime, yew and elm, a wire fence and some areas of shrubbery – possibly established by Brown, who had worked at Ashridge some 50 years earlier – was effectively a blank canvas. Repton's plan involved dividing this area into two sections. The eastern, the 'Ancient Garden', was designed in the eighteenth-century landscape tradition of Brown and his contemporaries and consisted of a wide lawn flanked by planting. The western half of the grounds, in contrast – the 'Modern Pleasure Ground' – comprised a collection of 15 distinct garden areas. Many of these were created in the form Repton proposed and others were partially implemented, subtle amendments being made as the gardens were laid out between 1813 and 1823 under the supervision of the estate steward, William Buckingham, and the architect Jeffry Wyatt. Buckingham noted the three visits of Repton to Ashridge in his diary, and describes how, following one of these on 31 March 1813, he sat down with Mr Atty, agent to the earl, and looked at 'Mr Repton's drawings'. These words were written in a gothic script, clearly a reference to the consciously archaic style of many of Repton's themed gardens, and perhaps an indication that the agent saw them as a little twee or affected in character.[5]

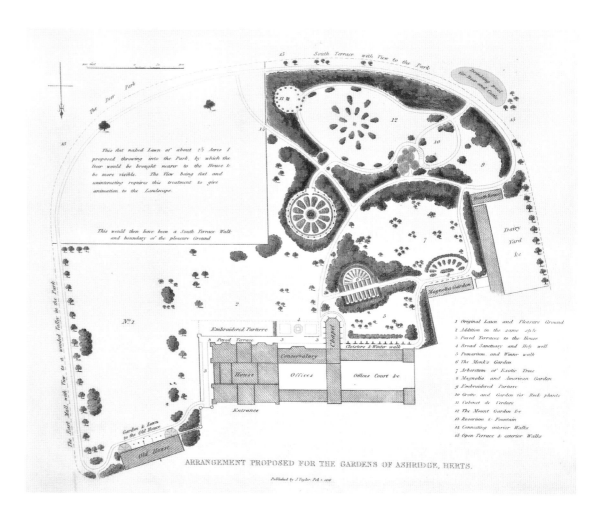

7   Plan of the gardens at Ashridge, published by Repton in *Fragments on the Theory and Practice of Landscape Gardening*, 1816.

THE ROSARY AT ASHRIDGE

London Published Feb 1st 1816 by J. Taylor

Peacock's *Polite Repository* in 1809, probably indicating an earlier involvement at Ashridge (the veranda attached to the house is very much in his style (Figure 6)). He now retained much of the existing layout, including the arrangement of shrubberies framing the lawn and the formal line of ancient limes adjacent to the east terrace. He proposed extending the lawn westwards, beyond the south front of the new mansion, so that it connected with his 'Modern Pleasure Ground', a suggestion that was carried out by Wyatt (Figure 7). The distant boundary was planted with shrubberies, complementing in style those already existing, thus providing a frame for the view south from the state rooms of the mansion.

It was the 'Modern Pleasure Ground' that was more innovative, not only because it contained a large number of distinct and specialised gardens but also in the liberal use of trelliswork to provide structure and support for climbers. In addition, while in some of the various gardens plants of different colours and forms were intermingled, as had been general in eighteenth-century pleasure grounds – and which continued into the nineteenth century, being advocated by, for example, Henry Phillips in his books of the 1820s[6] – in the Rosarium Repton employed a single type of plant, the rose, in blocks of uniform colour. This marked part of a significant shift in garden design that Paxton in 1838 was to describe as a change from the 'old practice of having a variety of plants in one large bed, and arranging them according to their height and colour' to the new system of 'grouping plants of one sort in small beds'.[7] Rose gardens in themselves were not entirely new. Brown's contemporary Richard Woods had created a 'Rosary Saloon' at Copford Hall (1784) and a 'Rosary' at Audley End (1780), both in Essex; more famously, a rose garden had been created for the Empress Josephine at the villa

The 'Ancient Garden', as named by Repton, extended southwards from the site of the earlier house at Ashridge (designed by Henry Holland for the third duke of Bridgewater), which became the location of an orangery designed by Jeffry Wyatt. Repton had made a drawing of this house that was published in

Malmaison near Paris in 1798. Repton himself had already created an example at Courteenhall in Northamptonshire in 1791, and was soon to design another at Endsleigh in Devon in 1814 – the latter with a circular arrangement of beds similar to that at Ashridge. But, because an illustration of the Ashridge Rose Garden was published in *Fragments*, it seems to have proved particularly influential, even in Europe (Figure 8). Prince Pückler-Muskau, a German admirer of Repton who wrote a book on landscape design, created a very similar garden at his home in Bad Muskau and another at the Schloss Babelsberg in Potsdam, Berlin.

Because most of the rose varieties available before the middle of the nineteenth century flowered for only one or two months of the year, and did not otherwise form attractive shrubs, early rose gardens were generally screened from the surrounding grounds by hedging or areas of shrubbery. Doubts have been raised over whether the colours and forms of the roses depicted by Repton in his illustration of the Ashridge Rosarium could have been achieved with the plants available at the time – about which Repton perhaps knew little.[8] Gallicas and Centifolias would have been suitable for the central beds, as they grow to a height of 70 cm and 130 cm, while the Portland rose (developed in 1790) could also be kept to around 60 cm in height if regularly pruned. But the red climbers shown were not yet available, nor were any climbers with such large flowers. Indeed, few red roses of any kind were yet in use, with the notable exception of Slater's Crimson China, which appeared around 1792; and bush roses were generally taller and leggier than those which Repton depicted, unless their branches were pinned down. The trellis would probably have been clothed not with climbers but with tall shrub roses, trained and tied – perhaps

vigorous varieties of Albas (white), Centifolias (pink) and Gallicas. Frankfurt roses (*Rosa x francofurtana*) such as 'Agathe' and 'Empress Josephine' (both pink), which are closely related to Gallicas, can reach 150 cm and could have been employed in the same way.

The enclosed, circular form of the garden can be viewed in two ways: in simple terms, as a continuation of the circular arrangements of flower beds seen in the work of Jacques Mollet, Thomas Wright, Capability Brown and Repton himself; or as another reference to the medieval past, its shape imitating the rose windows seen in many cathedrals. The Rose Garden was eventually laid out ten years after Repton had proposed it – by Jeffry Wyatt, as he was completing the work on the house – in the central position within the garden originally envisaged, but using the pattern of beds shown in the overall plan of the gardens provided by Repton, rather than as depicted in his specific illustration of the garden: that is, with eight beds, not twelve. It was also provided with a more elaborate fountain at its centre than Repton had envisaged and was enclosed by a yew hedge, rather than with the trelliswork originally proposed. By this time further varieties of rose had become available, and may have been employed. Additional Portlands, valuable for their repeat-flowering qualities, included 'Rose du Roi' (1815, also known as Lee's Crimson Perpetual) and 'Rose du Roi à Fleurs Pourpres' (1819).

Adjacent to the Rose Garden was the Monk's Garden, Repton's clearest attempt to evoke associations with the medieval monastic past. Here Repton had picked up on comments made by the antiquary Richard Gough about the discovery of medieval stone coffins in the area, and the garden comprised rows of beds, each with a false headstone, representing the graves of monks. As

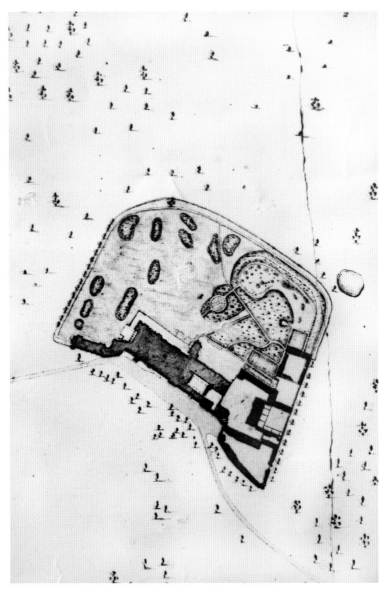

9   This Ashridge estate plan of 1823 confirms that most of the features proposed by Repton for the gardens were, in fact, created.

Repton put it: 'This Singular Spot, like the Stone at its Entrance, carries the mind back to former ages, when this little inclosure form'd the Retreat of the ancient inhabitants of the Monastery at Ashridge.'[9] Later, in *Fragments*, he quoted Mrs Erskine's description of the garden, with its:

> Close clipp'd box, th' embroider'd bed,
> In rows and formal order laid,
> And shap'd like graves.[10]

The entrance to the garden evoked an even earlier period of time, taking the form of a megalithic structure, 'The County Stone', that also served as a very specific reference to Ashridge's location astride the county boundary between Hertfordshire and Buckinghamshire.

Other gardens proposed by Repton similarly referenced the past. The Broad Sanctuary, the focal point of the whole pleasure ground, was to have a 'Holie Well' dedicated to St Benedict as its central feature. The latter, as drawn by John Adey Repton, was clearly based on traditional market crosses, and in particular on the elaborate medieval 'Eleanor Crosses' seen locally at Dunstable and St Albans. The well also acted as a conduit within a complicated set of waterworks linked to the well beneath the Chapel, in spite of the fact that Ashridge – located high in the Chiltern Hills – always suffered from problems of water supply.

The Broad Sanctuary was never in fact created and, while the County Stone was erected, it was in a less imposing and dramatic form than Repton had envisaged. Jeffry Wyatt did, however, lay out the Monk's Garden, albeit somewhat modified in appearance. It is clearly shown on an estate map of 1823 (Figure 9) and in the plan in H.J. Todd's *History of the College of Bonhommes at Ashridge*, published in the same year.[11] In addition, Wyatt created a garden to his own design, featuring a classical French parterre, that he called the French Garden, which was positioned immediately below the fifteenth-century Monk's Barn, with a version of Repton's Holie Well at its centre: confusingly, this area is today referred to as the Monk's Garden.

It is noteworthy that the illustration of the Holie Well included by Repton in *Fragments* includes (unlike that in the original proposals) a view of the Rose Garden and of the entrance to the Monk's Garden (Figures 10 and 11). All three features were references to Ashridge's monastic past, and all were connected by a circuit path that continued on from the Monk's Garden, via a covered walkway, to the Flower Stove, a heated greenhouse with another 'embroidered parterre' placed in front of it: maps of 1823 and 1857 show that these were, indeed, created.[12] The route continued through the 'Souterrein' – a subterranean passage – into the Countess of Bridgewater's Flower Garden, the layout of which was evidently influenced by the flower garden created by William Mason at Nuneham Courtenay, Oxfordshire, in the 1770s. These features, too, were created much as Repton had proposed, although the Flower Garden was never provided with the elaborate treillage shown on his drawing, Wyatt opting instead for a screen of laurel and yew. Other features proposed by Repton included an arboretum, an American garden and a rustic arbour, which was to have been placed where Wyatt laid out his French Garden, and which was created in 1996 in a different part of the grounds.

Much of Repton's design for the gardens at Ashridge was thus implemented, if in modified form, and even where Repton's

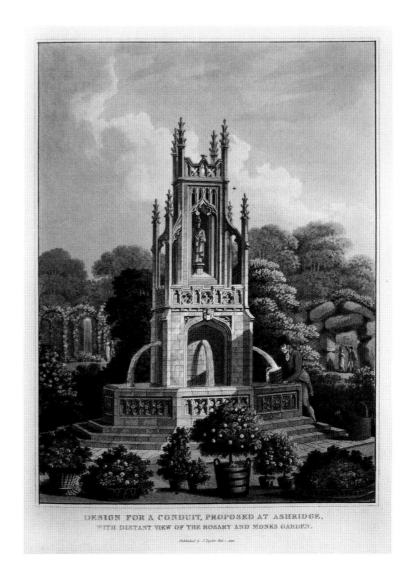

DESIGN FOR A CONDUIT, PROPOSED AT ASHRIDGE, WITH DISTANT VIEW OF THE ROSARY AND MONKS GARDEN.

Published by J. Taylor Feb.ᵧ 1816

10   The 'Holie Well', taken from *Fragments*.

FENCES, CALLED INVISIBLE

Published by J Taylor Feb 1 1816

11 The fences at Ashridge, taken from *Fragments*.

proposals were not adopted they often influenced the form of the gardens as these developed through the early nineteenth century. His proposed garden for magnolias and American plants, for example, was not established, but magnolias were planted against the house and a range of American trees and shrubs were placed throughout the gardens. Similarly, the terrace proposed by Repton was only partially created, but was added to in 1889 and now runs the length of the south front of the house; and, while the Broad Sanctuary never materialised, the Holie Well was constructed, broadly as designed by John Adey Repton, in Wyatt's French Garden. However, Repton's gardens were extensively modified in the course of the nineteenth century. The Monk's Garden was removed in 1829 by Charlotte, Countess of Bridgewater; a formal Italian Garden was created within the northern section of the 'Ancient Garden' around 1854; and the Flower Stove was replaced by a purpose-built Fernery, designed by Mathew Digby Wyatt, in the mid-1860s. Wyatt's French Garden was modified in the 1860s when the four quarters were planted by Lady Marian Alford as a floral representation of the coats of arms of the principal families involved with Ashridge.

The chief features of the gardens at Ashridge, especially the Rose Garden and the French Garden, have been carefully and extensively restored over the last two decades and work is continuing on the Souterrein, a significant feature on the main route through the gardens. In the absence of any plant lists, varieties described in a plan of 1799 for the flower garden at nearby Hartwell House, Buckinghamshire, have been employed, except in the Rose Garden, which is currently planted with nineteenth- and early twentieth-century repeat-flowering varieties.

Report Concerning the Gardens of Ashridge
Respectfully Submitted to The Earl of Bridgewater

&c &c &c

By his Lordship Most Obedient Humble Servant

H Repton

To The Earl of Bridgewater

My Lord,

When your Lordship first did me the honour to ask my opinion, I did not immediately see, by what expedients, a pleasure ground might be made to correspond with the Style & Importance of the Building; according to the modern practise of Landscape Gardening: The more I have since thought on the subject the more I am convinced, that something different from the meagre Serpentine Taste of Modern Invention, is imperiously call'd for at Ashridge & I hope therefore that Your Lordship will permit me, in the following pages to deliver my sentiments more fully on so important a Subject.

I must consider that I am adapting adequate Pleasure Grounds, to a Palace, which under Your Lordships auspices & Direction & the Cooperation of Correct Taste in the Architect, will be a lasting specimen of the happy combination of Ancient Grandeur & Modern Comfort: to both of these I now humbly hope to contribute something in my Department, and for the opportunity of so doing I have the honor to be

My Lord   Your Lordships much obliged
                 as well as very humble Servant

H. Repton

At Ashridge February 16 1813.
Plans made
At Harestreet near Romford March 20.

Introduction

After almost half a century, passed in the Parks and Gardens of England, and during much of that time, professionally consulted on their improvement; I am fully convinced that Fashion has frequently misled Taste by confounding the scenery of <u>Art</u> and <u>Nature</u>. And while I have acceded to the combination of two words <u>Landscape</u> and <u>Gardening</u> yet they are as distinct objects as the Picture and its Frame. The scenery of Nature called Landscape, and that of a Garden, are as different as their uses: one is to please the eye, the other is for the comfort and occupation of man: one is wild and may be adapted to animals in the wildest state of Nature, while the other is appropriated to man in the highest state of Civilization and Refinement. We therefore find that altho' Painters may despise gardens as subjects for the pencil, yet Poets, Philosophers and Statesmen have always enjoyed and described the pure delights of Garden scenery.

A Garden as the appendage to a place of such importance as Ashridge is no trifling consideration; and it ought well to be weighed before we sacrifice one of the most splendid and costly works of <u>Art</u> to the reigning rage for <u>Nature</u>, and all that is deemed <u>natural</u>. It will perhaps be said, that where we work with Nature's materials, the production should imitate Nature; but it might with equal propriety be asserted, that a house being built of Rocks and stones, should imitate a cavern.

In the vast edifice of Ashridge the Style and Costume of ancient date, of rich and purest Gothic, has been correctly preserved and imitated by the genius and classic taste of the Architect judiciously directed by his noble Employer; but we cannot with propriety go back to the same date in the style of the Gardens, because it has been justly observed by Lord Bacon "When ages grow to civility and elegancy men come to build stately, sooner than to garden finely, as if Gardening were the greater perfection".

Let us then begin by defining, what a Garden is, and what it ought to be. It is a piece of ground fenced off from <u>cattle</u> and appropriated to the use and pleasure of <u>Man</u>: it is or ought to be cultivated and enriched by Art, with such products as are not natural to this country, and consequently it must be artificial in its treatment, and may without impropriety be so in its appearance. Yet there is so much of littleness in Art, when compared with Nature, that they cannot well be blended. It were therefore to be wished, that the <u>exterior</u> of a garden should be made to assimilate with Park scenery or the Landscape of Nature, and the <u>interior</u> may then be laid out with all the variety, contrast, and even whim, that can produce pleasing objects to the Eye, however ill adapted as studies for a picture. This forms the basis of what I shall have the honour to suggest at Ashridge, and if my pencil has given inadequate representations of Scenes, not yet existing, I may plead in my excuse that I am not a painter, and if I were, my subjects could not be painted: yet they may serve better than mere words to realize and bring before the Eyes of others, those ideas which have suggested themselves to my own imagination.

"Segnius irritant animos demissa per aures.
Quam quæ sunt oculis subjecta fidelibus."
["What we hear, With weaker passion will affect the heart, Than when the faithful eye beholds the part"].[14]

Of Ancient Gardening

It fortunately happens at Ashridge, that the area proposed to be dedicated to Garden and Pleasure ground, is bounded both to the East and to the West, by a straight line of lofty trees: these give a character of antiquity and grandeur to the site, and prove it to have existed before serpentine lines were introduced. I cannot here omit mentioning, the having been told, that when Mrs Siddons objected to the straight braids represented in her celebrated picture in the Character of the Tragic Muse, and requested Sir Joshua Reynolds to let the hair flow in more graceful ringlets, that great Master observed, "that without straight lines there might be grace or beauty, but there could be no greatness or sublimity": and this same rule must hold in Gardening as in Painting. It is therefore with peculiar satisfaction I observed the straight lines of walks near the house, and that Mall to the East in a line with the trees: but I fear I may not have sufficient influence immediately to effect my line of boundary, and Walk to the South: from the common objection of what is call'd cutting up a Lawn; tho' in fact, if a Walk or a ha-ha be well made, they will both become invisible at a little distance when viewed transversely, as shown in this section.

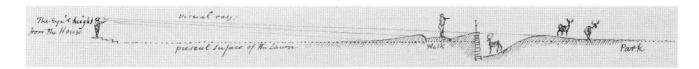

12   Red Book: cross-section of the lawn and ha-ha.

The eye should only see one continued surface of grass; this at Ashridge will be more easily accomplished, because from the nature of the substratum, there will be no water in the bottom of the fosse however deep it may be made.

I can hardly expect, that the line of wire fence should be immediately altered; but as it must very soon perish, it becomes my duty to point out a different line for the future more durable boundary of the Gardens: and this alteration will throw out at least three acres of ground, which must otherwise be kept mown; since no plantations can possibly be made on the same, without injuring the View of the Park. The only use that could be made of these three acres, would be an open Cricket ground, which may either be in the park or excluded from it: yet appear one surface with the intermediate space of Lawn which I have called the Bowling green. This is an appendage perfectly accordant with the ideal date and character of the building, and would be still more perfect by extending the walk from the East terrace to form the quadrangle complete. These Walks may all be considered as part of the original artificial, and truly magnificent style of Gardening in former times, when Art was avowed as artificial, and was no otherwise connected with Nature, than as a frame with a picture, its costliness bespeaking its value.

Of Modern Gardening

When the straight Walks and lofty walls of Ancient Gardening, had disgusted, by their sameness, prevailing in all places alike whether great or small, it was naturally to be supposed, that Fashion would run into the opposite extreme, by making every thing <u>curved</u> as the greatest contrast to <u>straight</u>. Thus because the winding footpath across the <u>uneven</u> surface of a field, was that line which Nature directed, every thing became <u>serpentine</u>, this was deemed the <u>line of beauty</u>, and was adopted as the model for all lines, whether of roads – of walks – of water, and even of fences to plantations: for it was asserted by some that "<u>Nature abhors a straight line,</u>" yet if we look at the surface of the ocean, or only at the extensive plain in the South front of Ashridge and its distant horizontal range of wood, we shall confess that there is a grandeur in straight lines which Nature does not abhor. There are situations "Where <u>Space</u>, not <u>Beauty,</u> spreads out its delights". It is only the Excess of any thing that ceases to give delight, for the mind of man requires variety. Now there can hardly be an object of less interest, after the first hundred paces, than a meandring Walk betwixt two broad verges of grass, at so great a distance from the beds of flowers and shrubs, that they are not to be distinguished; added to which we often see a uniform mixture of every kind of plant, so, that no one part of the garden differs from another. Of such Scenery, the Poet might aptly complain

Prim gravel walks thro' which we winding go
In endless serpentines, that nothing shew
Till tir'd I ask 'Why this eternal round?
And the pert gardener says 'Tis Pleasure Ground'.
                  *R P Knight

Yet there are many Pleasure-grounds of this kind, with Walks of a mile which I have shuddered to encounter & for this reason, I have never advised such Walks except as the connecting lines leading to other objects; and these should be contrasted with each other, and varied by the Style, Character, Growth and Selection of the different plants in different parts. Of this the Map will give some idea: and the Table describing the Walks with the objects to which they lead will show the variety proposed.

But I must first say a few words respecting <u>Water</u> and <u>Fences</u>.

Water

The water at Ashridge is by Art brought from a deep well or collected from rain in numerous Tanks, and this must be pumped up into reservoirs. Now it would be possible to lead pipes from such reservoirs, in such manner, that every drop of water used for the gardens, should be made visible in different ways: in one place as a <u>jet d'eau</u> in the rosary, in another as a falling shower or dropping well, near the Souterrein; and from hence the waste pipes might be led to keep up the water in the Park pool. But the greatest effect would be obtained from a conduit or apparent <u>holy well</u> near the Greenhouse: this might be thrown up from the well, and the surplus would find its way into the Tank beneath; thus with <u>actual scarcity,</u> there might be an appearance of great <u>command of water</u>. Perhaps a contrivance might be introduced to filter this water by ascent; and make an artificial bubbling fount of the purest and brightest colour. It is not necessary for me to describe the various expedients by which this could be effected, in a place where so much Taste and contrivance have already been evinced; all I wish to hint is the possibility of making much of a little water, at the same time losing none. In Garden scenery a fountain is more lively than a pool, and as the nature of a chalk soil will not admit of those imitations of rivers and lakes, which

---

*   The Modern Style has been very severely, though with some justice, ridiculed in the Landscape, a Poem by R. P. Knight Esq' in which my name has been traduced by mistake. Mr K. supposes me a servile follower of all Mr Brown's practice, because I ventured to defend some parts of it: but as his work speaks my own ideas on other parts, I take the liberty of quoting from it.

modern Gardening deems essential to a Landscape; and as in proportion as a thing is more rare, it becomes more valuable: it is the duty of the Improver to make every drop of water <u>visible,</u> that can be obtained; for besides the pleasure the Eye takes in seeing water, we cannot but consider it of the utmost consequence to a garden, where if the <u>labour</u> of <u>pumping</u> cannot be avoided, it ought to be <u>carried on unseen</u>; lest our choice of the site for a garden should be condemned in these words of Isaiah "And ye shall be confounded for the gardens that ye have chosen, for ye shall be as an oak, whose leaf fadeth, and as a garden that hath no water".[15]

Of Fences

The most important of all things relating to a Garden, is that which cannot contribute to its beauty; but without which a Garden cannot exist. The fence must be effective and durable, or the irruption of a herd in one night, would lay waste the cost and labour of many years.

Every thing at Ashridge is on a great scale of substantial and permanent grandeur, and the fence to the gardens should doubtless be the same. The deep walled ha.'ha' invented by Brown, was seldom used by him but to give a View thro' some glade, or to give security to a terrace walk, from whence (as my late friend Mr Windham used to say) "it is delightful to see two bulls fighting without the possibility of danger". This cannot be said of that wire birdcage expedient which has of late years been introduced to save the expence of a more lasting barrier; and though it may be sufficient to resist sheep or even cows for a few years in the Villas near London, yet the mind is not satisfied when a vicious Stag approaches it with undaunted eye and a mien not to be terrified. Add to this the misery of viewing a Landscape thro' a prison bar, or misty gauze veil, ranging above the eye; and also that iron is a material of which we have had but little experience, except that it too soon decays. For this reason a line is shewn on the map which may hereafter be adopted, for I must consider the present wire fence only as a temporary expedient. I might also add another argument against invisible fences in general (except in short glades) viz. that when they divide a park from a garden, they separate two things which the mind knows cannot be united, since it is evident that flowers cannot grow amongst cattle and that cattle ought not to be admitted amongst flowers and therefore such fence may, in parts be visible, to satisfy the Eye as well as the Mind.

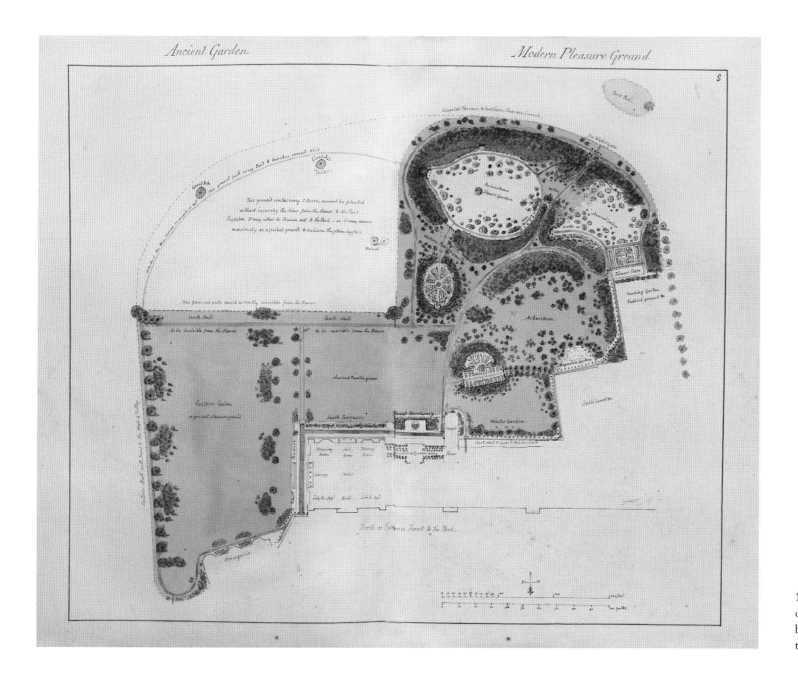

13   Red Book: Repton's overall plan
of the gardens, showing the distinction
between the 'Ancient Garden' and
the 'Modern Pleasure Ground'.

14   Red Book: view from terrace, looking south, 'before'.

15   Red Book: view from terrace, looking south, 'after'.

Walks (measured from the Scale)

		Length in yards	Breadth in feet
1	Straight Terrace attached to the House South front	80	12
	East front	55	10
2	Connecting line in front of Orangerie	100	8
3	Present Mall with View to the East	150	8
4	Proposed invisible Mall, with view to the South	180	8
5	Circular Terrace (including Winter Walk)	320	8
6	Covered Walk from the Chapel & the Flower stove	180	6
7	Leading line thro' Western pleasure ground	170	8
8	Branch from the same to the Water gate	70	6
9	Branch thro' Monk's garden and Berceau Walk	60	5
10	Path to the great Ash trees in the Park	200	4
11	Various Walks in the interior from	200 to 250	3 to 5

Variety of Objects to which these Walks lead

		Length in yards	Breadth yards	Area Square yards
1	The front Lawn, or ancient Bowling green Garden	85	x75	6,375
2	The Orangerie and present Eastern Pleasure ground	150	x100	15,000
3	The Arboretum, or open Grove of rare Trees	80	x65	4,800
4	The Western pleasure ground in glades and Walks	520	x20	10,400
5	The Flower Garden and American borders	80	x65	4,800
6	The garden for annual flowers	50	x35	1,750
7	The Garden for Rock plants &c	30	x7	210
8	The Souterrein Grotto and dropping well	17	x6	102
9	The Rosary a small area opening into larger	30	x20	600
10	The Monk's Garden and its Rock Entrance	25	x20	500
11	The great Berceau of Lime Trees	30	x8	240
12	The Magnolia Garden	25	x10	250
13	The home Winter Garden and Covered Walks	180	x9	1540
14	The Sanctuary and Holie Well of St. Benedict.	35	x25	875
	also including the Conservatory as being a coverd part of the same			

16 Red Book:
the 'Water Gate'.

WATER GATE

This Vignette gives some idea of the manner in which the Park Pool may be shewn to advantage from a walk in a plantation when by concealing its boundary the water is magnified in appearance but for this effect a Gate or wall are requisite, or the ends of the pool will be visible.

17   Red Book: the 'Park Pool'.

18   Red Book: the Flower Stove.

PARK POOL. [pencil note: vid. Repton Horse Pond – Bridgwater]

The effect of Cattle assembled in large herds, on the banks of a pool, however small; & the glitter of its Water in a South West exposure, are features not to be neglected in a Chalk soil, where a large expanse of water is not to be expected.

The Flower Stove.

It is impossible to represent such a subject in a Landscape yet in reality, it is one of the chief <u>agrèmens</u> [*sic*] of Garden Comfort and the formal embroider'd parterre is in Character with it. Perhaps an Apiary with Glass Beehives might be added.

19   Red Book: the Arboretum.

20   Red Book: the 'Souterrein'.

ARBORETUM

An open grove of choice trees, forming part of a Modern Pleasure ground this sketch shews the sort of Seat & Coverd-way composed of Yews, that (not too much exposed) may be applicable to such a Grove, altho' beneath the dignity of Ashridge to be seen from the House.

The Souterrein

This represents the Entrance from the West & forms part of an Assemblage of Flints &c for the culture of Rock plants. If not too fanciful, a Grotto-like appearance may be given.

21   Red Book: the 'Rosarium'.

22   Red Book: the Flower Garden.

ROSARIUM.

This sketch of the interior of a Rose garden, shews a lighter sort of Trellis, than that of the flower garden, but to secure its durability, the hoops may be formed of Iron.

Flower Garden

This sketch is supposed to be taken from the East Entrance of the Souterrein shewing the sort of <u>Cabinets de Verdure</u>, composed of more massive trellis, than that described in the Rosarium.

23 Red Book: the 'County Stone'.

24 Red Book: the 'Monk's Garden'.

The County Stone.

This ancient Boundary betwixt the Counties of Buck[s]: & Hert[s], is here supposed to be raised on other stones of the same kind, to form the Entrance to the Monks Garden & may be also enriched with Rock plants.

THE MONK'S GARDEN

This Singular Spot, like the Stone at its Entrance, carries the mind back to former ages, when this little inclosure form'd the Retreat of the ancient inhabitants of the Monastery at Ashridge.

25 Red Book: the
Winter Garden.

THE WINTER GARDEN.

To connect the Conservatory with the Flower stove & Winter Garden by a Coverd-Way or Walk (like that at Woburn) would not only be useful in Winter, but in Summer it would be the best expedient for hiding the Walls & buildings, which woud be seen from any walk near them. This may be compared to making a friend of a too powerful Enemy.

The Holie Well

Dictum Benedicti Bene dictum
Thus Holie Benedictus wel mote saye
An Holie Wel, shal rise in future daye.
Then Wyn unmixte, and Water shal unite,
To *merke* the *past*: and *fixe* the *future* Site.

26 Red Book: the 'Holie Well'.

THE BROAD SANCTUARY

This sketch shews the effect of St Benedicts well & the flowers on the Terrace, to enliven the Corner darken'd by the broad Shade, thrown from the Chapel by an evening Sun.

27   Red Book: the 'Broad Sanctuary'.

Hand-written notes that accompany the portfolio of drawings and text for The Gardens of Ashridge by Humphry Repton, March 1813 (see Figures 28–30)

The Outlines of the Skreens being markd on the ground it is only necessary to explain the sort of plants for which this General rule may be given. The small dotted green shews smaller plants as Laurels – Shrubs &c to the South Aspect & American Evergreens towards the North Aspect.

Where the Skreens follow the line of the Walks, there should be a verge of <turf> 18 inches & the border to be dug with Roses & herbaceous plants near the walk – but where the skreen is towards the lawn & no walk near – it should not be dug – nor any defined line – but some ornamental plants may be left out detach'd from the Mass of skreen.

Those parts of the plan where large blotches of Green appear are supposed to be forest trees intermixd with the Shrubbery.

Of the interiors

A – to be surrounded by a skreen of dwarf Plants only may have an inner border of roses & the area to be after wards thrown into beds for roses only in different small patches, as a Rosary.

B & C – are left open to let in the sunshine but they may be considerd as two separate gardens in point of Character – thus.

B will consist of small beds surrounded some with trellis – some basket work – some edgings of various kinds & each to contain one Class of flowers & all the seats – Berceaux &c should be of substantial Versails trellis. This Garden B to be connected <with C> by a Subterranious grotto like passage in a dell to be a place for Rock plants & all the small patches in this Garden C. to be borderd with flints & perhaps some masses of stone for the rock plants.

D – where this area is open'd & cleard of many or most of the trees it may <be> used for flowers or for the more rare exotic shrubs & trees as an open Grove or Arboretum.

E – will form a part of the Same Area but divided by a Shaded walk formd by a berceau walk of clipd lime trees & the seats, gate & ornaments of these areas may be of yew grotesque including the Barn & the fence towards the Back road which may be a coverd walk to the stables.

The Square Box area to have an iron gate in the Pudding stone & the great Boundary mark'd & at the other end a gate of Yew tree.

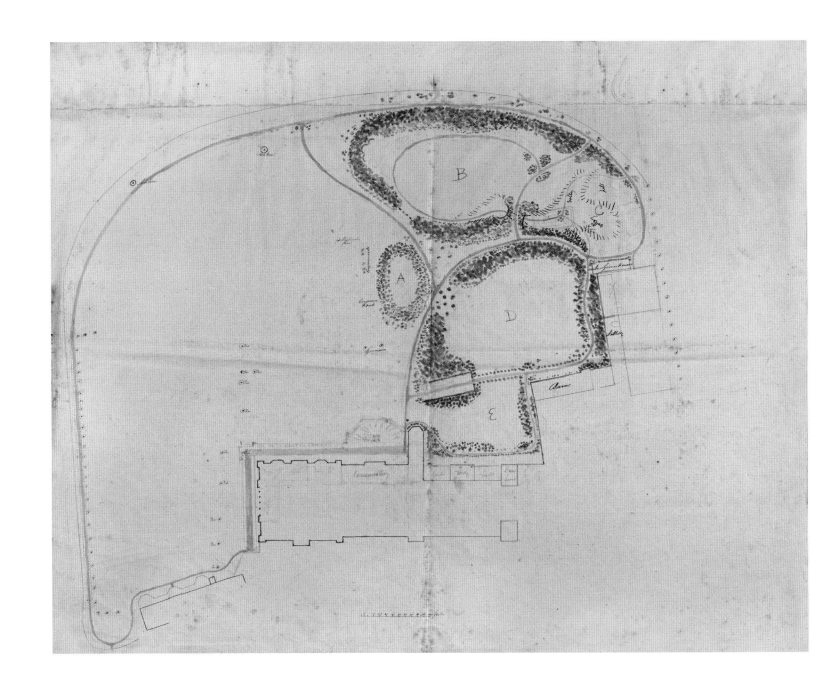

28 Repton's working plan of
the 'Modern Pleasure Ground'.

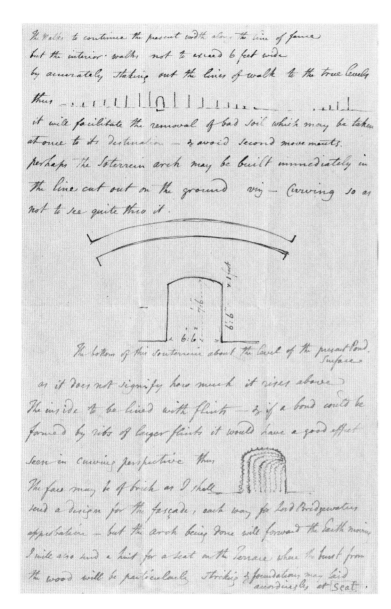

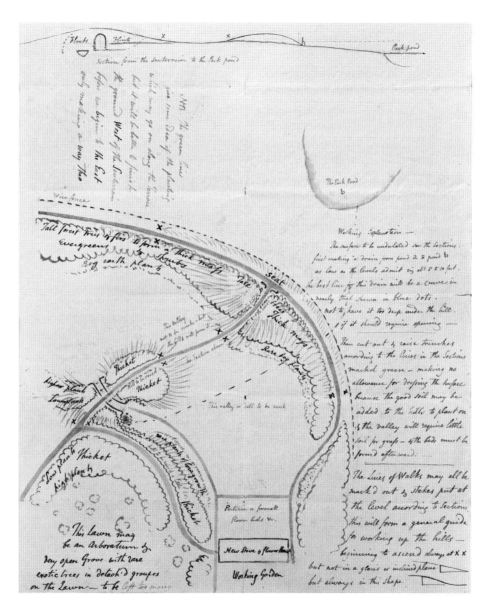

29   Illustrations included with the notes to accompany the working plan of the 'Modern Pleasure Ground', concerning construction of the 'Souterrein'.

30   Repton's annotated illustration of the 'Dell Garden'.

Notes

1 The editors are grateful to Professor Stephen Daniels for permission to use some of the notes from a lecture he presented at a conference celebrating the work of James Wyatt and Humphry Repton held at Ashridge in 2013. Our thanks also go to Dr Sarah Rutherford, for permission to use some of the notes from her Conservation Management Plan for the Gardens at Ashridge from 2011 and her introductory notes to a reproduction of the 'Red Book' for Ashridge produced in 2013.

2 Grid references relate to the mansion with which the designed landscape in question was associated.

3 Repton, *Fragments*, p. 147.

4 S. Daniels, unpublished lecture at Ashridge Summer School, August 2013.

5 HALS: DE/X230/Z1-3, diaries of William Buckingham, steward and agent to Francis, 3rd Duke of Bridgewater, 1813–14, 1822–27.

6 H. Phillips, *Sylva Florifera* (London, 1823) and *Flora Historica* (London, 1824). For a discussion of this transition see M. Laird, *The Flowering of the Landscape Garden: English pleasure grounds, 1720–1800* (Philadelphia, 1999).

7 *Paxton's Magazine of Botany*, quoted in D. Stuart, *The Garden Triumphant: a Victorian legacy* (London, 1988), p. 116.

8 The editors are indebted to Charles and Bridgid Quest-Ritson for their observations on Repton's rose garden and advice on the form and colours of roses available in the early nineteenth century.

9 Getty Research Institute, Los Angeles, California: 850834, H. Repton, *Report Concerning the Gardens of Ashridge*, March 1813.

10 Repton, *Fragments*, Fragment XXVII, p. 140.

11 H.J. Todd, *The history of the College of Bonhommes, at Ashridge, in the county of Buckingham, founded in the year 1276, by Edmund, earl of Cornwall* (London, 1823).

12 HALS: 56482, Ashridge estate plan 1823; Ashridge House archives: plan of 'Ashridge mansion and pleasure grounds', n.d. [1857].

13 Getty Research Institute, Los Angeles, California: 850834, H. Repton, *Report Concerning the Gardens of Ashridge*, March 1813.

14 From Horace, *Ars Poetica*, line 181.

15 Isa. 1:30.

Haileybury, Great Amwell

TL 358107

Haileybury is situated three miles (c.5 kilometres) south of Hertford, on soils formed in London clay and acid gravels.[1] In 1805 the Haileybury estate was placed on the market by its owner, William Walker, after he had inherited Swinnow Park in West Yorkshire.[2] It comprised a house with offices and outbuildings and an area of farmland, surrounded by properties owned by Charles Cowper of Goldingtons, Lord John Townshend of Balls Park and Colonel Charles Brown of Amwellbury. Walker had been a surgeon in the East India Company's service, and had purchased the house from Stephen Williams, a director of the Company. Haileybury was described in the 1805 auction advertisement as possessing 'extensive shrubbery walks, mount and grove' as well as pasture, meadows and paddocks. The site was flanked by heathland to the north and west, and by enclosed pastures on the other sides: Hailey Lane formed the southern boundary.

The Directors of the East India Company were looking for a freehold property to acquire as a site for a new college in which to train young men who were nominated to be 'writers', the junior administrators of the company. The premises they were currently using for the purpose, Hertford Castle, had become too small and was unsuitable in other ways. Having explored a number of possibilities, Haileybury was purchased on 23 October 1805 at auction for £5,900.[3] Soon afterwards, William Wilkins was chosen to design the new college, in preference to Henry Holland, the company's surveyor and architect. He was the son of William Wilkins senior, with whom Repton had worked in the early years of his career, and was a noted exponent of the Greek Revival style. He was later to design Downing College in Cambridge and University College, London. Haileybury was to provide accommodation for 100 students and their professors and to contain three public rooms (Figure 31). Humphry Repton was employed to design the grounds after the chairman, Edward Parry, was asked by the Committee of College in September 1808 to approach him.[4] In May 1807 the company's surveyor, Samuel Pepys Cockerell (who had succeeded Holland a few years earlier) had reported the lack of an adequate landscape setting for Wilkin's fine and imposing Greek Revival building.[5]

Repton visited the site in November 1808 and by January 1809 had completed his *Book of Plans, Sketches and Report*, which was presented to the Court of Directors (the governing body of the East India Company) on 25 January. It was then passed onto the Committee of College (responsible for running the college) for their consideration. According to a letter from Samuel Pepys Cockerell, dated 28 April 1809, and the Committee of College Minutes, all but one of Repton's initial recommendations for Haileybury were accepted.[6] He visited the site on six further occasions and produced two further reports during the course of 1809. He appeared before the Committee of College in

Overleaf
Left
31 Early nineteenth-century engraving of the south front of the East India College, Haileybury.

Right
32 Thomas Medland's aquatint of Haileybury College from the south, published in 1810. Repton's pools, which were in reality still under construction at the time, can be seen in the foreground.

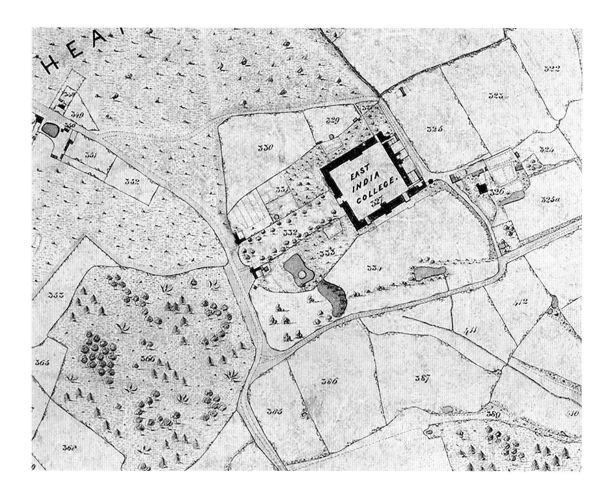

33 The earliest detailed map of Haileybury College and its grounds dates from 1836 and, while it shows the main features of Repton's work, may also depict subsequent additions and alterations.

of the East India Company held by the British Library.[7] The Haileybury and Imperial Service College Archive also includes the original Thomas Medland drawing of the south front of the East India College, on which the well-known 1810 aquatint of that title was based, and which was drawn as work on the building and its landscape was under way (Figure 32).[8] Although surveyed several decades later, a map of 1836 also shows what is probably the Repton landscape largely intact (Figure 33).[9]

Repton's design was conceived within a framework already agreed by the Committee of College: on 30 September 1808 the decision was taken to create an impressive western approach to the college along an avenue leading in from the London–Hertford turnpike road, and to divert Hailey Lane southwards in order to expand the grounds in that direction.[10] To realise this scheme it was necessary to exchange land with both Charles Cowper and Lord John Townshend, the latter for the southern extension and the diversion of Hailey Lane, the former to acquire land to the west of the college. Repton's main contributions were apparently to provide appropriate planting for the site, including the trees lining the western approach; to landscape the grounds to the south of the college; and to create the imposing terrace along the south side of the college, a feature partly intended to dispose of the large amounts of earth left after levelling the site but mainly, as he explained, because it was 'the only means worthy of the importance of such an Edifice' (Figure 34).[11] He also submitted proposals for creating an ornamental water feature – 'the Water'. These, after some deliberation, were rejected by the Committee, and Repton instead supplied a design for a more modest pool, created by extending some existing ponds (old brick pits) in the

January 1810 to make additional suggestions for the grounds and submitted a fourth report on the 22nd of that month, returning again in April to mark out some of his proposals on the ground. Unfortunately, the loss of the *Book of Plans* and of the second Report means that the full character of Repton's design remains unclear, but many of its principal features can be reconstructed from the material presented below, preserved among the records

34   Early nineteenth-century engraving showing Repton's great South Terrace.

south-western corner of the site (see Figure 36 below). This was provided with a central island and was fed by drains leading in from the turnpike road and from a sunken fence flanking the main western entrance. Interestingly, Repton also proposed erecting a tall boundary fence around the new southern boundary of the grounds, although with a 'sunk fence' performing this function to the south-east, presumably to avoid interrupting the view from the terrace (see Figure 35 below). This flanked a new service road, laid out to Repton's plan, which ran in from Hailey Lane. He was also involved in laying out the Principal's Garden, occupying the area immediately to the south of the entrance avenue; but not, apparently, in the design of the smaller gardens associated with the lodgings of the individual professors. Repton chose the Islington-based nurseryman Thomas Barr to provide plants and to oversee the landscaping work more generally, and he negotiated with the Committee on their joint behalf.[12]

A number of features of Repton's landscape survive at Haileybury:

1. The Terrace on which the college stands, offering a fine prospect to the south. The lawn below it, extending south to Hailey Lane, was substantially altered in 1863 and many of the trees were felled in 1865, following the 1862 re-opening of the institution as Haileybury College.

2. The boundaries of the Principal's Garden remain almost unchanged, although the pattern of walks designed by Repton has not survived.

3. The back road that Repton planned and Thomas Barr constructed is still in use, linking the London Road and Hailey Lane.

4. The Water, composed of two pools, designed by Repton remains and continues to be fed by the original system of land drains. The upper pool, located within the Principal's Garden, was partly silted up by 1862, leading to the loss of its original island.

5. The entrance avenue survives, but was altered in 1903 when the South African War Memorial was erected.

6. Little if anything of the planting proposed by Repton and executed by Barr survives, but the grounds retain a number of earlier trees – pollarded oaks – that were preserved by Repton when the landscape was laid out.

The full range of correspondence and other documents associated with Repton's activities at Haileybury, all in the British Library, is reproduced below. They provide both an unusually complete picture of his dealings with a client and detailed information about one of his only institutional commissions.

Letter from S. Cockerell, 18 May 1807[13]

To the Honourable the Committee of College

Gentlemen,

I beg leave to report to you that in considering the plans and specifications of the Works in the intended Buildings at Hayleybury, I am of opinion several Additions should be made thereto, to render the whole fully adequate to the purposes intended, in point of strength, security and other circumstances, incident to a Public Building of its extent and consequence; as any saving of any expense which occasions a slight and insufficient execution or a mean effect in the approach and principal apartments, is an eroneous economy unworthy of the subject, and inconsistent with the expence which is given to the principal exterior Front. The particulars may be comprized, under the following heads viz:

[…][14]

The dressing of Gardens and Ground, Fencing, planting and the restoring or leveling the Brick Grounds are not provided for, nor any Fence between the Gardens and Logias, so as to separate them from the Quadrangle.

The several Articles contained under the two last paragraphs do not interfere with the execution of the contract of the Building and may be provided for afterwards but the several preceeding observations are necessary to be decided upon before the works to which they relate are taken in hand.

I am

Honourable Sirs

Yours most obedient & faithful Servant

S Cockerill

18 May 1807

Extract from the minutes of Committee of College 30 September 1808[15]

That it will be very desirable to remove the road on the south side of the College Ground, further southward, if an exchange of land can be effected with Lord John Towneshend, in order to obtain more space in the South Front of the Building, and also to the Turnpike road to Hertford, if the same can be done, and that Dr Henley be desired to make such application to the Parties as may be necessary to obtain these Arrangements.[16]

That the Entrance to the College be by an Avenue from the Hertford Road to the Gate with two rows of Trees in each side – the sides whereof to be fenced with 6 feet oak palings.

That it would be expedient to procure a general design for laying out the Ground South of the College in the most judicious manner from Mr Repton, or some other person of reputation and skill in the practice of such Works to be laid before a Committee of College with an estimate of the expense of executing the same, and that the chairs be requested to apply of Mr Repton.

It is noteworthy that the entrance avenue, one of the key features of the grounds and one which – without this evidence – we might have been tempted to attribute to Repton, was clearly planned before Repton was commissioned.

Letter from S. Cockerell [to Mr Rundall, clerk to the Committee of College], 7 November 1808[17]

Dear Sir,

On survey of the Buildings at Hayleybury on Friday last, I found that the progress made since the last advance entitles Mr W Wilkins to the Instalment of £2,500 due on the 2nd Inst. & enclose my Certificate accordingly. I have added the request for my commission thereon, & will trouble you to prepare the warrant accordingly.

I will trouble you to acquaint the Committee that I attended Mr Repton at Hayleybury on Friday last, when we met Dr Henley, & went over the whole of the Ground together, explaining to Mr Repton every circumstances necessary for his consideration in forming a design for the Ground round the College; Mr Repton intends to take another View of it in the course of ten days after some levels have been taken of the Ground, & he will then recommend what occurs to him as fit to be done there, keeping in View the points suggested to him by the Chairman; and also the Ground proposed to be exchanged with Lord John Townshend & that to be enclosed from the Waste of Hertford Heath.

I am Dear Sir Your most obedient humble Servant.

S Cockerell

Saville Row 7 November 1808.

Extract from the minutes of Committee of College 10 November 1808[18]

A letter from Mr S. P. Cockerell dated the 7 instant representing the result of his and Mr Repton's inspection of the Grounds belonging to, and surrounding the new College, with a view to the Plan, for the laying out and planting the same, to be made by Mr Repton was read.

Letter from S Cockerell, 27 January 1809[19]

Sir,

I beg leave to lay before the Committee of Colleges when they take Mr Repton's design into Consideration the Plan of the Company's property at Hayleybury, which I had surveyed some time ago, for ascertaining the Exchanges to be made; a Copy of the outlines of this Plan was passed to Mr Repton by me, to assist in explaining his design, for forming the Grounds, to the committee – it will show more particularly the parts proposed to be taken, in exchanges, and to be enclosed.

It will also shew the present dispositions of the Grounds round the School Houses, which by the Committee's order is to be divided into two Dwellings for the Married professors & I have marked thereon in Pencil the division of Ground which I understand will be most acceptable to them, & may be most convenient in this arrangement.

I have also accompanied that Plan, with a plan of the several Stories of the School Houses, and of the manner in which it may more conveniently & cheaply be divided into two dwellings & shall be glad to know the pleasure of the Committee thereon, that Estimates may be formed of the Expence of executing it.

I observe that Mr Repton's dissertation does not take any Notice of the intended stables, & I presume the Committee will direct me to make designs for them, the situation decided by the Committee on the spot, seems to be marked out by Mr Repton in his Plan, & I presume the Committee will approve the Idea of forming one or two fives Courts at the back of the Stables & an Exercise Ground between them along the North side of the College.

I am Sir

Your most Obedient Humble servant

S P Cockerell

27 January 1809

Extract from the minutes of Committee of College 27 January 1809[20]

A letter from Mr Repton read and referred in Court the 25th Instant submitting his plans for forming and laying out the College Grounds at Haylebury being laid before the Committee. Ordered that it lie for further consideration.

'Heads under which Mr Barr has made his calculations for carrying into effect the plan delivered by H. Repton', February 1809[21]

Labour in Grubbing old hedges, making new, planting Quick.

Destroying the old road, forming new, finding faggots & gravel for the same.

Making Walks in the President's Garden, draining the Land where necessary, making brick drains across the Roads, ploughing & levelling the ground to the south & west, finding plants, barrows and tools.

Trenching for the Plantations, furnishing trees, shrubs, carriage & Labour in planting, Foreman & Expences of Journeys &c including a Reasonable profit for time & Responsibility   £1160 0s 0d.

Forming the water from 2 to 400 [cubic yards] – according to the extent of the Pool & the nature of the Soil & levels, which may be ascertained previously to its being begun.

Verso Read in Committee of College 24 February 1809

This is an interesting and rare example of Repton himself directly subcontracting the execution of a commission. The plans he prepared for private landowners were normally implemented using estate workers and/or with labour hired by the estate. This deviation from normal practice may in part be due to the fact that the College had no large pool of labourers in its employ and, given that it was still under construction, little in the way of staff of any kind.

Extract from the minutes of Committee of College 24 February 1809[22]

The Committee being met for the purpose of examining the Plans sent in by Mr H Repton, pursuant to the committee's resolution of the 10 November 1808, and which Plans were also referred by the Court of the 25 ultimo as to laying out the College Grounds at Hayleybury. And Mr Repton attending the Committee and delivering in an Estimate, prepared by Mr Barr, of the Expense of carrying the said Plans into effect.

Letter from H. Repton, 13 March 1809[23]

Hartford. March 13th 1809

Sir,

I have this morning been at Hayleybury College to examine & measure on the Spot the detail of that Estimate which I had the honor to state to the Committee as a General Amount & which I now inclose with such additional Specification as may enable the Committee to form a Contract for the due execution of the same if they should think proper – but on comparing this statement with that which I had before the honor to deliver a difference will appear, for which it is necessary to account & which I hope will be found explained by the following Items:

1st It was very properly suggested by the Committee that the avenue trees should be planted by trenching the ground instead of digging holes.

2nd It was suggested that the trees should be staked & I have added that any trees which may fail in the first two years, shall be replaced & made good.

3rd It has been proposed by the Company's Surveyor that the publick road should be gravel'd 9 inches instead of 7 Inches deep & that the private <Avenue> roads should be 12 feet instead of 10 feet wide – & the gravel a little deeper to which I readily assent from its propriety.

4th A very serious additional expence has been incurred by the quantity of earth wheeld out from the interior of the quadrangle & which must all be moved to a greater distance & which amounts to not less than 2,620 Cubic Yards at 14d (the price already paid by Mr Wilkins) would alone amount to £152 16s 4d – a circumstance which has taken place since Mr Barr made his first estimate. To all this might be added the difference between the actual measurement now taken with precision on the spot & the former which was taken from the map, & I trust the Committee will think the difference between the former Conjectural sum of £1,160 0s 0d & the present actual sum <of £1,350> for which the Contractor is ready to bind himself to do the whole, will be sufficiently explained – I have the honor to be Sir

Your most obedient

Humble Servant

H Repton

P.S. I am now on my way into the North of England, but shall return the middle of next month – when I shall be happy to give any further explanation in person – on the receipt of the Commands from the Committee.

'An estimate of Groundwork & Planting at Hayleybury College agreeable to Mr Repton's Plan' by T. Barr, 14 March 1809[24]

Grubbing & taking down old hedges, leaving the best trees & Masses of brush wood & levelling the banks – 320 Rods

Making new banks and ditches with good Quick; Ditches five feet wide & three feet six inches deep; banks three feet high – 315 Rods

New Publick road forming & graveling fifteen feet wide with brush wood under the road & the gravel nine inches thick in the crown – 106 Rods

New Avenue road forming gravel 12 feet wide with brush wood under seven inches thick in the crown – 114 Rods

New road within the premises & over the heath to join the Hertford road ten feet wide & six inches thick in the crown – 177 Rods

New walks in the Principal's garden six feet wide & six inches thick in the crown – 72 Rods

Digging up the old road & levelling it down – 102 Rods

Trenching the avenue rows ten feet wide – 81 Rods

Planting 420 Horse Chestnuts or Elms or Planes, good healthey trees from 11 to 12 feet high & having them properly staked & any trees to be replaced that shall fail in the first two years

Trenching for new Plantations & planting good healthey trees and shrubs of proper sorts for different situations agreeable to Mr Repton's directions in size & sorts & not more than five feet apart – 120

Removing into the valley at 150 yards distance a large quantity of clay brought out of the Quadrangle & laid on the west side of the College – 1,733 Cubic yards

Solid earth in the west front to be removed into the Valley to show the plinth of the Building & bring the roads to a proper level to the Gateways – 185 Cubic yards

Levelling and Ploughing the south & west side of the College & laying it down with Hay seeds, Dutch Clover, Trefoil & Rye Grass – the three acres on the Common to be Ploughed three times in the summer in order to kill the rushes

Hornbeam & Quick hedge on each side the avenue the ground to be trenched two feet wide

Two large heaps of earth on the south side the College will require to be removed – 700 Cubic yards

Shaping the sides of the sand Pit and Planting it

Hollow Draining the land & making brick Drains under the Roads where wanted

The following work is not taken into this Estimate viz:
Wooden Fences of all Kinds, Brick walls, Fruit trees, nor any work on the East or North of the college, except the new Private road leading through the Premises & over the Heath.

The whole of the work to be done as here specified in a good & workman like manner agreeable to Mr Repton's Plan & subject to his Approbation when finished for the sum of one Thousand three Hundred & Fifty pounds.

By me Thomas Barr
Balls Pond Nursery
14 March 1809

Thomas Barr founded his nursery at Balls Pond in Islington, on the west side of Newington Green Road, in 1791. It gradually increased in size and by 1806 covered around 11 acres (4.5 hectares).

Letter from S. Cockerell to Edward Parry, 16 March 1809[25]

Dear Sir,

I return you Mr Repton's letter with Mr Barr's estimate. I believe Mr Barr has intended a fair estimate, but I am not a judge that it is actually so, it is true that there is a great deal of Ground carried by Mr Wilkins out of the Quadrangle to the West, which must be moved again, & also to the South, the latter would form the Terrace if you decide to have A Terrace, Walk there but the Walk itself seems not to be included in the Estimate; nor does it seem to be decided upon, whether the Terrace shall be supported against the Lawn by a Wall with a Stone Coping upon it, & two very large flights of Steps equal to the breadth of the Logias, as described in Mr Repton's designs (which would cost at least £600) or whether the Terrace should be united with the Lawn by a steep Turf bank with two or three shallow flights of steps not above 10 feet wide each, the forming of which might cost £100 instead of six.

These sums also to be omitted in the Estimate: a fence to the Quick Hedges on each side as is customary in all new enclosures & which cannot cost less than 7s per rod for both sides of them or £110, and there must also be an addition of £600 for about 200 rods of Park pale fencing – these things brought together (exclusive <of pieces> of Water) in all add from Eight to thirteen hundred Pounds, according the Terrace may be expected for Works to the Grounds only forming a part of Mr Repton's design Estimated at £1,350.

I wish to receive Your directions as to what should be presented to the Committee on this occasion for their information.

I am Dear Sir Your faithfull, Humble Servant

Saville Row 16 March 1809

S P Cockerell

Edward Parry Esq

This letter is important in making clear that the idea of placing the College on a substantial formal terrace came from Repton, rather than from the architect William Wilkins.

Extract from the minutes of Committee of College 22 March 1809[26]

A letter from Mr J. Repton [*sic; recte* H. Repton] dated the 13th instant, advising his having examined on the spot, the detail of the Estimate he has before delivered as a general Account of the Expense of laying out the College Grounds etc and now submitting such additional specification as may enable the Committee to form a Contract for the due execution of the same if they should see proper, and stating the Amount at £1350 – also submitting Mr Barr's Estimate for executing the said Work, conforming to Mr Repton's plans, and a letter from Mr Cockerell the Company's Surveyor dated the 16th Instant, containing his Observations on the preceeding letter and Estimate, and requesting the Committee's directions in consequence.

Letter from S. Cockerell, 28 April 1809[27]

Dear Sir,

I have not been able to lay my hand on the Paper I had sketched out of the subject of the Secretary's letter to Mr Repton but the purport of it was, to inform him that the Court having adopted his design for the Grounds at Hayleybury reserving the Water for future consideration, the Committee has agreed with Mr Thomas Barr, Nurseryman according his Mr R's recommendation for executing the same at the sum of £1,350 under Mr Repton's direction, and the Committee desired to be informed of the amount of Mr Repton's charges for the design already delivered & his trouble therein and what further charges will be incurred by his undertaking the trouble of directing the execution of the work and for the whole of the Journeys he may have occasion to make to Hayleybury during the progress of the Work.

　　I have not recieved from you the Copy of the Schedule of Items determined on to be added to the Buildings at Hayleybury with the accounts of them respectively.

In margin: *Delivered*

I am Dear Sir
Your most Obedient Humble Servant
S P Cockerell
Saville Row 28 April 1809

Letter from H. Repton, 10 May 1809[28]

Hare Street near Romford Essex
May 10 1809

Sir,

I have received the honor of your letter dated 3rd Inst & beg to express my thanks for the honor done by the Court of Directors in adopting my plans for Hayleybury College & according to their desire have stated the account as follows:

1808

Nov 3 & 4 first visit & Expenses	£21s 0s 0d
Nov 24 – Visit & expences with Assistant to collect materials for the Survey or Plan	£21 0s 0d
Book of Plan, Sketches & Report	£52 10s 0d

1809

Feby 24 & March 13 – Attendance & visit with the Contractor to explain the Plan on the
Spot & take measures for the Estimate   £21 0s 0d

£115 10s 0d
Since the work was begun

1809

April 23 Visit & expences without assistance	£15 15s 0d	£31 10s 0d
May 9 Visit & expences the same	£15 15s 0d	£31 10s 0d

£147 0s 0d

And I suppose 4 or 5 More such visits <as the 2 last> will conclude the whole business of super intending the due execution of the Contract I have the honor to be
Sir Your most obedient humble Servant
H Repton

Certificate issued to T. Barr by H. Repton, 9 May 1809[29]

May 9th 1809. Having been at Hayleybury College this day & examined the progress of the work done according to the Specification of a Contract with Mr Barr I hereby certify that he is intitled to receive the first Payment by Instalment of Two hundred Pounds according to the said specification of Contract.

H Repton

To the Honourable The Court of Directors

of the East India Company

Letter from T. Barr, 17 May 1809[30]

To Mr Rundall, Clerk to the Committee of College

East India House.

Sir,

With this I beg to submit a Certificate of Mr Repton, that the Sum of Two hundred Pounds is due to me, on account of Work done at the E I College at Haileybury, under my Contract for laying out the College Grounds &c conformably to Mr. Repton's Plans.

I am sir

Your Obedient Servant

Thomas Barr

Ball's Pond Nursery

Newington

17 May 1809

Extract from the minutes of Committee of College 19 May 1809[31]

On Reading a Letter from Mr H. Repton dated the 10th Instant, stating in reply to the letter from the Clerk to this committee the amount of his Claim for his Book of plans for laying out the College Grounds and superintending the execution of the same by Mr Barr, being to the present time £147 also stating the further expense likely to be entailed by his superintending the due execution of Mr Barr's Contract. Resolved that this Committee approve the same.

The Report entered at the end of these minutes was then drawn up and signed.

Mr Repton entered certificate for the work done by Mr Barr, so far, in part of his contract for laying out the College grounds, by which it appears that he is entitled to an advance of £200, being laid before the committee.

Ordered That Mr Barr be advanced the Sum of £200 accordingly, on account of the said work, and that a warrant be made out for that sum to Mr Barr.

Letter from H. Repton, 2 July 1809[32]

Harestreet near Romford
July 2nd 1809

Sir,

Having heard from the Contractor that there are now some hopes of the original line of road being adopted I conclude there has been a Committee of College since I had but the pleasure of seeing you – and as I hope to be at home all this week – if you think there will be a Committee on Wednesday or Friday next I would go to Town to attend it because I meant to see the works the week following before I go into a distant part of the Kingdom & should be glad to leave full directions for the contractor how he is to proceed during my absence & to do as much as possible before the harvest takes off his men. I have the honor to be Sir
Your most obedient servant
H Repton

Certificate issued to T. Barr by H. Repton, 13 July 1809[33]

Hayleybury College July 13 1809

Having examined the progress of the work done at this place according to the Contract made by Mr Thomas Barr I do hereby certify, that the whole is in great forwardness that it is performed in a workmanlike manner & that he is intitled to receive Two hundred Pounds on account – being the second payment by Instalment

H. Repton

To the Honourable the East India Company

Letter from T Barr, 14 July 1809[34]

Sir,

I have to request you will have the goodness to lay the enclosed Certificate before the Honourable East India Company for payment for work done at Hayleybury College agreeable to contract being <for> the second payment of Two Hundred Pounds by instalment.

I am Sir Your Obedient Humble servant

Thomas Barr

Balls Pond Nursery

14 July 1809

Letter from T. Barr [to H. Repton], 16 August 1809[35]

Sir,

I have to request you will have the Goodness to lay the enclosed Account before The Honourable East India Company for payment for Extra work done at Haileybury College by Mr Cockerell's directions & which are not specified in my Contract.

I am Sir Your Obliged

Humble Servant

Thomas Barr

Balls Pond Nursery

16 August 1809

Account of T. Barr for extra work done at Haileybury, July 1809[36]

Extra work done at Hayleybury College agreeable to Mr Cockerell's directions & not specified in my Contract:

1809

April 22	150 Cube Yards of earth taken from Lecture room in Coal Yard @ 1s 2d	£8 15s 0d
May 13	30 Cube Yards of earth taken from Lecture room & Well in the Principal's Yard @ 1s 2d	£1 15s 0d
May 20	Man 2 Days stoping gaps against Cattle	7s 0d
May 24	20 Cube Yards of earth from foundation of Lecture room in Coal Yard @ 1s 2d	£1 3s 4d
July 22	2,361 Cube Yards of earth taken from the North side of the College & removed above 300 Yards @ 1s 10d	£216 1s 6d
		£228 1s 10d

Endorsed by S P Cockerell

The whole of the above Work is extra from Mr Barr's Contract & is reasonably charged

Letter from S. Cockerell, 17 August 1809[37]

Sir,

I enclose an Account of Mr Thomas Barr for moving Ground at Hayleybury more than contracted for by him under the direction of Mr Reptons amounting to <u>£228:1:10</u> which he is entitled to be paid if the Committee of College will please order the same.

I am sir

Your most Obedient

Humble Servant

S P Cockerell

17 August 1809

**Report to the Chairman & Directors of the East India Company
from H. Repton, 7 November 1809**[38]

Harford November 7 1809

The Terrace to the South of the College appears to be the only means of dividing the ground & protecting the building from Cattle in the front lawn – at least the only means worthy the importance of such an Edifice – & the fall of the ground makes it very easy to be executed. It is proposed to be 3 ft 6 inches high – with a dwarf iron rail on the top of about 18 inches.

The Boundary fence – To complete the inclosure already begun a line is marked & described on the annexed sketch by a dark brown line of which the stable building may form a part – this being the fence against a publick Road no gates will be necessary except one or a small wicket opposite the House A [see Figure 35] for the walk under the trees to the college – of which the professors would keep the key – and a gate into the kitchen Court which would be locked up at night.

Coal Yard – The present situation of the Coal yard is very inconvenient for the use of the Kitchen being at the extremity of the quadrangle & at the opposite corner & there being no access to this Coal yard but by the Avenue roads which are cut up by the Coal wagons. It would be a great improvement if a Coal yard nearer to the kitchen Court were to be made – to which access would be more properly had by the back road & thus the avenue roads would be reserved for light carriages only by right be kept as neatly as gravel walks.

Lodges – The parts of these buildings intended to be concealed by planting may be had by trees without any <other> fence, if the old boundary ditch were deepen'd as described to the Planter to form a sunk fence – which would also serve as a Channel to lead the Water into the ponds.

The Water – The original large piece of water being now given up it will be the more advisable to increase the size of the pools below the Principals garden – by raising the lower head & uniting the two into one Pool. Another pool might be made in the ground below when the New line of the road is form'd but till the Exchange of land

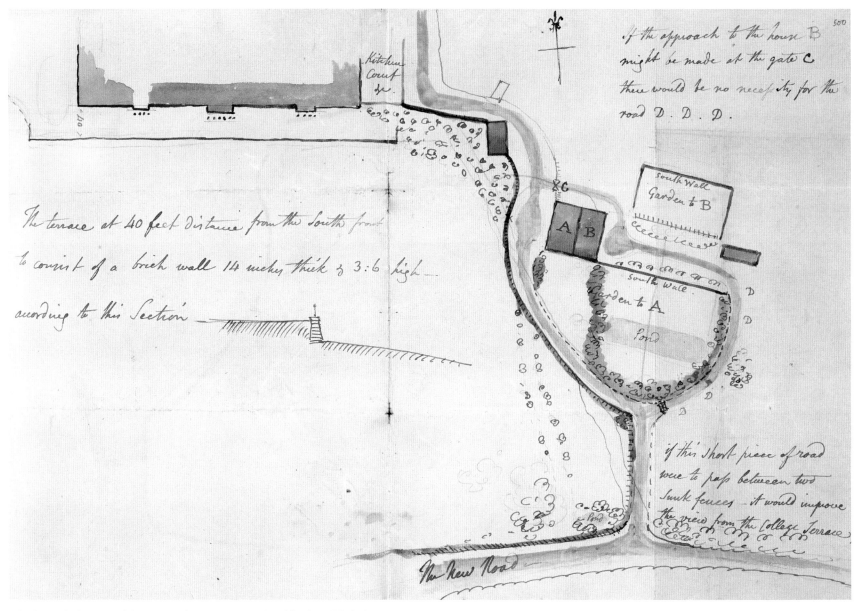

If the approach to the house B might be made at the gate C there would be no necessity for the road D. D. D.

Kitchen Court &c.

South Wall Garden to B

South Wall Garden to A

Pond

The terrace at 40 feet distance from the South front to consist of a brick wall 14 inches thick & 3:6 high according to this Section

if this short piece of road were to pass between two sunk fences it would improve the view from the College Terrace

The New Road

35   Repton's drawing of the proposed new service road and ha-ha at Haileybury.

was completed I could not with propriety mark out the exact lines or levels of these pools & shall wait the further directions of the Honourable Company on this subject.

This is the first clear reference to the abandonment of Repton's original idea, for a small lake or pond of some kind in the area to the south of the college, and its replacement by a new and less ambitious plan for creating conjoined ponds from abandoned brick pits lying to the south-west. These ponds were created, and still survive, although in modified form, and with that to the north now surrounded by modern buildings.

Letter from H. Repton, 9 November 1809[39]
Harford November 9 1809
Sirs,
I have this day visited the College at Hayleybury mark'd out several matters – of which the annexed sketch & Report may explain the uses.

I regret that I did not know the intention of [the] Directors to hold a Committee of College on the Spot or I would have had the honor of attending them next Thursday but am unfortunately obliged to go from hence into Yorkshire – I must also express my regret, that I have not occasionally received my instructions from such authority as would justify any departure from the Original Letter of the Contract with Mr Barr – as I do not feel myself empowered by my instructions to superintend his execution of the same – to give any orders for forming or planting any gardens, belonging to the professors, which were not mentioned in the original map & Report & must therefore beg to know, how far I may go in giving such necessary orders, as the alteration from the original Contract may require.
I have the honor to be Sirs
Your most obedient
Humble Servant
H. Repton

If the annexed map & instructions be approved & confirmed by the Committee, I will beg that it may be given to the Clerk on the Ground Mr Cleverly who is the Deputy of Mr Barr the Contractor & <who> will explain any thing on the Spot.
Endorsed
Read Committee of College 24 Nov 1809.

Letter from T. Barr, 11 November 1809[40]

Sir,

I have to request you will have the goodness to lay the enclosed Certificate before the Honourable East India Company, for work done at Hayleybury College agreeable to Contract being for the Third Payment of two Hundred Pounds by Instalment.

I am Sir Your Obedient. Humble Servant
Thos. Barr
Balls Pond Nursery
11 November 1809

Letter from S. Cockerell, 2 December 1809[41]

Dear Sir

I received your communication on the Subject of the reference undertaken by Dr Henley as to the assessment of the College, & immediately wrote to him thereon. I submit to Your consideration that the Resolution passed at the College Committee on Wednesday as to the Terrace be inserted in the Schedule as follows Viz: "That a Terrace be formed along the South Front of the College 40 feet wide elevated above the Lawn faced with a Brick wall & Coped with Stone, and that two flights of Stone Steps from the terrace to the Lawn be placed opposite to the Logias".

And that the article in the Shedule respecting the fence between the Married professors Gardens, have interlined between the word "proper" and "fence" the words "Oak pales".

I am Dear Sir
Your most obedient
Humble Servant
S P Cockerell
Saville Row 2 December 1809

Certificate issued to T. Barr by H. Repton, 21 December 1809[42]

To the Chairman & Directors of the Honourable the East India Company.

This is to certify that from the progress made in the Execution of the Contract at Hayleybury College Mr Thomas Barr is intitled to receive the further Sum of Four hundred Pounds being the 4th & 5th Instalments of £200 each due to him.

H Repton
Harestreet near Romford
21st December 1809

Letter from T. Barr, 23 December 1809[43]

Sir,

I have to request you will have the goodness to lay the enclosed Certificate before the Honourable East India Company for Payment being the 4th and 5th Instalments of £200 each on my Contract for Work done at the East India College.

I am Sir Your Obedient Humble Servant
Thomas Barr
Balls Pond Nursery
23 December 1809

Extract from the minutes of Committee of College, 10 January 1810[44]

Mr J Repton [*sic; recte* H. Repton] attending the Committee and stating verbally some suggestions of his; as to certain alterations in the College Grounds, the general plan for the laying where of by Mr Repton was approved on the 5 April last. Mr Repton was desired to state the same in writing.

Letter from H. Repton, 22 January 1810[45]

Harestreet near Romford

January 22 1810

Sir,

I have enclosed a report to which I hope you will be able to return me a speedy answer – that I may give the necessary orders when I go next to Hayleybury. I have also inclosed my account being at this time engaged in making out all my accounts to the end of last year. I have the honor to be Sir

Your most obedient

Humble Servant

H Repton

Report concerning Hayleybury College submitted to the East India Company by H. Repton, 22 January 1810[46]

Laid before Committee of College 9 February 1810

Gentlemen

This is in obedience to your instructions that I should <u>deliver in writing</u> the substance of the Report I had the honour to make personally at the East India House.

1st The business of the Contract has been nearly compleated & the work done in a proper manner but the Contractor complains of the roads having been torn up by Coal Carts before they had time to settle sufficiently. This arises from the improper situation of the Coal Yard in the West front of the College, to which no access can be had from the back road & I beg leave to suggest the necessity of removing it to a more proper situation for which Mr Cockerill, your Surveyor, has in some degree provided a yard nearer to the Kitchen.

2ndly: The pits at the bottom of the Principals Garden made by digging clay for bricks remain in an unsightly & unfinished state, never having been puddled to hold water, & being on two different levels. I beg leave to propose that the two pits be formed into one pool on the same level by raising the lower head & partly destroying the upper one in the manner shewn by the annexed sketch.[47] To level the Edges & cover the bottoms of these pits with vegetable soil would cost as much, as to form them into the pool here described-viz – from 60 to 100 pounds according to the mode of doing it.

3rdly: There are other excavations below these which will require the same treatment & may be converted into Water with <almost> as little cost, as made dry pasture. This might be made a very material improvement to the Scenery and would not exceed £120 – if it can be done immediately & before the contractor removes his foreman and labourers from the Spot. I have therefore to beg that I may receive my instructions on these Subjects before I close their accounts & dismiss them.

I have the honor to be Gentlemen
Your most obedient humble servant
H. Repton
Harestreet near Romford
January 22 1810

Account submitted to the East India Company by H. Repton with his letter dated 22 January 1810[48]

1809

June 7th visit to Hayley Bury College to collect materials for 2nd Report	£21 0s 0d
Report & plan No 2 curtailed in consequence of difficulties in the exchange of land adjoining	£10 10s 0d
June 15 & 16 – visit to meet committee	£21 0s 0d

NB: the above is not included in the 4 or 5 visits which I said would be sufficient for superintending the Contract of which only 3 have been made Viz:

July 13 – visit	£15 15s 0d
Octr 13 – ditto	£15 15s 0d
Novr 7 – ditto	£15 15s 0d
	£99 15s 0d

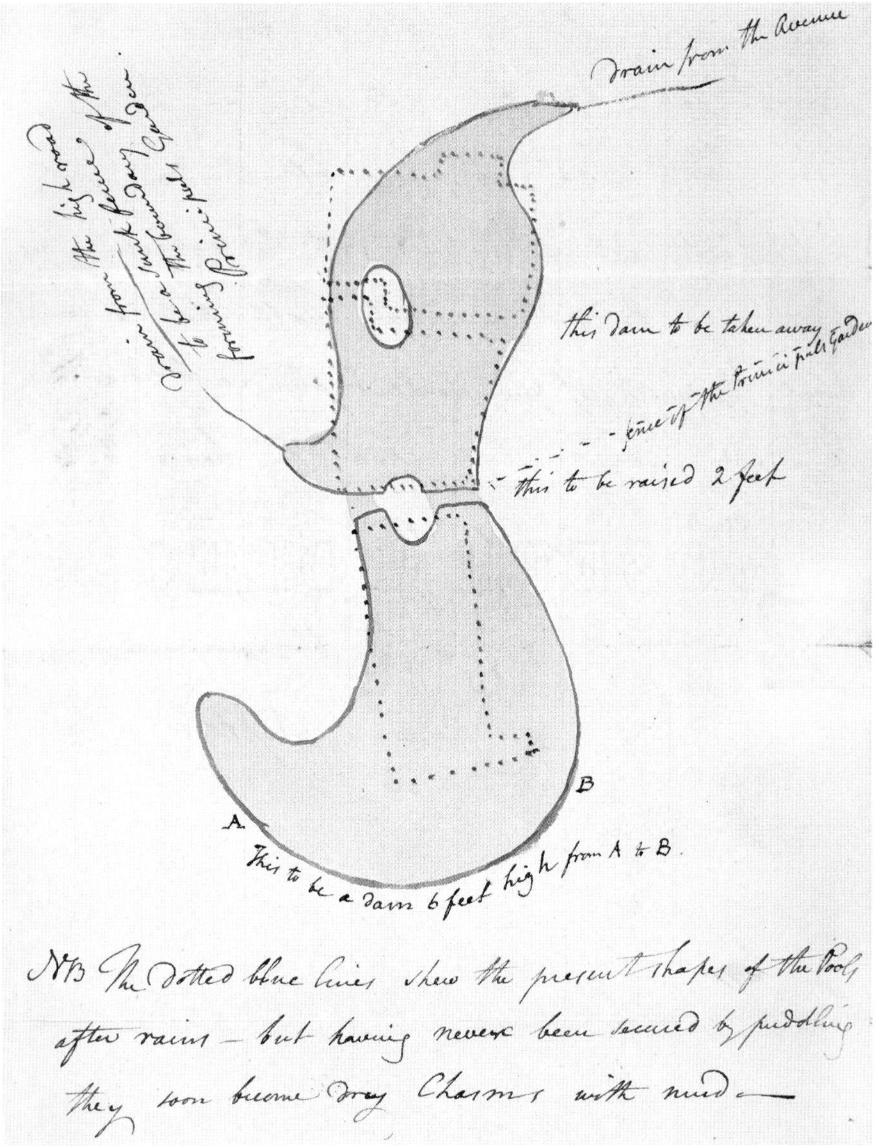
Drain from the Avenue
This dam to be taken away
This to be raised 2 feet
A
B
This to be a dam 6 feet high from A to B.
NB The dotted blue lines shew the present shapes of the Pools after rains – but having never been secured by puddling they soon become dry Chasms with mud –

36 Sketch by Repton showing the design for the two ponds, formed from old brick pits, in the south-western area of Haileybury's grounds.

Extract from the minutes of Committee of College, 9 February 1810[49]

A report from Mr Henry [*sic*] Repton dated the 22 Ultimo proposing some further Alteration to his plan for laying out the College Grounds at Haileybury.

Letter from H Repton, 4 April 1810[50]

To the Chairman etc etc etc of the Honourable East India Company
April 4 1810 Woburn Abbey

Gentlemen,

Having understood that a Committee of College would be held at Hayleybury this week, I thought it my duty to mark out on the ground, the lines laid down in the annexed Map, which I have the honor to submit to Your Consideration, as the best expedient for levelling & finishing the unsightly chasms made by excavating for brick earth – which are sometimes dry pits & sometimes overflowing pools after sudden rains. Instead of removing all the present dams & levelling the banks I propose to remove only a part of the upper dam & to raise the two others so as to form two irregular shaped pools to have the appearance of one piece of Water.

This will in a great degree realize the affect of Water represented in the drawings which I had the honor to deliver with my original Report & Opinion. I am happy to state that the whole expence will not exceed 40 or 50 Pounds according to the depth of the Pools while, from the quantity of Labour required to remove the old dams & level the edges, it would cost almost as much to make it dry land, as to produce this beautiful mirror, in which the College will be reflected in the most favorable point of View. As I am now in my way into the North & shall not return before the next month I have left such instructions with the Contractor & his foreman on the spot as will enable them to compleat the whole, if you should be pleased to command It to be done, I have the honor to be Gentlemen

Your most obedient

humble servant

H. Repton

Letter from T. Barr, 7 May 1810[51]

Sir,

I shall be very much obliged to you if you will request Mr Cockerill to have the goodness to give me a Certificate for <u>two</u> or <u>three</u> Hundred Pounds for extra work done at the East India College which is not specified in my Contract, this will not be more than half the sum due to me for Extra work done there.

I am Sir Your Obliged

Humble Servant

Thomas Barr

Balls Pond Nursery

7 May 1810

Endorsed by S.P. Cockerell, 9 May 1810

I beg leave to Certify that Mr Barr Is Entitled to the sum he requires, if the Committee think proper to Order the same

Certificate issued to T. Barr by H. Repton, 7 July 1810[52]

Harestreet near Romford
July 7 1810
To the Chairman & Directors
of the Honourable the East India Company

This is to certify that Mr Thomas Barr is intitled to receive the further sum of Two hundred pounds being the Sixth Instalment due to him on his Contract for works performed at Hayleybury College.

H. Repton

Letter from T. Barr, 10 July 1810[53]

Sir,
I have to request you will have the goodness to lay the enclosed Certificate before The Honourable East India Company for Payment for work done agreeable to contract at Hayleybury College

I am Sir Your Obliged,
Humble Servant
Thomas Barr
Balls Pond Nursery
10 July 1810

I shall take it as a favor if you will give me a line when you have got a warrant in my favor & I will call on you.

Letter from T. Barr, undated[54]

Sir,

I have to request you will have the goodness to lay the enclosed before the Chairman of the Honourable the East India Company for Payment making a reserve of such a part of it as the Honourable Board may think proper, till I have made good the trees & shrubs this Autumn agreeable to my Contract.

I also shall be much oblig'd to you to lay before the Chairman My account for extra Work done by order of Mr Cockerill which is not specified in my Contract, the Ballance due to me is £604 12s 9d & I believe Mr Cockerell has past my account.

I am Sir your Obliged Humble Servant
Thomas Barr

Letter from S. Cockerell to Mr Rundall, 26 September 1810[55]

East India House
26 September 1810

Sir,

I beg leave to inform the Honourable the Committee of College, that I have received from Mr Barr who executed the alterations in the Ground work at Hayleybury & other Works there, in part by Agreement under the Superintendence of Mr Repton & other parts by the Instructions of the Committee on the Spot & directed by me, An account of the Several Extra Works so done by him, amounting to above one thousand Pounds, on which he has received £300 on Account & has Credited for works which were intended to have been executed under Mr Repton's superintendance but were omitted to give place to part of the Works in his present Account. And as I cannot certify the balances due to him without Reference to Mr Repton, I beg leave to recommend the Honourable Committee to advance to Mr Barr the further sum of £400 until the balance can be ascertained.

I am Sir Your most obedient servant
S P Cockerell
Mr Rundall

Letter from S. Cockerell to Mr Rundall, 17 December 1810[56]

Sir,

I beg you will please to lay before the Committee of College the Enclosed account of Ground Works, Terrace, and Gravelling, done by Mr Barr at Hayleybury, during the last and present Year, more than was comprized in the Work done under the direction of Mr Repton, amounting to £1,016 0s 9d the whole of which appears to be reasonably charged and may be comprized under the following Heads:

Digging & Levelling the Ground for placing the Lodges and ditching & Grubbing for the Park Pale fencing.
Improving the Entrance to the College & Gravelling the sweep.
Carting and spreading Gravel in The Quadrangle & dressing the Grass Plats.
Levelling, draining & fencing the Cricket Ground and fives Court.
Forming and Gravelling the Roads & Entrances to the Kitchen, Offices, Professors' Houses, and to the Courts and Stables attached to them and to the College.

Mr Barr has given Credit for £700 received on Account and for Trees Grubbed and Sold £39 8s 0d leaving the balance of £276 12s 9d due to him.

Mr Barr states to me that the Terrace Walk intended in Mr Repton's design, altho' included in the Specification was entirely omitted in his Estimate of £1,350 – for which he undertook to do the whole of the work; and it appears by refference to the Original Particulars of that Estimate, that it was so omitted. I have not therefore made any deduction for the same, which I presume the Committee will approve in consideration of the full performance of his Contract.

I am Sir
Your most obedient
Humble Servant
S P Cockerell
17 December 1810
Mr Rundall

Account submitted to the East India Company by T. Barr for 'Ground Works, Terrace, and Gravelling', 1809-10[57]

Draft To Thomas Barr

For Work done at the East India College & not specified in his Contract by Order of Mr Cockerell

1809

July 15	Digging out foundations of the two Lodges 260 yards @ 3d	£3 5s 0d
	8 Rod of Grubbing hedge rows for upper Lodge @ 3s	£1 4s 0d
	Man 6 Days levelling in lower Lodge	18s
	Grubbing up 7 Large trees @ 3s 6d	£1 4s 6d
October 14	1,523 Cub. Yards of earth removed from upper Lodge @ 1s 3d	£95 3s 9d
October 28	Digging a new Ditch in front of Lodges & wheeling away the earth – 17 Rod @ 2s 6d	£2 2s 6d
	2 men levelling about the Lodges 3 days each	18s
	Grubbing hedge Rows on the north side the College – 77 Rod @ 3s	£11 11s 0d
	Grubbing 3 Pollard trees	6s
	63 Cub yards of earth taken out of the Coach sweep opposite the grand entrance @ 1s 3d	£3 18s 9d
	70 load of Gravel & carting into the above sweep @ 6s	£21 0s 0d
	18 Rod of Ditching on the north side of College 4 feet wide & 3 feet 6 Inches Deep @ 2s 6d	£6 1s 6d
	Carried forward	£147 13s 0d
	8 Dozen Hurdles as for bill & receipt	£7 4s 0d

1810

March 17	1,902 Cub Yards of earth taken away from south front to form a Terrace as per estimate @ 1s	£95 2s 0d
	73 Rod of Terrace Walk levelled for Graveling as per estimate @ 1s 6d	£5 9s 6d
	73 Rod of Graveling to do @ 5 load to the Rod & per Load Estimated @ 7s per load, but being brought from Hoddesdon Charged 8s	£146 0s 0d
March 31	1,033 Cub Yards in large hill in Cricket ground removed @ 9d per Yard	£38 14s 9d
	221 Cub. Yards on the west side of ponds @ 6d	£5 10s 6d
	311 Cub. Yards on South Side ditto @ 8d	£10 7s 4d

	488 Cub. Yards on east side of ditto 8d	£16 5s 4d
	881 Cub. Yards large holes north side the field @ 6d	£22 0s 6d
	333 Cub. Yards in 6 small ponds @ 6d	£8 6s 6d
	Taking up 20 Rod of Quick & levelling the banks @ 1s 6d	£1 10s 0d
	55 Rod new Ditch & Planting with strong Quick on south west side of field @ 2s 6d	£6 17s 6d
	Grubbing 15 Elm trees @ 1s 3d	18s 9d
	180 Rod of Land draining straw &c @ 1s 3d	£11 5s 0d
	Ploughing 5 times the 6 Acres and laying it down with grass, Clover & Trefoil	£24 10s 0d
	183 Rod of Laying old hedges & ditching round the Fields @ 1s 3d	£11 8s 9d
	72 Rod new ditching & hedging @ 2s	£7 4s 0d
	Carried forward	£566 7s 5d
	14 Rod of new Ditching & planting strong Quick in Col Brown's Field @ 2s 6d	£1 15s 0d
	44 Rod of new Ditching across the meadow to convey the water from the Cricket ground @ 1s 6d	£3 6s 0d
	Grubbing 50 Poplars & Fir Trees @ 1s 6d	£3 15s 0d
	135 Cub Yards of earth removed from Kitchen door @ 1s	£6 15s 0d
	Digging for a brick Drain from upper Lodge to the pond & filling in the same 48 Cub Yards @ 1s	£2 8s 0d
	2 men 5 Days each taking up old fences	£1 15s 0d
June 9	4 men 3½ Days each levelling in the Lodge Yards @ wheeling the earth from the wells	£2 9s 0d
	46 Loads of Gravel <from Hoddesdon> for the Lodge Yards @ 8s	£18 18s 0d
	4 Men a Day each wheeling in ditto	14s 0d
June 16	4 Men 5 Days each levelling each side of College	£3 10s 0d
	105 Load of Gravel for the sweep by the Kitchen door @ 8s	£42 0s 0d
	6 Load of Gravel to the Revd Mr Luton & Hamilton back doors @ 8s[58]	£2 8s 0d
	6 Load Gravel to the Revd Mr Bridges ditto @ 8s[59]	£2 8s 0d
	184 Loads Gravel into Quadrangle @ 8s	£73 12s 0d
	6 Men 15 Days each wheeling in	£15 15s 0d
	5 Men 5 Days each leveling yard and & forming Road to the Revd Mr Maltus House[60]	£4 7s 6d

	275 Loads Gravel to the Revd Mr Maltus Road, Yard & north of the stable @ 8s	£110 0s 0d
July 14	6 Men 6 Days each levelling the Yard & ground at the Revd Mr Battons[61]	£6 6s 0d
	Carried forward	£867 18s 11d
	60 Load of Gravel for Revd Mr Battons Coach Road & yard @ 8s	£24 0s 0d
	2 Men 2 Days each repairing the Walk from the end of Terrace to the Revd Mr Battons House	14s 0d
	18 Loads of Gravel for the same Walk @ 8s	£7 4s 0d
	4 Men 2 Days each sloping the ground round the Revd Dr. Henleys Coach House	£1 8s 0d
	56 Load of Gravel for ditto @ 8s	£22 8s 0d
	5 Men 6 Days each digging foundations & levelling Grounds for five Courts	£5 5s 0d
	120 Load of Gravel for ditto @ 8s	£43 0s 0d
July 20	6 Men 5 Days each wheeling @ ditto	£5 5s 0d
	4 Men 3 Days each forming a Walk from the Revd Mr Bridges House to the Cricket ground	£2 2s 0d
	26 Loads of Gravel for ditto @ 8s	£10 8s 0d
	5 Men 10 Days each Digging out foundations for Terrace Wall & the drain	£8 15s 0d
	6 Men 2 Days each & a Team 1½ Day removing the earth from the foundation of Terrace Wall & Drain	£3 12s 0d
	2 Men 2 Days each digging foundations for Laboratory	14s
	6 Men 6 Days each Mowing & cleaning the Quadrangle & the grounds of the south & west side the College	£6 6s 0d
	Carried forward	£1,008 19s 11d
	2 Horses Rolling the ground one day	10s
	2 Horses Carting of rubbish one day	10s
	Man a day digging foundations for a wall in the Revd Mr Bridges Yard	3s 6d
	176 Rod of Ditching round the Park Paling @ 8d	£5 17s 4d
		£1,016 0s 9d

Deductions:

1809

July 22	Received for 7 Oak trees, bark & fagots	£9 10s 0d
	Received for 3 Pollard trees	£1 10s 0d

1810

March 17	Received for Poplar trees & Firs of Mr Chiffins	£23 3s 0d
May 21	Received on Account	£300 0s 0d
August 20	Received for 15 small Elms of Mr Chiffins	£5 5s 0d
Sept 26	Received on Account	£400 0s 0d
		£739 8s 0d
	S P Cockerell	£276 12s 9d

This is an extraordinarily useful account of the work involved in creating the grounds at Haileybury. Many of the activities alluded to would have taken place when private parks and pleasure grounds were laid out under Repton's direction, including the removal of hedges and old pollards, the planting of trees and shrubs and the gravelling of carriage drives. The extent of ground levelling, however, is unusual, and reflects the fact that much of Barr's work was directed towards preparing the sites of lodges and other buildings.

Letter from H. Repton, 21 January 1811[62]

Harestreet near Romford

January 21. 1811

Sir,

At the Close of the year I now send in my Account to the Honourable East India Company & will be obliged to you to do the needful to have it passed & will call on you the first time I come to Town.

I remain Sir

Your obedient humble Servant

H. Repton

Account of visits to Haileybury made by H. Repton in 1810 enclosed with his letter dated 21 January 1811[63]

Mem: of Visits to Hayleybury College from H. Repton

1810

January 16 & 17 – Attendence	£21:0:0
April 3rd – Ditto	£15:15:0
July 23rd – Ditto	£15:15:0
	£52:10:0

Notes

1 Repton's involvement at Haileybury was first highlighted by R.G. Desmond, 'A Repton garden at Haileybury', *Garden History*, 6 (1978), pp. 16–19.

2 BL: IOR L/L/2/1351–1373, property records for East India College, Haileybury, 1806–1861.

3 *Ibid.*

4 BL: IOR J/2/1, Committee of College Minutes, Reports and Papers, 1804–1813, pp. 248–9.

5 BL: IOR J/1/22, correspondence and papers addressed to the Committee of College, 1807–1811, fol. 430; architect Samuel Pepys Cockerell was surveyor to the East India Company from 1806 to 1824. See P. Meadows, 'Cockerell, Samuel Pepys (1753–1827)', *Oxford Dictionary of National Biography*, Oxford University Press, 2004 <http://www.oxforddnb.com/view/article/5783>, accessed 15 September 2017.

6 BL: IOR J/1/24 fol. 405.

7 BL: IOR J/1/22–26, correspondence and papers addressed to the Committee of College, 1807–1811 and IOR J/2/1, Committee of College Minutes, Reports and Papers, 1804–1813. For more detailed information concerning the surviving East India Company records relating to Haileybury see A. Farrington, *The Records of the East India College Haileybury & Other Institutions* (London, 1976).

8 The artist and engraver Thomas Medland was the drawing and oriental writing-master at Haileybury until his death in 1833. He also engraved Humphry Repton's trade card. See E. Tollfree, 'Medland, Thomas (*c*.1765–1833)', *Oxford Dictionary of National Biography*, Oxford University Press, 2004 <http://www.oxforddnb.com/view/article/18498>, accessed 15 September 2017.

9 HALS: DP/4/29/18, 'Map of the Parish of Great Amwell in the County of Hertford 1836', surveyed by John Griffin.

10 BL: IOR J/2/1, pp. 248–9 and IOR J/1/23, fols 403–405.

11 BL: IOR J/1/24, fol. 501.

12 R. Desmond, *Dictionary of British and Irish Horticulturalists* (London, 1994), p. 48.

13 BL: IOR J/1/22, fol. 430

14 The sections not included here concern stone work and interior fittings required for the new building.

15 BL: IOR J/2/1, pp. 248–9.

16 Until his death in 1815, Revd Samuel Henley was the first principal of Haileybury. See G.P. Moriarty, 'Henley, Samuel (1740–1815)', rev. John D. Haigh, *Oxford Dictionary of National Biography*, Oxford University Press, 2004 <http://www.oxforddnb.com/view/article/12933>, accessed 15 September 2017.

17 BL: IOR J/1/23, fol. 408.

18 BL: IOR J/2/1, p. 252.

19 BL: IOR J/1/24, fols 339–340.

20 BL: IOR J/2/1, p. 252.

21 BL: IOR J/1/24 fol. 322.

22 BL: IOR J/2/1, p. 323.

23 BL: IOR J/1/24, fols 341–342.

24 BL: IOR J/1/24 fols 343–44.

25 BL: IOR J/1/24, fol. 347.

26 BL: IOR J/2/1, p. 323.

27 BL: IOR J/1/24, fol. 405.

28 BL: IOR J/1/24, fol. 407.

29 BL: IOR J/1/24, fol. 417.

30 BL: IOR J/1/24, fol. 419.

31 BL: IOR J/2/1, pp. 351–2.

32 BL: IOR J/1/24, fol. 445.

33 BL: IOR J/1/24, fol. 449.

34 BL: IOR J/1/24, fol. 447.

35 BL: IOR J/1/24, fol. 460.

36 BL: IOR J/1/24 fol. 464.

37 BL: IOR J/1/24, fol. 462.

38 BL: IOR J/1/24 fol. 501.

39 BL: IOR J/1/24, fols 498–500.

40 BL: IOR J/1/24, fol. 505.

41 BL: IOR J/1/24, fol. 521.

42 BL: IOR J/1/24, fol. 544.

43 BL: IOR J/1/24, fol. 542.

44 BL: IOR J/2/1, p. 487.

45 BL: IOR J/1/25, fol. 349.

46 BL: IOR J/1/25 fols 333–4.

47 The sketch of Repton's proposals for the ponds referred to here is a draft version of the plan at BL: IOR J/1/25, fol. 375 reproduced at Figure 36.

48 BL: IOR J/1/25 fol. 351.

49 BL: IOR J/2/1, p. 489.

50 BL: IOR J/1/25, fols 374–375.

51 BL: IOR J/1/25, fol. 384.

52 BL: IOR J/1/25, fol. 413.

53 BL: IOR J/1/25, fol. 411.

54 BL: IOR J/1/25, fol. 417.

55 BL: IOR J/1/25, fol. 419.

56 BL: IOR J/1/25, fol. 456.

57 BL: IOR J/1/25 fol. 457.

58 The Revd Edward Lewton was professor of classical and general literature at Haileybury from 1806 and later registrar and librarian until 1830 (see lists of staff in A. Farrington, *The Records of the East India College Haileybury and Other Institutions* (London, 1976); Alexander Hamilton was professor of Hindu literature and history of Asia from 1807 to 1818 (see R. Rocher, 'Hamilton, Alexander (1762–1824)', *Oxford Dictionary of National Biography*, Oxford University Press, 2004 <http://www.oxforddnb.com/view/article/12044>, accessed 15 September 2017).

59 The Revd Bewick Bridge was professor of mathematics and natural philosophy from 1806 to 1816 and registrar from 1814 to 1816. See T. Cooper, 'Bridge, Bewick (1767–1833)', rev. J. Tompson, *Oxford Dictionary of National Biography*, Oxford University Press, 2004 <http://www.oxforddnb.com/view/article/3386>, accessed 15 September 2017.

60 Thomas Robert Malthus, the author of *An Essay on the Principle of Population* (London, 1798) was professor of history and political economy until shortly before his death. See J.M. Pullen, 'Malthus (Thomas) Robert (1766–1835)', *Oxford Dictionary of National Biography*, Oxford University Press, 2004 <http://www.oxforddnb.com/view/article/17902>, accessed 15 September 2017.

61 Joseph Hallett Batten was professor of classical and general literature from 1806 to 1815 and principal from 1815 until his death in 1835 (see lists of staff in A. Farrington, *The Records of the East India College Haileybury and Other Institutions* (London, 1976)).

62 BL: IOR J/1/26, fol. 317.

63 BL: IOR J/1/26 fol. 319.

Lamer House, Wheathampstead

TL 18111607

LAMER IS A DIFFICULT SITE to interpret. Repton prepared a Red Book in 1792 but this is peculiarly vague, in part because he failed to include a plan of the site (claiming that no accurate survey existed which could be adopted for this purpose). He also produced the drawing on which an engraving, published in Peacock's *Polite Repository* in 1793, was based (Figure 37). Lamer House stands just over a mile (around two kilometres) north of Wheathampstead village. It occupies a spur of land from which the ground slopes away to the west and, rather more gently at first, to the south, in the direction of the Lea valley. On this side, according to Repton, the 'hill … is so broad in front of the house; that in many respects it must be treated as if the situation were flat'. Lamer Wood, an area of semi-natural ancient woodland, lies a little to the north of the house. The soils are formed in clay-with-flints overlying chalk.

Lamer became a manor in its own right in the fourteenth century, when it formed part of the extensive properties of Westminster Abbey, and the Garrard family resided there from 1553, initially renting it from Sir John Brocket before acquiring it outright.[1] An imposing new manor house was erected by Sir William Garrard in 1555 and a deer park was in existence by 1589, an early seventeenth-century document describing how it covered 110 acres.[2] The Garrards were prominent city businessmen, and several served as Lord Mayors of London or as members of parliament for the pocket borough of Amersham (Buckinghamshire), although none seem to have held major offices of state. The family remained in occupation until 1947, although on two occasions the property did not pass directly, heirs being obliged to add the name of Garrard to their existing surnames. One of these was Charles Drake Garrard, formerly Charles Drake, who commissioned Repton to make improvements some time around 1790.

The Tudor mansion, which featured tall crenellated towers, was substantially rebuilt by Sir Benet Garrard between 1761 and 1767, at considerable expense, as a Georgian red brick building of an 'elegant simplicity', with interiors designed in part by Robert Adam.[3] The stables to the east of the house may also have been rebuilt at this time. Part of the original mansion still survived when Repton first visited in 1790, but now only the walls of the kitchen garden, lying to the north of the house, remain from the Tudor period.

On the accession of Charles Drake Garrard in 1780 the noted landscape designer Nathaniel Richmond (who had already worked on his father's estate at Shardeloes in Buckinghamshire) was commissioned to remodel the grounds.[4] The estate accounts record cutting down trees, clearing undergrowth, levelling ground, sowing grass and making a new road as well as much activity in the gardens.[5] By the time that Munford prepared a map of the estate in 1799 (Figure 38) the only geometric feature to remain from the design shown, somewhat schematically, on Dury and Andrews' county map of 1766 was the main avenue, planted with limes, which served as the principal approach from the east – from the Ayot road.[6] One of Richmond's main changes was the construction of a new principal approach leading to the house from the south. There had long been a bridle way or lane on this side, leading off the Wheathampstead road in the south-western corner of the park, but Richmond seems to have constructed a replacement that began in the same place but then ran on a more westerly line, near to the western edge of the park, passing first along low ground before climbing the slope to approach the house. Above all, Richmond laid out elaborate pleasure grounds to the west of the house that included a fine summer house (which still survives). He also created a meandering or serpentine walk flanked by a strip of woodland, which led from the western edge of the pleasure grounds, incorporating an existing dell, and then continued on to Lamer Wood, which was itself partly planted up in ornamental fashion.

From 1788 the estate accounts feature payments for 'work on Lamer Ho.', signalling the fact that the architect Thomas Fulcher of Ipswich had been employed to make further modifications to the mansion, including the addition of a bay window on the western façade, much classical ornamentation and a round portico.[7] It was at this point that Repton was called in to make further improvements to the grounds, first visiting in September 1790, charging for two days' work in November and for providing a plan (now lost) of the 'stable yard etc' and, finally, producing the Red Book in 1792.[8] The current whereabouts of the latter is unknown:

37   Lamer House, as illustrated in Peacock's *Polite Repository* for 1793.

fortunately, a photocopy exists, although the illustrations are of poor quality.[9] We have attempted to restore one of them, with and without its 'slide' or flap, as Figure 39.

Repton's proposals for Lamer were limited in part because, as he put it in the Red Book, he considered himself 'rather called in to compleat the plan suggested by the late Mr Richmond, than to take up the whole from the beginning'. He suggested breaking up the wide sweep of lawn to the south ('too great an expanse of uninteresting Lawn') with judicious planting, and proposed altering the main southern approach by abandoning Richmond's new drive and taking the main approach along the line of the existing bridleway, but beginning at a point a little further south on the Wheathampstead road. The entrance would be provided with a new lodge: he included a sketch of a 'small simple cottage' that was to fulfil this role and which

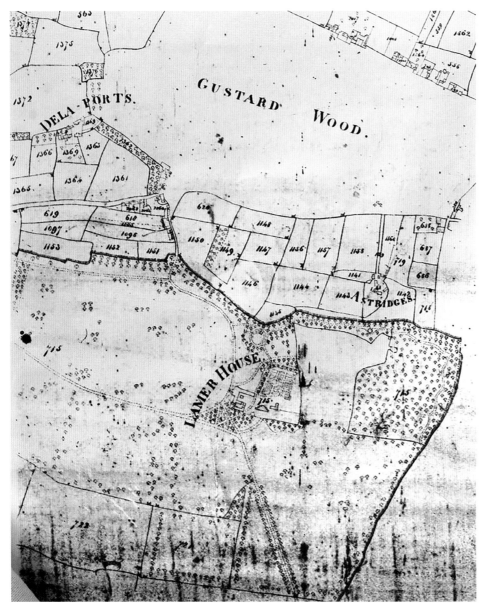

38 Lamer House and its grounds, as shown on an estate map of 1799 (north to the right).

'would have a pleasing effect'. He stressed that the entrance should be so constructed so that it gave the impression that the road was heading straight for the house, and that travellers for Kimpton and Hitchin would have to bear left. Another new approach, which he had staked out on the ground, was also made to replace the avenue leading to the house from the east, from the direction of Ayot St Lawrence.

Repton made no proposals for the pleasure grounds. He was a great admirer of Richmond's work and considered that they 'had been made with so much good taste by Mr. Richmond that I should advise no alteration in what is already done'. But he did recommend extending the main walk further into Lamer Wood and suggested that 'to avoid returning by the same ground it may be beautifully conducted under the irregular line of beeches'. He also recommended that there should be 'a shed half buried in the wood, the front of which is composed of the present portico of the house', and a 'reposoir' or shelter placed nearby, made of an old Gothic porch that he hoped had been saved for that purpose – probably the seventeenth-century portico from the old house, which was eventually, at some later date, incorporated into the entrance to the walled kitchen garden.

Repton also proposed a number of alterations to the architecture of the house, venturing 'to depart from Mr. Fulcher's design in some particulars'. He suggested altering 'the colour of the house from red to white; or rather stone colour; and breaking the parallel line of [the] roof by a pediment', as well as enlarging the central window, substituting a square for a circular portico 'more proportional to the house' and simplifying or removing ornamental details 'for the sake of that simplicity which should be the leading character of Lamer'.

It appears from the evidence that few of Repton's proposals were implemented. The Ordnance Survey 6-inch map suggests that the main pleasure ground walk may have been extended further into Lamer Wood, but it was not made into a circuit path as he proposed. The lodge was not built (although one was erected in the 1850s close to this position) and Richmond's approach road remained in place until at least 1827, to judge from an estate map of that date,[10] although the old road, whose line was preferred by Repton, still survives to this day. Comments made by Mary Snead in 1831, that the view to the south of the house comprised 'a sight of green parkland stretching without incident as far as the eye can see', suggests that Repton's advice about planting here had not been heeded. As the Red Book does not include a plan of the site it is unclear whether any of the clumps he proposed for the park were established. Payments are recorded in the estate accounts for 'trenching the ground for a new plantation' in 1791, after Repton's visit, and some of the clumps shown on the 1799 map have a vaguely Reptonian look, but overall there is little evidence that his proposals for the park were implemented. In contrast to all this, the illustration made of Lamer House by John Chessel Buckler in 1834 shows that his suggestions for modifying Fulcher's plans for the house probably were largely adopted: the house is shown faced in stucco and displays the raised pediment, enlarged central window and modified portico much as proposed in the Red Book (Figure 40). Indeed, Fulcher himself provided sketches for alterations to the south and the library fronts that appear to follow Repton's advice,[11] and supplied the materials for the stucco rendering.[12]

There were many subsequent changes to the grounds in the course of the nineteenth and twentieth centuries, before the Garrards finally sold the property. In 1947 it was acquired by Sir Nicholas Cayzer, who sold the following year to Grenville Hill. Hill demolished most of the house in 1949. In 1953 the property was bought by George Seabrook, who built a new 'modern labour saving residence'[13] on the site, in part using materials from the previous house. But in 1954 the estate was split up and the park subdivided. A tall hedge was established to provide privacy and to break up the great expanse of lawn, cutting off the views over the park to south and east. A new lime avenue was planted, approaching the house from the south. The main area of the park became a golf course in 1996, leading to the loss of many old trees and the establishment of much typical golf-course planting, the creation of a large pond for irrigating the greens and the erection of a club house. This has since gone out of business. The main areas of woodland survive, together with fragments of the pleasure grounds. The most interesting remains relate, in fact, to Richmond's activities, and include his serpentine walk (now a public footpath), with fine displays of snowdrops in early spring; the summer house in the pleasure grounds; and some of the trees planted here, including several mature specimens of Portuguese laurel (*Prunus Lusitanian*), cherry laurel (*Prunus laurocerassus*) and evergreen oak (*Quercus ilex*). Whatever Repton may have contributed to the landscape has now been lost.

Lamer Hertfordshire
A Seat of C Drake Garrard, Esq[r]

Introduction

Sir,

Yours is the only place of any consequence for which I have not delivered in writing a general plan to be compleated at leisure: an omission I must thus account for, first, the pressure of business which sometimes induces me to evade a practice becoming every day more difficult to continue; secondly the want of an accurate survey on which I might mark my intention and make my ideas more easily understood, and thirdly that I considered myself rather called in to compleat the plan suggested by the late Mr Richmond, than to take up the whole from the beginning: it is this latter consideration that now induces me to submit the following pages to your perusal, in which I shall not only deliver my opinion without being fettered by what has already been done; but assign such reasons for that opinion as I hope will be allowed satisfactory; since I am convinced that no alteration can be deemed real improvement, unless a reason can be given for adopting it.

    I have the honour to be Sir

    Your most obedient & very

    humble Servant

    H Repton

The premises first viewed November 7th 1790
Plan delivered in January 1792

Character

The antient stile of the house, which from one tower only remaining when I first visited Lamer, seems to have borne the Character of those important Mansions built in Elizabeth's reign; had been too far changed by rebuilding to recover that dignity which it formerly possessed.

There is so much picturesque beauty and importance even in the worst species of what is called Gothic architecture, that I am always an advocate for preserving its character wherever it is possible: in this instance however I had not the honour of being consulted till it was too late to preserve any part of the original structure*; and consequently a <u>New</u> Character must be imposed upon the place: It is <not> possible from the appearance of the present house to excite the idea of Baronial importance but the more modern Architecture still may be made conformable to picturesque beauty; and from the size both of the House and surrounding Lawns, I think the Character to be aimed at, is, an elegant Simplicity: this I mean to form the basis of all that I shall have occasion to suggest concerning the improvement of the House and grounds at Lamer.

Situation

The summit of that hill on which Lamer is situated, is so broad in front of the house; that in many respects it must be treated as if the situation were flat; because the distant views seen from the lower apartments, tho' in some directions extensive and very interesting in themselves, are seen over too great an expanse of uninteresting Lawn. However beautiful the distant scenery may be, it is necessary that what is seen from the windows of a mansion should please by that portion of Landscape which is nearest The dwelling, and most appropriated to it, otherwise the house appears to situated in the worst part of a <u>fine</u> country: This is in some measure the case with Lamer if we confine ourselves merely to the views southward, the few scattered clumps of Lime Trees are not sufficient to counteract the general nakedness of the Lawn over which the distant country is presented. Such an exposure was not more applicable to the antient stile of the House when our Ancestors thought of nothing less than Landscape, and were sometimes content to look on an inner court, or a scene incumbered with Stables barns & walls in every direction: to this fashion succeeded the rage of laying everything open, but rational Taste has taught us that there is often more beauty in concealing than in displaying the most delightful objects, it is not the Eye, but the Imagination that must be gratified. "Esperer c'est jouire, promettre c'est donner" ['To hope is to enjoy, to promise is to give'].[15]

---

* It is an act of justice, to record in this place, that the Change of Character & Stile, of which I have complained, was not only prior to my being consulted, but to any plans adopted by the present possessor of Lamer.

The House

The external appearance of a house is so immediately connected with my profession that I consider it as no act of presumption if I hint my opinion on the subject.

Several very neat designs have been made by Mr Fulcher for ornamenting the south front of this house; one of them I have here inserted No II, in all the other designs an enrichment of columns or pilasters was proposed.

The most experienced Architect finds so much difficulty in making the doors and windows of a modern new house accord with the proportions of Grecian Architecture, that it is generally safer not to attempt the introduction of Columns than to offend by a false intercolumniation: and this difficulty is much increased when they are to be adapted to a house already built. Pilasters, are I think always introduced with impropriety on the outside of a House; except as accompaniments to Columns, or in such situations where a building cannot be seen from a distance, or where there is no room for Columns; as we frequently see them introduced to enrich public edifices in the streets of a City; but the lines formed by the shadows of a pilaster are little seen at a distance; from whence the general effect of a building in the Country is always to be studied.

39   Digital redrawing of one of the illustrations from the lost Lamer House Red Book, now surviving only as a photocopy.

40   Lamer House, as illustrated by John Chessel Buckler in 1834, showing that many of the improvements suggested by Repton to the architecture of the house had been implemented.

Altering the colour of the house from red to white; or rather stone colour; and breaking the parallel line <of> roof by a pediment, will alone produce a very pleasing effect, yet as the jambs on each side the centre window are wider than the others, it will be necessary to enlarge that window and support it by a portico more proportionate to the house the present portico being too low for its situation. As I have ventured to depart from Mr Fulchers design in some particulars, it will be proper, to give my reasons for having done so. I have omitted the vases and the pateras for the sake of that simplicity which should be the leading character of Lamer, and if the semi-circular breaks in which the lower windows are placed, were also omitted, I think it would be better: the architraves and mouldings round the windows would increase the expence without adding to the general effect at a small distance. This as I have before observed should be the first consideration in all external Architecture; and it is by the disposition of the windows, and those bold projections which make deep shadows, that we are to produce general effects: it is with this view, that I propose a square portico in preference to a round one; because the shadow of one will be more conspicuous than the other; and tho' considerably larger it will be less expensive than the round one.

The House will derive great importance from being shown at an angle presenting two fronts, and if no where looks so well as at the spot from whence the following drawing No IV is made, even the present house from that spot is not displeasing.

It is not uncommon to see a good house disfigured by white window shutters or blinds, which used in a white house are apt to blot out so many of the windows, this effect on a red house offends less, yet it gives the building a motley appearance as shewn in the slide of the drawing.[16]

Approach

Having already so frequently delivered my opinion on this subject in other places I shall here only sum up the principal requisites of a good approach to a house.

1st It is and ought to be a <u>Road to the House</u> and to that principally.

2ndly If it is not naturally the nearest road possible, it ought artificially to be made impossible to go a nearer.

3rdly The artificial obstacles thrown in the way to make this road the nearest ought to appear natural.

4thly Where an Approach quits the high road, it ought not to break from it at right angles which robs the entrance of importance (except it be a long skreen like that at Sion House) but rather at some bend of the public road from whence a lodge or gate may be more conspicuous and the high road may appear to branch from the approach rather than the approach from the high road.

5thly After the approach enters the park it should avoid skirting along its boundary which betrays the want of extent or unity of property.

6thly The house should not be seen at so great a distance as to make it appear less than it really is.

7thly It is particularly desirable that the house should be at first presented in a pleasing point of view, and if it is possible it should be all shewn at once, and not be displayed by degrees.

8thly As soon as the House or any part of it is visible from the Approach, there should be no temptation to quit the road, which will certainly be the case if, the road be at all circuitous, without sufficient obstacles to justify its course; such as water, or inaccessible grounds &c.

Mr Richmonds Road

There is no part of my profession so painful to me as the occasional necessity of condemning or altering what has already been adopted by the advice of a predecessor, and I have always considered the late Mr Richmond as the only person since the immortal Brown whose ideas were at all correct on the subject: he understood perfectly how to give the most natural shape to artificial ground, how to dress walks in a pleasure garden, and how to leave or plant picturesque groupes of trees, his lines were generally graceful and easy, but his knowledge of the Art was rather technical and executive; than theoretical; he could stake out the detached parts of a place with much taste, but of the great outline he had so little idea that he never delivered any general plan, and indeed I have frequently heard his employers complain 'that they seldom understood what were his intentions till they were executed'. It is perhaps for this reason, that I so frequently meet with discordant parts in places improved under his direction, and I have hardly ever seen an <u>Approach</u> made by Mr Richmond, which could be fairly justified, they are all circuitous and consequently generally neglected.

If the rules I have laid down in the preceeding page have any foundation in reason, I have only to desire that the present lines of approaching Lamer be tried by that standard.

[No V Drawing of the approach and the cottage. *Not reproducible.*]

A Comparison

The only plausible reason for skirting along the edge of a park, with an approach, is the objection to what is called 'cutting up the Lawn by a line of gravel across it'. This at Lamer is at once answered by observing that a foot path and a bridle way* must cut across the park, and that a road from the house and stables to the farm must be provided for: it will therefore surely be better to make one road serve all these purposes and at the same time form the most interesting and natural line of approach. I propose instead of going to the place of the present gate, to

_____

*   There is no right of bridle way.

make the entrance where the park first joins the road, and at this spot a small single cottage of the kind I have described in the foregoing sketch N° 5 would have a pleasing effect: the absolute necessity of a Lodge here I have myself twice experienced, by having been obliged to stop at the gate till a key could be procured from the house.

I think the pale should be continued from the road, and perhaps the plantation at the corner a little increased by a continuation of the skreen eastward.

In the drawing which represents the lodge I have shewn the pale dividing the park from the adjoining arable land, for tho' the appearance of a park pale is always to be avoided <u>within</u> <u>side</u>; yet whenever it is seen on the <u>outside</u> of a park it gives importance to the place.

[No VI Drawing of the house with suggested alterations. *Not reproducible.*]

Plantations

The too great expanse of Lawn which I have already mentioned, requires to be broken by certain plantations, which having no map I cannot describe on paper; but they may be so disposed as not only to enrich the view to the south without excluding any material distant objects, but also they may be made subservient to the new approach, by hiding all view of the house till we arrive at the spot I have described and represented in the drawing No VI.

This is not to be done by one continued skreen, but by such separate clumps as may produce the same effect without giving an air of confinement. A plantation will also be necessary to the east, it will hide the hedge in this approach and give height to the opposite side of the valley leading towards the farm house. There is a corner of a field which should be thrown into the park, because it makes an unpleasantly acute angle when seen in the Road leading to St Albans, from whence the House is displayed to great advantage, well backed by wood: in the following sketch I do not pretend to that minuteness of portraiture which may delineate every object, but the general appearance of the house is shewn in its altered state, at such a distance as to depend for its effect, entirely on the great masses of light and shade, since the feeble projection of pilasters or Architraves would be invisible: yet the pediment, the portico, and the larger window over it will sufficiently enrich the front without any unnecessary expence: in this sketch I have faintly marked the acute angle of the hedge which I before mentioned as necessary to be removed.

[No VII drawing of road with carriage and pedestrians. *Not reproducible.*]

Approach from Ayott

Great part of this already marked upon the ground, it is less necessary to describe it, especially as without a map it is very difficult to explain by words its direction; but I shall just mention it to assign my reasons for the change.

The single avenue is not of sufficient consequence in the size of its trees to justify the roads continuing <along> it, especially as the Character of the house has been totally changed.

An approach thro' a venerable double avenue to a Gothic mansion is often allowable, but in this instance the avenue should be hid by a plantation in the spot where the road is to quit it, and <from whence it> takes an easy curve across the corner of a field, which must belong to the park as far as the high trees.

Thus instead of an uninteresting flat we gain a view of the rich valley and country towards Hatfield, and tho' the Stable front will be the first object that presents itself, yet this being a subordinate and not the principal approach and the stables themselves being ornamental, I see no objection to their being seen amongst the trees, but rather an advantage. This road may now very fairly come forwarder than would otherwise be allowable, because its union with the principal approach is a full justification.

Walks

The pleasure ground has been made with so much good taste by Mr Richmond that I should advise no alteration in what is already done; but the walk should be continued thro' the wood, and to avoid returning by the same ground it may be very beautifully conducted under the irregular line of majestic Beeches. In the little sketch which by way of a Vignette concludes this volume, I have attempted to show these beeches, and in the distance have inserted a shed half buried in the wood, the front of which is composed of the present portico to the house. I do not mean that it is to be placed in that situation, but it will be a handsome object seen from the outside of some part of the wood, and a reposoir may also be made elsewhere of the old gothic porch which has I hope been saved for that purpose, but this should be entirely buried withinside, and in some sequestered spot, where its different character may not appear incongruous with the modernised front of the Mansion and Offices.

[No VIII Drawing of the beeches and portico. *Not reproducible.*]

Notes

1   D. Stern, *A Hertfordshire Demesne of Westminster Abbey* (Hatfield, 2000); L. Stone and J. Fawtier-Stone, *An Open Elite: England 1540–1880* (Oxford, 1984), pp. 200–6.

2   HALS: D/EB2102/T20 deeds of house, orchard and land near Lamer Park gate, 1589–1676; HALS: 27362, undated 'particuler of the Mannor of Lamere', but probably late sixteenth- or very early seventeenth-century in date, records 'a faire brick house w[i]th orchard and gardens, court yards & all other out houses w[i]th a dovehouse' valued at £1,500, together with a 'well paled' park of 110 acres which included 20 acres of wood ground.

3   HALS: 27424/1–10, Lamer Account Book, 1767–1783 and other papers, 1665–1780; C. Oman, *Ayot Rectory* (London, 1965), p. 157.

4   D. Brown, 'Nathaniel Richmond (1724–1784): "One of the gentleman improvers"', unpublished PhD thesis (University of East Anglia, 2000), p. 25.

5   HALS: 27424/1–10; 80232(a)–80238, Book of Estate Rentals & Accounts, 1787–1916.

6   HALS: CP109/29/2, 'A Plan of the Manor of Whethampsted in the County of Hertford belonging to the Dean and Chapter of the Collegiate Church of St Peter Westminster', surveyed by D. Munford, 1799.

7   HALS: 80232(a).

8   NRO: MS10.

9   Two of these have been digitally redrawn – see Figure 39.

10 HALS: DE/Gd(Add)/P1, volume of maps of the Lamer Park estate, surveyed by E. Johnson, Hatfield, 1827.

11 HALS: DE/Gd(Add)/P6, undated sketch of proposed improvement to the old Library front.

12 In 1806 Robert Fulcher advertised a particular of his new stucco in *The Ipswich Advertiser* and said it could be seen at Lamer.

13 HALS: DE/X269/B58, sale particulars, 1953.

14 Red Book lost; photocopy in private collection.

15 J. Delille, *Les Jardins, en Quatre Chants* (Paris, 1780).

16 'Slide' is Repton's term for the flaps used in his 'before and after' drawings. The drawing referred to here is that reconstructed as Figure 39.

New Barnes, St Peter and St Stephen (St Albans)

TL 156054

New Barnes lies to the south-east of St Albans, adjacent to a flour mill on the river Ver. It originally formed part of the Manor of Sopwell, granted by Henry VIII to Sir Richard Lee after the Dissolution of St Albans Abbey in 1539, but it became a separate property in the following century, when it was sold by Sir Harbottle Grimston to Robert New, a member of a wealthy St Albans family.[1] The estate was of modest size, never much more than 300 acres (*c*. 120 hectares), and comprised a combination of low-lying meadows along the river and productive arable fields on the rising ground to the east. An estate map of *c*.1660 shows New Barnes as a relatively modest timber-framed house with a small formal garden on the north-east (entrance) side and a large area of orchard to the south.[2] It was approached along a lane from the east.

By the time Humphry Repton arrived at New Barnes in 1802, considerable changes had been made to this original house, probably by Edward Strong, Master Mason of St Paul's Cathedral and a relative of the New family, who lived there until his death in 1723.[3] A drawing made by Oldfield around 1800 shows the entrance front of a five-bay, three-storey, red-brick building in typical early eighteenth-century style, with a two-storey extension to the side (Figure 41). Dury and Andrews' county map of 1766 suggests that significant developments had also taken place in the immediate vicinity of the house. The original garden to the front had disappeared and, in its place, a rather larger garden had

been laid out to the rear, facing the river, one element of which appears to have been a formal water feature, linked to another pool and fed by a spring in a field to the north-west. The orchard still remained, although now somewhat smaller; there had been some adjustment to the pattern of field boundaries; and a bridge had been constructed across the river Ver, beside the mill, linking New Barnes more directly with Sopwell and St Albans.

In 1797 the then owner of New Barnes, a widow named Ann Horn, died. The estate, described as a 'Freehold Residence and Farm', was advertised for sale in *The Times*:

> A very desirable FREEHOLD ESTATE, advantageously situate adjoining the High Road, within one mile of St Alban's in the county of Herts, and 29 from London, called New Barnes, comprising a commodious Brick Dwelling-house, with all convenient offices, pleasure-grounds, fish-ponds, gardens and orchard, and the surrounding inclosures of excellent meadow, pasture, arable and woodland, a spacious farm-yard, with every necessary outbuilding, the whole comprising 192 acres, lying very compact, rounded and intersected by the River Coln, and well watered.[4]

The property was bought by Matthew Towgood, the third son of an extremely successful businessman of the same name.[5] Matthew

senior, who came from a nonconformist background, had made a large amount of money as a merchant trading with the West Indies from Bridgewater in Somerset before moving to London to set up the banking firm of Langston, Towgood and Amory.[6] When he died in 1791 his will instructed that his five children should receive equal shares of his fortune, enabling Matthew to move his already large family to New Barnes and his elder brother William to buy the nearby estate of Organ Hall, just outside Radlett (q.v.).[7] It is possible that Towgood's interest in purchasing New Barnes had a commercial aspect. In 1795 a plan to build a canal linking St Albans and Watford had gained royal approval and, although this never materialised, it was intended to go via Sopwell and New Barnes Mills.[8] A more promising project financed by the Towgood family bank in Hertfordshire concerned the Frogmore paper mill on the river Gade, where one of the first mechanised papermaking machines was installed by the Fourdrinier brothers in 1803.[9] This involvement in papermaking ultimately took Matthew Towgood away from Hertfordshire: after the Fourdriniers were declared bankrupt in 1810 he moved his family to Little Paxton, near St Neots (then Huntingdonshire, now Cambridgeshire), and took over the running of a more advanced paper mill there, which the bank had held from them as security.

Towgood's decision to employ Humphry Repton to improve his new estate may have been inspired by the example set by his eldest brother's business partner John Langston MP, who had done the same at his Oxfordshire home, Sarsden House, in 1795.[10] Matthew's other brother, William, also used Repton's services at his Hertfordshire estate around the same time (q.v.). The New Barnes Red Book, like that for Woodhill, is much concerned with establishing the 'character' of the place as a gentleman's residence, as opposed to a working farm. The key proposals were the conversion of the fish ponds to the south-west of the mansion into a diminutive serpentine lake (with the water brought closer to the house and made more visible by the removal of existing trees and shrubs); the creation of a new park to the east of the house, extending up the valley side and bounded to east and south by perimeter belts; and the construction of a new approach drive, running through the middle of the park from an entrance on what is now Napsbury Lane although continuing beyond it, to the east, to meet the London Road.

The period immediately after Repton's visit was not an easy one for Towgood. His first wife Margaret died in December 1803 and, although he married a second wife, Ann Gibson, in September 1804, by 1807 New Barnes was on the market again.[11] It was advertised in the *Morning Chronicle* in very similar terms to those used a decade earlier, although interestingly this time the reference to fishponds is omitted, and a 'green-house' is an added feature. The estate is now described as covering 319 acres, and there is more emphasis on the potential income to be made from 'three most eligible farms … the greatest part of which are free of tithes'.[12] No mention is made of any recent changes to the landscape. Exactly when the Towgoods left New Barnes is unclear – a new daughter, Frances, was baptised at St Peter's Church in St Albans in May 1809, so the initial attempt to sell the property may have been unsuccessful – but they had certainly taken up residence at Heddings Manor in Little Paxton by 1812.[13]

Many of Repton's recommendations for New Barnes appear to have been implemented. The Ordnance Survey draft drawings

Left
41   New Barnes house, as illustrated by Henry George Oldfield, *c*.1800.

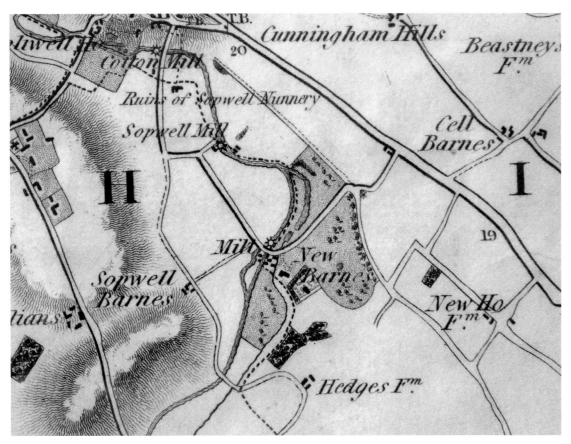

42   New Barnes and its grounds, as depicted on Andrew Bryant's county map of 1822.

of 1805 show the serpentine area of water to the south-west of the house and suggest that the fields to the east of the house had been thrown together to form the new park. All these features, together with the perimeter belt around the park, are more clearly depicted on Bryant's map of 1822 (Figure 42); and, in much greater detail, on a map which accompanies sale particulars of 1886, based on the Ordnance Survey first edition 25-inch map (Figure 43).[14] This clearly shows the curving 'fishpond' to the south of the house, which eventually flows into the river Ver, and which is described in the particulars as 'a small lake divided into upper and lower portions, which afford an agreeable diversification of Scenery close to the Residence'. It is noteworthy, however, that this feature directly replaced the original formal pond and had not, as Repton recommended, been moved any closer to the house, probably because the topography would have made this prohibitively expensive. The park to the north and east of the house is clearly shown, although the belt had not been established quite as Repton had proposed, and many of his clumps had not been planted. It is described as 'upwards of 40 acres of rich pasture' planted with 'oak, elm, chestnut, fir, pine, beech, hornbeam, in clumps and belts': comparison with the 1660s estate map shows that it had been formed by throwing together four fields, and that a curving spinney to the east and a small circular copse had been retained as woodland areas: many of the parkland trees had similarly once stood in the dividing hedges.

The new driveway across the parkland, designed to meet the high road and display the estate to best advantage, was never created. Instead, a shorter curving driveway, linking the house to the lane which Repton so disliked at an entrance lodge, appears on the 1886 map, but not on Bryant's survey of 1822. A pair of lodges and an archway still exist here, the design matching that of an archway at the house end of the drive.

The original house and some of the outbuildings are now absorbed into the complex of Sopwell House Hotel, while much of the former estate land is occupied by Verulam Golf Club. Repton's perimeter belt survives, although much replanted and, in places, extended; the serpentine watercourse has dried up, although traces of its route are preserved along a boundary. The park is now occupied by fairways, separated by typical golf-course planting, although some fragments of Repton-period planting may survive, together with the remains of an earlier spinney. The eastern margins of the park are now bounded by the main railway line from London. Repton's proposals for New Barnes may, in large measure, have been implemented, but they survive in only fragmentary form today.

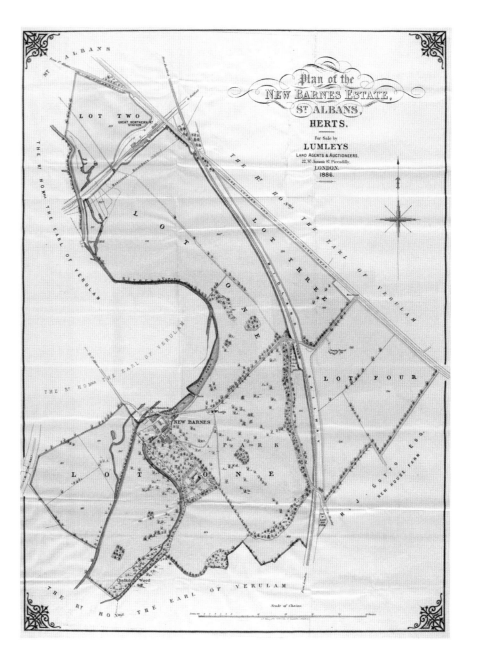

43 The grounds of New Barnes, as illustrated on a sale map of 1886, based on the Ordnance Survey First Edition 25-inch map.

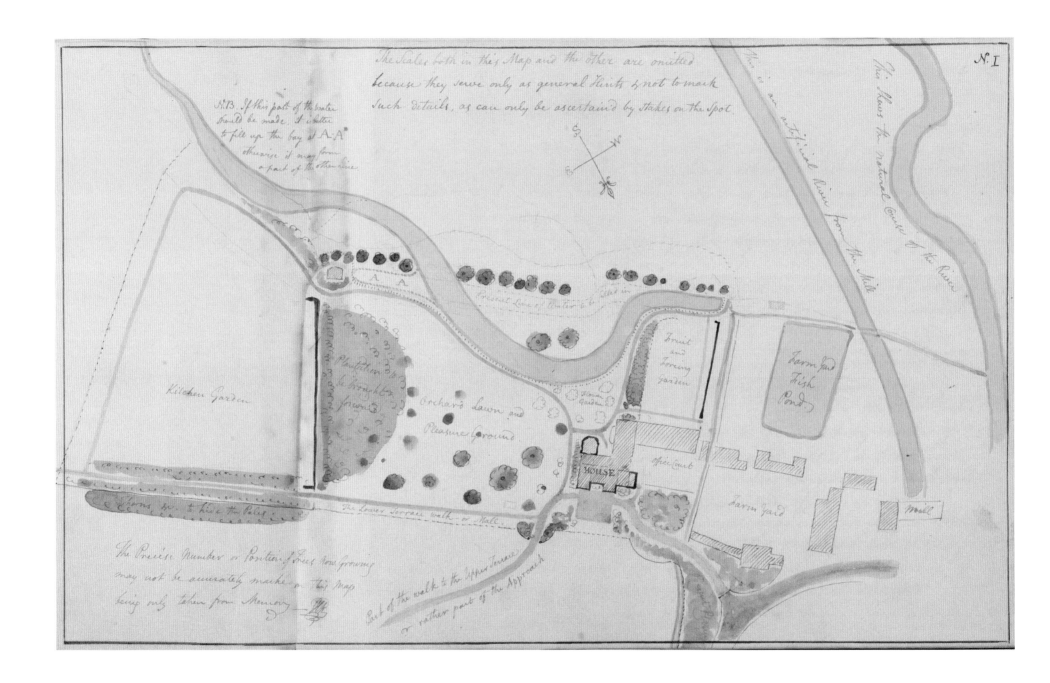

The Scales both in this Map and the other are omitted
because they serve only as general Hints & not to mark
such details, as can only be ascertaind by stakes on the spot.

This shews the natural course of the River

This is an artificial River from the Mill

N.B. If this part of the water
should be made, it is better
to fill up the bay at A.A.
otherwise it may form
a part of the other line

Present Line of Water to be filled in

A A

Kitchen Garden

Plantation
to brought to
forward

Fruit
and
forcing
Garden

Farm Yard
Fish
Pond

Orchard Lawn and

flower
Garden

Pleasure Ground

HOUSE

Office Court

Farm Yard

Thorns &c. to hide the Pales

The lower Terrace walk or Mall

Mill

The Precise Number or Position of Trees now growing
may not be accurately marked on this Map
being only taken from Memory

Part of the walk to the Upper Terrace
or rather part of the Approach

New Barnes in Herts:
A Seat of Matthew Towgood Esq[r]

Introduction

Sir,

The following remarks for the Improvement of New Barnes will in some measure have been anticipated by our conversation on the spot, and as a Volume of my general opinions is now actually in the press it is the less necessary to explain my reasons for the hints I now suggest. Yet there remains one point which I have not before noticed, because it never before occurred in the course of my practice, viz Your objection to the Approach, because it shewed the most beautiful part of the place. I would allow some weight to this objection if the road were to be circuitous, but if it happen to be the nearest line possible, I cannot see any reason for going round to avoid shewing, what half the persons who visit the place may perhaps never be shown at all unless they see it in the approach.

I have the honour to be, Sir,
Your most obedient Humble Servant,

H. Repton.

September 1802
Harestreet near Romford Essex

Left
44   Red Book: plan of
the pleasure grounds.

45 Red Book:
illustration II,
view to the south
east, 'before'.

N.º II.

46 Red Book:
illustration II,
view to the south
east, 'after'.

Character.

In delivering my opinion of the improvement of a place, I must suppose that certain general principles of good Taste exist, on which a rational plan may be founded; for otherwise the whole business of my profession would be useless, and every hint for improvement might be contradicted or at least disputed. I shall therefore premise with respect to the Character and Situation of New Barnes that it is to be rendered as cheerful, beautiful, and interesting as may be consistent with economy, utility, and the natural advantages of the Situation; without sacrificing too much the value of the land, or the convenience of the Place, to the appearance it may have to strangers: yet bearing in mind that True Taste teaches us that we do not live for ourselves alone.

If profit were only to be considered, the lawn in front of the House must continue to be sown with corn, and the flower garden at the back with potatoes and cabbages; but the Character of the Mansion being distinct from that of the Farm, the ground should partake of the same Character.

It is therefore my duty to point out under these circumstances, what advantage may be taken of the natural beauties of the Situation.

Situation.

When this Mansion was a mere farm-house, its situation was unobjectionable; but as the residence of a Gentleman it might have been better placed on the estate. At present while it unites the convenience of the former, with the appearance of the latter, it is necessary to take some advantages of the Views from the house which have been hitherto neglected.

In arranging the apartments of a new house, I have frequently asserted as a general principle, that if consistent with objects of greater importance in point of utility, the windows of all the best rooms (except the dining parlour) should be rather towards the south than towards the north, and that they should command the most interesting features. This induces me to turn my attention immediately towards those points of view where the greatest improvement can be effected; and whether two new rooms be added to the south, as originally proposed; or only the drawing room be enlarged in that direction; I must begin my plan of improvement with considering <u>that side</u> of the house, especially as the views towards the North are along an inclined plane*, which altho' it is actually a steep hill yet it appears to disadvantage from the low situation of the house.

---

* In a Work now in the press I have explained the effect of views taken from different heights and also the difference between Views to the North and to the South.[16]

The Water and View South-East.

The County of Hartford exclusive of its beautiful inequality, possesses two other circumstances in greater perfection than most other Counties in England viz. Wood and Water, and altho' of the former there is but a small portion belonging to this Estate, yet the richness of the hedgerow Timber, and the abundance of Woods in the neighbourhood, make up this deficiency, and only require to be shewn by opening views towards them.

With respect to the Water, altho' the house is surrounded on every side by a copious supply of brilliant coloured water, yet it is so disposed as hardly to be visible from the house; and in the only part where it is seen, it appears raised above the level of the adjoining ground. A very small quantity of water illumined by a South or Western Sun makes a great feature of beauty in the home scenery, and with very little trouble the straight canal may be changed to the natural course of a river, which by going off in a line from the Eye, and by making its way thro' the opening proposed in the row of trees, will reflect a brilliant sky instead of the dark foliage of the lofty Elms. Of this the sketch Nº II of part of the View towards the South-East will best explain the effect. And here I shall observe that I have supposed the old channel leading to the thatched seat entirely filled up, because the surface of the proposed new line of water should be rather below than above the level of the ground, and serve as a drain to the land, rather than be pounded up above its natural surface.

View South-West.

The row of tall trees and the line of Yew hedge, at present form a Curtain between the eye and all that is worth seeing. Yet from the Aspect being Westerly, this Curtain must be undrawn with caution or we shall open the house to the glare of a setting Sun and the power of driving winds and rain, which are always to be guarded against in a Western Exposure. For this reason I have in the sketch Nº III supposed more trees to be left than I otherwise should have done, to open the View into the valley.

And by leading the course of the water much nearer to the house we shall not only see more of it, but it will lessen the quantity of dressed ground, and increase the quantity of feeding ground; bringing the cattle nearer to the windows yet making a natural boundary between the meadow and the garden which in this instance should I think be entirely dedicated to flowers and flowering shrubs.

These two sketches with the help of the map Nº I [see Figure 44] will, I hope, sufficiently explain all that I think advisable to improve the Views from the house.

47   Red Book:
illustration III,
view to the south
west, 'before'.

48 Red Book: illustration III, view to the south west, 'after'.

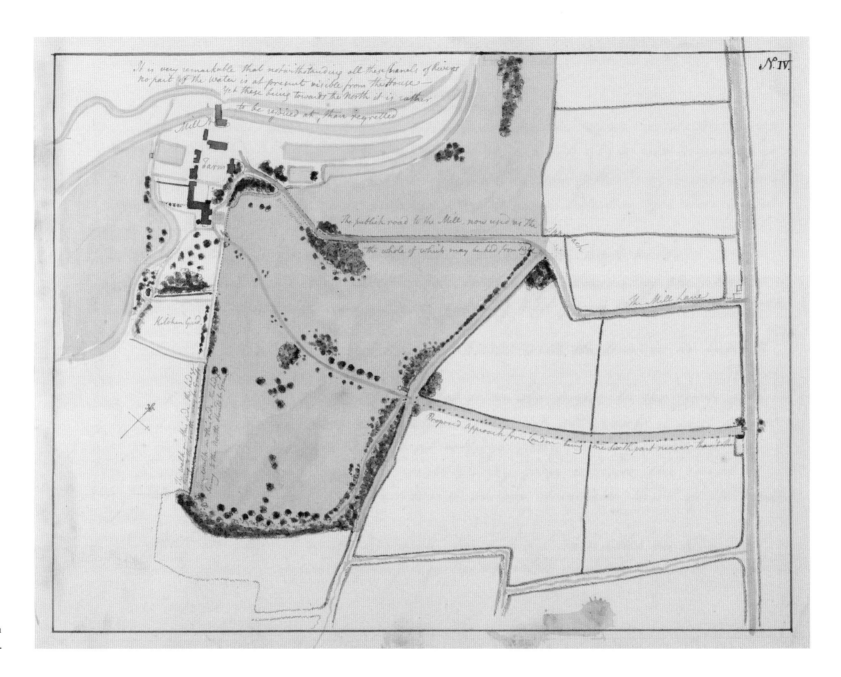

49   Red Book: illustration
     IV, plan of the park.

View to the North.

In considering the Views towards the North, I must suppose the land immediately in sight of the house to be laid down in grass, and some plantations to enrich its surface and make it look more like a park and less like a farm. But before I should recommend any dots or clumps to be meagrely scattered over this comparatively naked hill, I should first advise an ample plantation along its brow, and when this has acquired the growth of a few years, the intermediate space may be enriched with more effect and more certainty of success, by transplanting some of the trees from the necessary thinning of these plantations, after they have become naturalized to the soil, and after some shelter towards the North and East shall have been formed by this skreen. But it is not only in the View from the house that such a plantation is necessary, it will form a most interesting Walk and improve that natural terrace which is doubtless the greatest beauty of the Place. I do not here mean <to recommend> the narrow belt of shrubbery which might be advisable in places where ground is valued by the foot, not by the acre: but such a breadth of forest trees as may in time form a Wood not less respectable than that towards the East of which I shall take advantage in connecting a Walk to the Terrace.

The Approach.

Having so fully explained my intentions on the Spot, and the map Nᵒ IV shewing the precise line of the proposed Approach, it is not necessary to enlarge much on this subject, yet I will mention the following reasons for it.

1st It is nearer from London by one sixth of the distance between the Turnpike and the house.

2nd It shews the extent of the place and connects it with the high road.

3rd It avoids the lane in the hollow way which is the opprobrium of the place and which with very little management may be entirely hid from the house and from the Approach.

4th It forms a Walk immediately connecting the house with the Terrace or makes a return walk from that thro' the Woods

and lastly. As it only requires to be gravelled from the house to the first gate; from thence it may be used or not at pleasure. But at all events a seat, which I supposed to form the back of a Labourer's cottage may be so placed as to answer the double purpose of ornament and Utility from whence the most interesting view of St. Albans may be shewn in one direction and of the house &c in another.

With a sketch of the latter I shall conclude these brief remarks on a subject which I rejoice to find so capable of improvement, with so little expense or difficulty.

50 Red Book:
view of the house
from the east,
across the park.

Notes

1   A. Wares, 'Sopwell House – from Tudor Shed to Luxury Hotel', *Herts Advertiser*, 22 August 2013.

2   HALS: XIII/30, Gorhambury archive.

3   J.T. Smith, *Hertfordshire Houses: A selective inventory* (London, 1993), p. 156.

4   Sales by auction, *The Times*, London, 27 January 1797. The river Ver flows into the river Colne.

5   S. Norman, *Sopwell, a history and collection of memories* (Sopwell Residents Association, 2012), p. 20, based on research by Anne Wares. In 1799 Towgood is recorded paying 6s 8d land tax as proprietor.

6   A. Gordon, 'Michaijah Towgood', *Dictionary of National Biography*, 1885–1900, Vol. 57, <http://www.like2do.com/source?s=Towgood,_Michaijah_(DNB00)>, accessed 21 October 2017.

7   TNA: PROB 11/1202/74, will of Matthew Towgood, banker, Clements Lane, City of London.

8   Norman, *Sopwell*, p. 45.

9   D. Broad, *The History of Little Paxton: The story of a Huntingdonshire village on the banks of the river Great Ouse* (Little Paxton, 1989), p. 253.

10 S. Daniels, *Humphry Repton: Landscape gardening and the geography of Georgian England* (Yale, 1999), p. 265.

11 *Gentlemans Magazine*, 28 September 1804, p. 976.

12 *Morning Chronicle*, 2 September 1807 and subsequent dates up to the sale on 11 November 1807.

13 HALS: DP/93/1/3, St Peter St Albans baptism register, 1796–1812; Towgood's next daughter Ellen was baptised at Little Paxton in July 1812: Broad, *Little Paxton*, p. 254.

14 HALS: DE/Hx/E740, sale particulars for New Barnes Estate, St Albans, Lumleys Land Agents and Auctioneers, Piccadilly, London, 22 June 1886.

15 Gorhambury House archives.

16 Repton is here referring to his book *Observations on the Theory and Practice of Landscape Gardening*, published in 1803.

Panshanger, Hertford St Andrew

TL 290132

WILLIAM COWPER, SON OF THE second baronet, was born at Hertford Castle in 1665, served as Lord Chancellor from 1707 and became the first Earl Cowper in 1718.[1] He established the Cowper family at Cole Green in the parish of Hertingfordbury in c.1704 and in 1719 bought the neighbouring house and farm at Panshanger.[2] The mansion at Cole Green was separated from Panshanger by a broad valley occupied by the diminutive river Mimram, flowing south-east towards Hertford and marking the parish boundary between Hertingfordbury to the south and Hertford St Andrew to the north. Cole Green mansion stood within its park on a broad plateau lying to the south of the Mimram. To the north, on land sloping down to the river, lay the open fields of Hertingfordbury, while the flood plain itself was occupied by hay meadows, likewise divided into strips.[3] Panshanger House stood to the north of the river and around a mile (1.6 kilometres) to the north-east of Cole Green, amidst almost 400 acres (c. 160 hectares) of enclosed land, and (unlike Cole Green mansion) enjoyed fine views across the valley.

There had been a notable house at Panshanger from at least the late sixteenth century and it was grand enough to be described as a 'mansion' by 1712.[4] There were gardens and walks cut through an adjacent grove and in 1719 the tenant, Sir Gregory Page, proposed to lay out an ornamental canal in the valley 'at the bottom', although whether he did so is not known.[5] A plan of the Panshanger estate drawn at the time of its purchase by Earl Cowper in 1719 shows a landscape of fields and meadows,[6] and a contemporary timber survey recorded strips of trees between the fields west of the house, one of which contained the 'Great Oak', which was twice the size of almost all its neighbours.[7] The county map by Dury and Andrews of 1766, however, indicates that extensive ornamental grounds had been laid out to the east and south of the house, in place of the earlier fields.

For much of the later eighteenth century Panshanger was the home of Lady Caroline Cowper, daughter of the second earl, and her husband Henry Seymour, who was Groom of the Bedchamber to George III and an MP.[8] The Seymours may have commissioned the architect James Adam (younger brother of the more famous Robert Adam) to draw up plans to improve 'Panshanger villa' and an illustration by H.G. Oldfield shows a house with at least two phases of building history (Figure 51).[9] When Lady Caroline died in 1773 Henry seems to have leased the house to some high-class tenants, including the sister of the duke of Manchester, Lady Caroline Montague.[10] In 1798 the fourth Earl Cowper, who had inherited the family estates in 1789, agreed to pay Henry Seymour £150 a year for the right to use Panshanger, but just a few months later in February 1799 the earl died (at Panshanger) at the age of 22. He was succeeded as fifth earl by his younger brother, Peter Leopold Francis Nassau Clavering-Cowper (1778–1837),

51 The old house at Panshanger, illustrated by Henry George Oldfield in the 1790s.

52   Engraving of Panshanger, based on a sketch by Repton, published in Peacock's *Polite Repository* for 1801.

who, following his brother's lead, decided that he would live at Panshanger in preference to the ancestral seat of Cole Green. A few months later he commissioned Humphry Repton to submit plans for laying out a new landscape there, which was to be created out of Cole Green park, the grounds of Panshanger and land that was then being enclosed from the open fields of Hertingfordbury, to the south of the Mimram. Repton visited Panshanger in June 1799 and delivered his Red Book eight months later in February 1800, although the creation of the new landscape began in July 1799, just a few weeks after his visit. An illustration of the house and its landscape, based on a sketch by Repton, was published in Peacock's *Polite Repository* for 1801 (Figure 52).

In the opening to the Red Book Repton records his first impressions of 'that delightful Valley which extends from Hartford to Welwyn', stating that 'there is no part more beautiful or interesting than the Ground near the present House at Panshanger', which he thought could not 'be better situated'. But he considered the view south from Panshanger House to be too confined by the 'narrow dell' below the house to make it a suitable location for the more stately – and considerably wider – residence that the earl planned to build. Much of the Red Book is in fact concerned with the siting, layout and style of the new mansion, and its relation to the valley landscape. Until its precise location had been decided Repton felt unable to make detailed proposals for improvements and his Red Book consequently contains few written specifications for laying out the new parkland. He deliberately left the first page of the book blank, writing on it in pencil: 'for the Map to shew the general Extent & boundary of the Park – The several approaches from Harford – Colegreen & Tewin with the Plantations – Drives &c'. Unfortunately no map was ever added and the Red Book thus remains, in a sense, incomplete.

Repton's proposals for the design of the 'water' or lake are largely described in a plan which he drew 'to shew the shapes of Ground … Wood & situations for a House', and his scheme for converting farmland into parkland by removing 'cross hedges and cornfields' is illustrated in various 'before and after' views. Of the massive programme of tree planting which Repton instigated there is almost no mention except in regard to his proposals for the 'views towards the south', which, he states, 'I shall defer mentioning in detail, till I can shew their improvement by the plantations which must be made to cloath the opposite bank'. The approaches to the house and the removal of public roads from the new park are also barely mentioned, the last section of the Red Book merely containing an oblique reference to moving the high road away from the north side of the house. Despite this lack of clear evidence in the Red Book itself, the surviving estate records, family papers and Repton's own publications leave no doubt that a great deal of the work undertaken to create the landscape of Panshanger park from the summer of 1799 was carried out in accordance with his advice, presumably delivered verbally during visits made in June 1799, September 1800 (three days) and March 1801 (four days).

Repton's proposal to divert the course of the river Mimram to the north side of the flood plain, where it could be made into a broad, sinuous sheet of water visible from the house, was accepted, and work started straight away. The Panshanger estate accounts record that in July 1799 'about 60 hands [were] at work' digging and 'wheeling out' the 'moory' or marshy soil, as well as huge quantities of the underlying 'gravel soil', in the valley bottom. In August another 20 men joined the workforce and by September no fewer than 110 men were employed on the project. Work continued through the winter, spring and summer of 1800 and included widening the water to the south and north, 'wheeling and spreading earth' and 'altering and slopeing'. By September 1800 the 'Piece of Water' was nearing completion and Repton was on site to supervise the final levelling on the north and south sides of the water, on the island and below the cascade.[11] The total cost of making the 'piece of Water below Pansanger' recorded at Michaelmas 1800 was £2,030 2s 1d and a full transcript of the ledger entry is presented below, after the transcription of the Red Book.[12] The lake featured two islands. The larger of these, the 'Broadwater island', is located at the great bend at the west end of the upper Broadwater: the plan in the Red Book shows that Repton's initial ideas for this were less well defined than those for the smaller island, which was carefully placed to conceal the weir in the view from the house, especially once it had been planted with trees.

Earl Cowper kept his own record of the tree planting in the park, which started in November 1799 on 'the Island by the Boat House'.[13] The following September Repton wrote to the earl, stating his intention to visit for 'a day or two' some time 'after the 16th or 17th Instant' (see transcription, below p. 154).[14] The earl's younger brother Edward Spencer Cowper recorded the two-day visit of Mr Repton and his son in his diary.[15] They arrived on Friday 19 September and the following day they 'Walk'd about the grounds the whole day marking plantations'. A few weeks later, in November, 1800 trees were planted in three locations: 'The great Plantation in Nether Street Common' (the arable field facing the house across the valley); 'between the Kitchen garden & the Road'; and 'on the Panshanger side of the new Piece of Water &c'. In November 1801 trees were planted in three further areas: on the south side of the new road 'descending the Hill from Panshanger to Poplar's green'; 'on the South side of the new Piece of water, & immediately opposite to that done last year'; and 'a small one on the other side of the Cascade by the Island'.[16] On 23 September 1802 the earl's brother 'Rode to Pansanger & Mark'd out some new Plantations', and on 8 November he 'Mark'd out the plantation destin'd to screen the Offices at Pansanger'. Earl Cowper recorded planting in November of that year 'All the Plantations intended to conceal the approach to the Carriage Bridge in the approach from London – that close to the offices at Panshanger & intended to conceal therefrom the approach - & that to the north of the Road between the great Oak & Panshanger House.'

Planting was to continue throughout the lifetime of the earl, who died in 1837, and beyond.[17] The early phases included the tree belt along the northern perimeter of the park 'to hide the paling', two small round plantations in Brocket field (across the valley south-west of the house), plantations and small round clumps on the slopes around the house and many acres of plantations on the valley sides south of the river. Many of these new plantations and clumps are depicted on estate maps of 1809 and 1810.[18]

On 3 November 1800 a writ was issued at Westminster commanding the sheriff of Hertfordshire, Justinian Casamajor, to hold an inquest into Earl Cowper's plans to divert highways and footpaths around Panshanger; four days later Edward Spencer Cowper recorded in his diary that 'the Jury met for turning the road & din'd at Panshanger', the latter being a common courtesy in such circumstances.[19] The public roads linking Hertford to Welwyn and Tewin and the road from Hertingfordbury to Welwyn, together with a number of footpaths, were duly diverted or closed, and over the next few years the earl paid for the construction of replacement roads that are still in use today: the B1000 from Hertford to Welwyn and Panshanger Lane between Cole Green and Poplars Green. In May 1801 he also built a new brick bridge to replace the ford across the river Mimram at Poplars Green.[20] In a note about road diversions in *Observations* Repton included Panshanger in a list of seven examples where, unusually, the alterations were supposedly advantageous to both landowner and public.[21] The changes were recorded by the assiduous diarist and local farmer John Carrington in two entries in 1800:[22] the second included a note that the third new road ran from 'Bramfield to Hatfield or Essington [Essendon] streight from Popler Green,

threw his old park close by his mansion house called Colegreen House, now pulled down'. A new carriage drive was constructed through the park from Cole Green to Panshanger, for which a bridge was constructed west of the new lake.[23] Repton submitted a plan for this, probably after his visit in March 1801, but it does not appear to have met with the earl's approval because in October 1804 the architect Samuel Wyatt was taken 'to the Water at Panshanger, with relation to a design for a new Bridge', which was built the following year.[24]

Given that almost all of the Red Book is concerned with the site and architectural style of the proposed new house at Panshanger, the plans for which were drawn up with the assistance of Repton's son John Adey, it is ironic that none of their suggestions were actually taken up.[25] Indeed, it seems likely that none of the building proposals submitted in the Red Book were accepted, including the conversion of the site of the old Panshanger House into stables and farm buildings and the removal of the walled kitchen garden from Cole Green to a position near the new mansion.[26] Repton's letter to the earl in January 1802 also mentions a plan for an 'Entrance Cottage', or lodge, for which he was owed £5 5s.[27] This plan does not survive: nor do his plans, also referred to in this letter, for a bridge and a boathouse. The 'cottage' may have been built, perhaps at Cole Green: in *Observations* Repton mentions Panshanger as an estate where well-maintained cottages adjoining the gates conferred 'adequate propriety' to the entrance from the public road.[28] With this possible exception, Samuel Wyatt (with whom Repton had long worked) appears to have been the earl's architect of choice, designing the alterations to Panshanger House as well as the carriage bridge over the Mimram, together with a

'New Lodge for the Keeper', which was constructed in the park from 1805.[29]

The payment of Repton's outstanding charges was recorded in Earl Cowper's bank pass-book in 1803: 'January 19 To Chas Cowper's bill to Forster Co for Humphry Ripton £32 11s'.[30] But it was to be another three years – and nearly seven years after work had started on the park – before the construction of the new house at Panshanger got underway. At the end of March 1806 John Carrington recorded: 'This month Lord Cowper begun Diging the foundation for Building a New house ajoyning the other at Pansanger';[31] and in April 1808:[32]

Thursday 28, … to Pansanger to See Lord Cowpers New House Building their. Joyneing to part of the old House, something Like a Castle, & all New Stables, But the simpletons Begun the foundation too Low in the Ground, abliged at a Great Expence to Lower the Ground above for the Howses better appearance … .

In contrast to his failed designs for the buildings, Repton's proposals for laying out the new park landscape *were* accepted and initiated with great enthusiasm and alacrity. The transformation of the valley started within weeks of his initial visit and was to continue for many decades, as his vision of 'rich hanging woods' rising above an elegant 'piece of water' was gradually realised. The results of the work undertaken in the first decade after Repton's initial visit are recorded on the estate maps of 1809 and 1810 referred to above (Figure 53). It is particularly noteworthy (especially with reference to sites such as Wall Hall – below, pp. 186–91) that the Red Book for Panshanger contains only a part of Repton's proposals for the landscape.

Panshanger house was demolished in the 1950s and the gardens largely dismantled, and the only buildings remaining today are the stables and the ruins of an orangery and conservatory, none of which owe their existence to Repton. Much of his landscape design, however, can still be recognised – despite decades of gravel extraction in the valley – and Panshanger Park is widely regarded as the finest example of Humphry Repton's work surviving in Hertfordshire today. The tranquillity and beauty of this section of the Mimram valley owes a great deal to the removal of the public roads in the early nineteenth century: the extensive views of grassy slopes fringed with woodlands and scattered with former hedgerow pollards all derive from Repton's Red Book, as does the sinuous Broadwater lake, whose reflections of the sky and valley sides continue to enliven the scene. The lake still contains two islands, the larger of which – the Broadwater island – was accessed by footbridges and formed part of the circuit of walks from the house. It was planted up with bulbs and flowering shrubs to produce a succession of colour throughout the year and carpets of snowdrops and aconites can still be seen, heralding the end of winter.

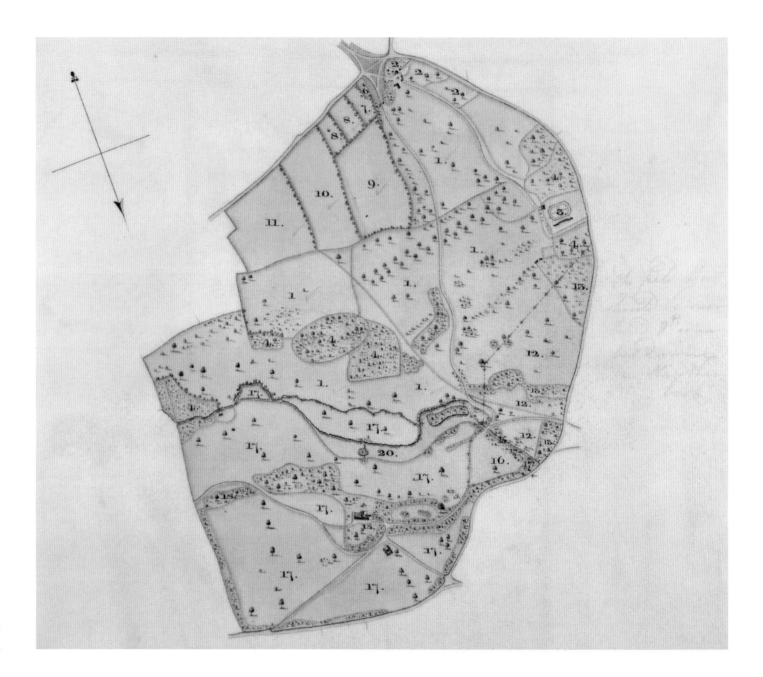

53 An estate map
of 1810, showing the
grounds of Panshanger
largely completed.

Panshanger in Hertfordshire
a Seat of the Right Honourable the Earl Cowper

&c. &c. &c.

My Lord

It is with peculiar satisfaction that I have the honour to submit to your Lordship's perusal, the following pages, in which I hope to prove that the Art I profess is not more founded on Caprice or fashion, than the Arts of Music, Poetry, Painting, or Sculpture; yet while few persons pretend to great Excellence in them who have not made these several Arts their peculiar study; it seems as if Landscape Gardening was so easy, that every Land Surveyor thinks himself competent to deliver an Opinion in that Art, though I confess, after many year's close Application, and the most extensive experience I still find it encompassed with Difficulties. The subject which your Lordship has been pleased to submit to my Consideration, is of no small magnitude; since it ought to comprehend a general plan for the future residence of your Lordship's family, with due attention to its Comfort, Convenience, and Magnificence; and at the same time that every advantage should be taken of the natural beauties of the situation. For the opportunity which your Lordship has given me of delivering this opinion, by consulting me on the subject, I beg to express my Gratitude and I have the honour to be My Lord

Your Lordships

Most obedient humble Servant

H Repton

At Panshanger the first Visit June 1799
Plan deliverd in February 1800 ---

This Page is left for the Map to shew the general Extent & boundary of the Park. The several approaches from Harford, Colegreen & Tewin with the Plantations, Drives &c

Character

It is impossible to do justice to the beauties of any Place, unless the whole be taken into Consideration, and its Character be duly ascertained; since that which may be adviseable in the Neighbourhood of a Cottage, will be totally inconsistent with the Environs of a Palace: and in Landscape Gardening as in every other Art, there must be a Consistency and Unity of character preserved, or the whole will be made up of discordant parts.

It was therefore impossible for me to advise how a piece of Water should be made at Panshanger, without at the same time considering under what circumstances that Water was to be chiefly viewed. The regular order of improvement seems to class points of view under three distinct heads.

1st From the house, or from given Stations which are permanent, such as Seats erected on favorite spots &c

2nd From the Approaches, or in the natural roads to the house, where an object ought to be made <to> appear to advantage, because it must be seen.

And **3rd** From the Drives or Walks which should shew the beauties of a place, and which may be so managed as to avoid those points of View, where any feature does not appear to advantage.

From hence it is evident, that no rational improvement can be suggested, without knowing from whence it is to be seen; and without previously determining where a house is to be built, it is absurd to fix the Situation of any great feature to be seen from the house: I shall therefore begin my plan for the Improvement of Panshanger by delivering an opinion concerning the situation for a house.

Concerning proper Situations for a House

This Page is quoted from the Work I published, which is now out of Print, and therefore cannot <easily> be referred to.

"However various opinions may be on the Choice of a Situation for a house, yet there appear to be some certain principles on which such choice ought to be founded, and these may be deduced from the following considerations.

First, The natural Character of the surrounding Country.

Second, The Aspects or Exposure, both with regard to the Sun and the prevalent Winds of the Country.

Third, The Shape of the Ground near the House.

Fourth, The Views from the several apartments.

Fifth, The Style, Character, and Size of the house itself.

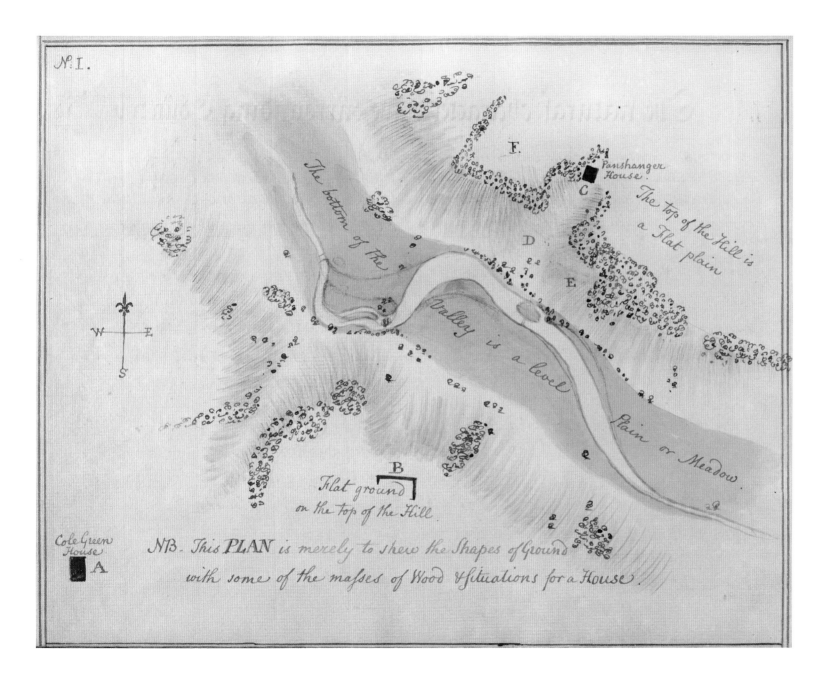

No. I.

The bottom of The

The top of the Hill is a Flat plain

F.

Panshanger House.

C

D

E

Valley is a level

Plain or Meadow

W — E

S

B

Flat ground
on the top of the Hill.

Cole Green House.

A

NB. This PLAN is merely to shew the Shapes of Ground
with some of the masses of Wood & situations for a House.

54 Red Book: illustration I, a
plan showing 'Shapes of Ground'.

Sixth, The numerous objects of Comfort, such as a dry Soil, a supply of good Water, proper space for Offices, with various other conveniences essential to a Mansion in the Country, and which in a town may "sometimes be dispensed with, or at least very differently disposed of.

It is hardly possible to arrange these six considerations according to their respective weight or influence, which must depend upon a comparison of one with another, under a variety of Circumstance, and even on the partiality of Individuals, in affixing different degrees of Importance to each consideration. Hence it is obvious, that there can be no danger of sameness in any two designs conducted on principles thus established, since in every different situation, some one or more of these considerations must preponderate, and the most rational Decision will result from a combined view of all the separate advantages or disadvantages to be foreseen from each".

I shall now proceed to consider these several Objects as they relate to Panshanger.

1st: The natural character of the surrounding Country

The chief Beauty of the Estate consists in the Valley, or rather the two hanging banks which form the Valley, because the Summits of the Hills on each side are flat, or what is called <u>Table Land</u>; and unless the House were to stand very near the Edge of the slope, it would command no View of the Valley: this is the Case with respect to the present Mansion at Cole Green A which stands so far back on the Hill as to make the views from it appear flat and uninteresting. It was I believe once proposed to bring the house forward towards the Brow at B on the same side of the Valley. This spot commands the most ample View, but its aspect would have been to the North, and much of the Landscape would have consisted of Land which does not belong to the Estate: either of which circumstances would be sufficiently objectionable, since in this Climate, the aspect or exposure of the principal rooms should be the first object of consideration; and the power we have over all the Ground seen from the House, is not of much less consequence: since both the Beauty and the Convenience of a Situation, depend more on what is <u>seen</u> from the house, than the actual extent of property; and it is better to have a Neighbour at less distance <u>behind</u> a house, than to see a great house though much farther off yet within such a distance of the front as tends to destroy the Unity of property, and of course to lessen the importance of the Place.

View from the sites C. and D. looking across the Valley towards Colegreen to shew the effect of the Water & Park.

55 Red Book: illustration II, view from sites C and D, looking across the valley towards Cole Green, 'before'.

Nº II.

View from the sites C. and D. looking across the Valley towards Colegreen to shew the effect of the Water & Park.

56   Red Book:
illustration II, view from
sites C and D, looking
across the valley towards
Cole Green, 'after', (a).

View from the Sites C. and D. looking across the Valley towards Colegreen to shew the effect of the Water & Park.

57 Red Book:
illustration II, view from
sites C and D, looking
across the valley towards
Cole Green, 'after', (b).

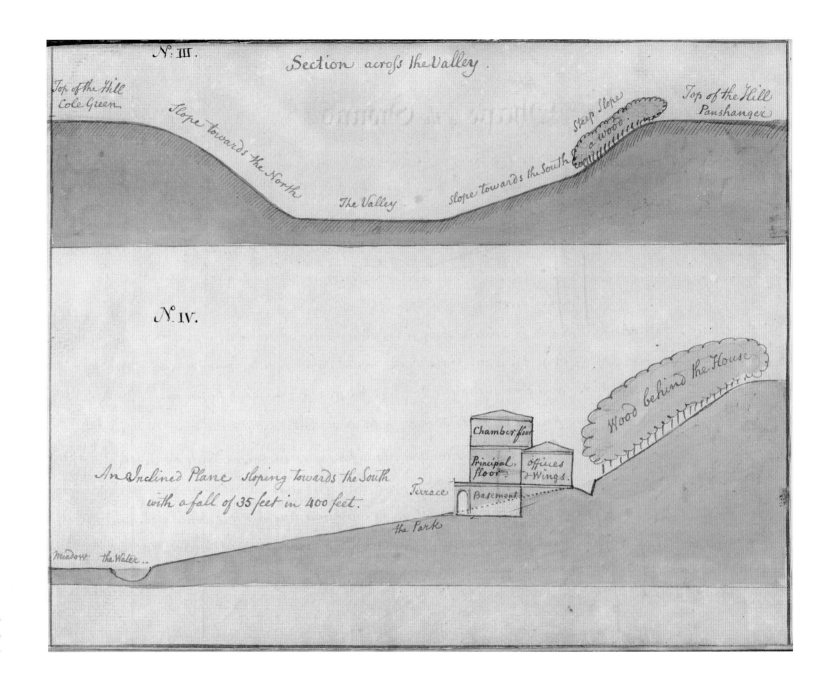

Nº. III.

Section across the Valley.

Top of the Hill Cole Green

Slope towards the North

The Valley

Slope towards the South

Steep Slope

a wood

Top of the Hill Panshanger

Nº. IV.

Wood behind the House

Chamber floor

Principal Floor

Offices & Wings

An Inclined Plane sloping towards the South with a fall of 35 feet in 400 feet.

Terrace

Basement

the Park

Meadow the Water

58 Red Book: illustration III,
section across the valley; and IV,
the same with the proposed house.

2ndly: The Aspects or Exposure

If it were possible in all cases to fix a house as I could wish, I should assert, that the best aspect for the principal Rooms is due South, or rather a few points towards the East, for various reasons, first, the South Sun is cheerful in Winter when it is low in the Horizon, and in Summer it is so much elevated as seldom to be troublesome: secondly the Views from a large house should consist of Wood, Water, and Lawn, all these objects appear best with the light behind them*, and thirdly the ornamental parts of Architecture are in a great degree lost on the North front of a house, which is never lighted up by the Sun; and though I have seen Grecian Porticos so placed, yet a Portico to the North is absurd; because both useless and invisible at a little distance while the front towards the South is strongly relieved by light and shade during every part of the day, and there is no object more beautiful, than a large building illumined by the rays of the Sun and contrasted by rich hanging Woods in which it appears to be embosomed and surrounded.

If the Aspect is to be consulted we are under the necessity of fixing on some spot across the Valley which runs from West to East, and this brings us to some Situation near the House at Panshanger C.

In that delightful Valley which extends from Hartford to Welwyn, there is no part more beautiful or interesting than the Ground near the present House at Panshanger C, and therefore at the first View of it, we should pronounce that a house cannot be better situated; but the beauty of this View is very confined, and is only seen along a narrow Dell which falls into the Valley at right angles: of course it would hardly admit of a house twice as large as the present, unless it were brought lower down the Dell, and this I confess was my first idea for the situation at D. I therefore considered that the Water would produce nearly the same effect from both stations, and would be well placed both with regard to the present house and to a new one to be built in the same line. But when I reflected ~~that~~ that the present pleasure Ground might be rendered equally interesting to a new house, it seemed unpardonable to choke up the mouth of this small Valley or Dell, by placing a house directly across it, and this determined me to seek for another situation. The top of the hill is as flat as the table land on the opposite side the Valley, with the additional objection that the slopes being planted, we could not see into the Valley without cutting down the Wood, and therefore I am compelled to seek a situation below the Wood, either to the East or West of the Dell, or short Valley already mentioned.

---

*   as I shall shew or endeavour to prove in the course of this volume

View from the Site E towards the West — with the Effect of removing the present hedges — & also of

...ter in the Meadow ⸺ This Landscape is supposed to be lighted up by the Morning Sun.

59 Red Book: illustration V, view from site E towards the west, 'before'

View from the Site E towards the West — with the Effect of removing the present hedges — & also of

V .

ter in the Meadow ——— This Landscape is supposed to be lighted up by the Morning Sun .

60   Red Book: illustration V,
view from site E towards the
west, 'after'.

3rd: Shape of the Ground

This leads me naturally to the 3rd consideration, of the shape of the Ground near the house, which does not admit of a flat surface, because there is no level Ground except on the summit of the hills which has already been described as table-land; or in the flat Meadow which would be too low: and thus no choice seems left, but to build on the side of the hill, where the Ground every where falls with a considerable descent, and there is both to the East and to the West of the Dell already mentioned, about 1 foot fall in 10 which I shall describe by the opposite section No. III.

Under such circumstances it is evident, that a house with its offices which would extend a hundred feet in depth from the front to the back, would have ten feet difference of level between the front and back floors; and consequently that either the front rooms must be ten feet out of the ground, or the back rooms ten feet below the surface, or at least that the difference must be in some way divided between them: but as in such a situation the difficulty is increased with the depth of the house, so it is lessened by extending the length of front; and if it were in other respects adviseable the whole might be drawn out from east to west in one continued line, but this would reduce all the rooms to one aspect; and increase the expence of building. There seems therefore no plan so adviseable for an inclined plane, as that which I have mentioned in my printed work, viz. to set the house on a terrace in the manner described by the section, which will furnish a variety of aspects as well as a variety of views from the several apartments. as explained in Section No. IV.

4th: View from the House

By this plan of putting the Body of the house on a basement story, it will project beyond the wings, and thus obtain Views to the East and West as well as to the South, and by referring to the Map No. I it will be seen, that the water is so contrived as to be shewn <to> the greatest advantage from the situation E which upon the whole appears to the best possible for the house. The view to the East will consist of an open grove and the water going off in a long strait reach to a considerable distance; which is contrasted by the View towards the West where the great bend of the Water is the leading feature, this latter view which I suppose to be from the Picture-Gallery is shewn in the Sketch No. V. which represents the effect of taking away the cross hedges and corn fields, and also shews what the meadow was before the new river had been formed.

There are several reasons for preferring the East to the West side of the Dell. 1st. the Mass of wood behind the House will be far richer in the view from the opposite bank, 2ndly the effect of the water is better, and the line of communication with the island is shorter and easier, and 3rdly the view towards the west is far better because a few trees in cross hedges may be preserved to break the glare of a western sun, and the line of wood when the hedge before it is removed will be a beautiful feature across the Dell. In this sketch I have shewn a hint of a bridge at the extremity of the Water near the great Willow, as I suppose the road from London will pass in that direction.

The views towards the south I shall defer mentioning in detail, till I can shew their improvement by the plantations which must be made to cloath the opposite bank: but as a general remark I will observe, that from the centre of the house the effect of the Portico will be useful in breaking the straight line of horizon, which must continue to be rather naked for some years to come: though trees planted on a declivity will sooner produce their effect than on a level surface; and as the centre of this view will be enriched by the projecting part of the building, the eye will of necessity be directed <obliquely> towards the south-east or south-west along the course of the water, and the valley; in both which directions the views are so perfect as to need little improvement and consequently the view towards the south will be unobjectionable, because it will consist of Wood Lawn and Water which are always best seen with the sun behind them.

In this place I shall take the liberty to insert a digression concerning the effect of <light on> Landscape which I trust will not be deemed irrelevant, when speaking of the aspects of rooms, and the views to be seen from them.

Digression

In passing along the banks of the Thames between the town of Reading and Wallingford, I observed the different effect produced by the same objects under different lights. In the morning when the sun was in the East, the Wood was in a solemn repose of shadow, the water which reflected a brilliant sky was strongly illumin'd and I could trace the whole course of the river: and the Grass was of a vivid green very strongly contrasted by the opposition of dark trees in shadow, while the distances were seperated by the brightness of the Atmosphere: I could hardly distinguish any other objects: but these formed an interesting Landscape from the strong contrast of light and shade. Coming by the same spot in the evening, when the sun was in the West, I was surprized to see objects which I had not before observed; the whole scene was changed, the dark

61   Red Book: illustration VI, morning view of a river valley.

Nᵒ VII.

EVENING.

62   Red Book: illustration VII, evening view of a river valley.

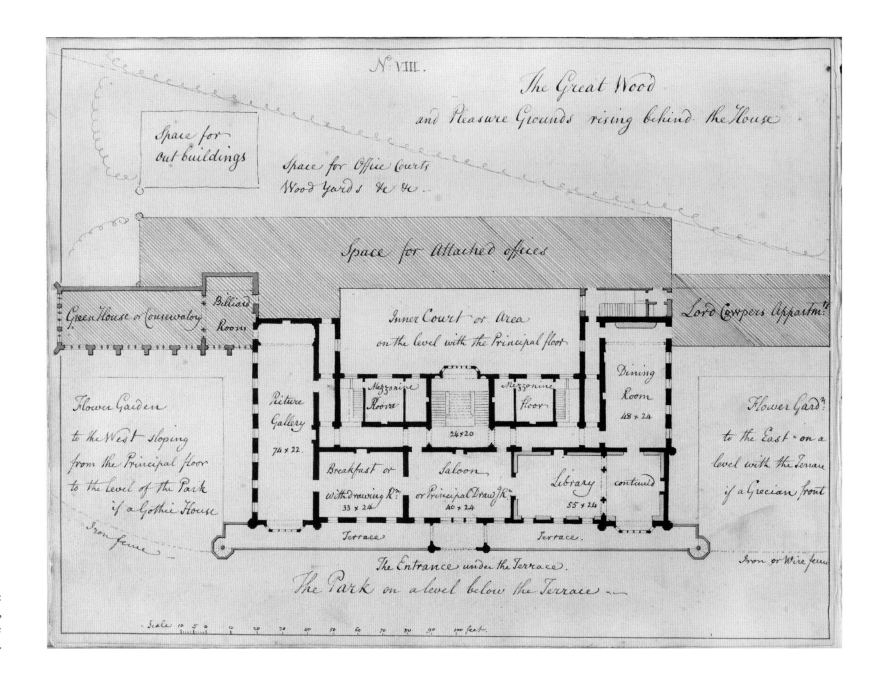

N.° VIII.

The Great Wood
and Pleasure Grounds rising behind the House

Space for
out buildings

Space for Office Courts
Wood yards &c &c

Space for Attached offices

Green House or Conservatory

Billiard Room

Inner Court or Area
on the level with the Principal floor

Lord Cowpers Appartmts

Flower Garden

to the West sloping
from the Principal floor
to the Level of the Park
if a Gothic House

Iron fence

Picture Gallery
74 × 22

Mezzonine Rooms

Mezzonine floor

Dining Room
48 × 24

Flower Gardn

to the East · on a
level with the Terrace
if a Grecian front

24 × 20

Breakfast or
Withdrawing Rm
33 × 24

Saloon
or Principal Draw Rm
40 × 24

Library
55 × 24

contained

Terrace

Terrace.

Iron or Wire fence

The Entrance under the Terrace.
The Park on a level below the Terrace

Scale 10 5 0   10   20   30   40   50   60   70   80   90   100 feet.

63 Red Book:
illustration VIII,
ground plan for the
proposed house.

clouds reflected in the water rendered it almost invisible, the opposite hanging wood presented one glare of rich foliage, but was not so beautiful as when only the tops of the trees were relieved by small catching lights; but the most striking features were the buildings, the boat, the path, and even the distant town of Reading, which I had not seen till they were strongly illumed by the opposite sun: and on comparing this effect with others of the same kind frequently since observed, I think I may pronounce, that all natural objects such as Wood, Water, Lawn, and distant Hills or Mountains, appear best with the sun behind them: and all artificial objects such as Houses, Bridges, Roads, Boats, Arable Fields, and even distant Towns and Villages appear best when the sun shines full upon them. And consequently in point of beauty, the grounds consisting of natural objects towards the south will appear to greatest advantage from the house when the sun is behind them and of course the house itself being an artificial object will appear to the greatest advantage from the grounds when the sun shines full upon it.

5th: The Stile Character and Size of the House

It has been objected to my predecessor Mr Browne[*] that he fancied himself an Architect; but I am convinced from experience that some knowledge of Architecture is inseperable from the art I profess. I do not mean those necessary but inferior branches of the art, which relate to the practical construction, and which the builder or mere House joiner may perhaps understand better than Palladio himself; but those higher requisites of the art which relate to Forms, and Proportion, and Character, and Arrangement, all which are to be acquired by observation without serving a regular apprenticeship to the trade of building, as we have seen exemplified in the designs of certain noblemen, who like Lord Burlington had given their attention to the art. It is therefore with some confidence (because not without practical assistance) that I venture to deliver an opinion on the 5th consideration necessary to be consulted in deciding on the proper situation for a house, since it is impossible to place a thing without knowing what form it will bear, or what space it will occupy; and after looking through all the houses in the 5 Volumes of Vitruvius and all the other designs which have been published by Architects, I will venture to assert that it would be impossible to fit any house that ever was built to the spot I conceive to be the best at Panshanger.

---

[*]   In the dispute betwixt him and Pain the Architect, the latter seemed to have the advantage, because Brown has left nothing in writing; but if we compare the houses built by each, we shall discover that Brown has left many good specimens of his Skill, while Pain never built a house that was comfortable without great alteration.

64   Red Book: illustration IX,
view of 'Grecian' (classical)
house.

The Principal Entrance of a house seems to have puzzled all architects who have studied in Italy, because they generally introduce a flight of steps which are never used in this Climate, leading to a Portico which opens into a Hall, and this destroys the comfort of a house by cutting off that connection which ought if possible to be preserved uninterrupted, ensuite, from one room to another through the whole of the principal floor: this may be done where the entrance can be made at the back of a house which is sometimes practicable, or at the side which seems hardly admisible, except the sides are equal to the front in Length and Character. And it's always observable that in those houses where the entrance is made in a very large and lofty hall, the rooms appear low and gloomy: one of the ablest authors on the subject of taste has remarked, that the entrance can hardly be too dark if we wish to impress the idea of cheerfulness and grandeur on the rooms which are to be seen afterwards. I have therefore supposed the entrance to be in a Subhall receiving its light from the great Window on the stairs, which is not to be considered as a common staircase, but as an ample flight of steps leading only to the principal suite of Apartments, of which [only] a general hint is annexed in the plan No. VIII which with a little alteration of Doors Windows &c. may be rendered applicable to either of the two designs.

Very great indeed would be the comfort and convenience of a terrace on the same level with the Ground about the house, but which looks down on the road and park below, and this seems the only means of raising the house to a proper level, as the principal floor would then be nearly fifty feet perpendicular above the Water, and therefore being a running stream it cannot be deemed two [*sic*] near at a hundred yards distance.

Concerning Grecian and Gothic.

There exists so great a difference in opinion betwixt the two characters of Architecture, that I will not say which of the two designs I should prefer for this situation, but in the first it seems necessary to continue the Terrace as far as the wings, which must be regular and of equal Length. In the other the terrace <u>may</u> finish with the body of the house, and the wings be of different lengths and on a different level, because a certain degree of irregularity is always observable in old mansions.

Of Gothic Houses

If the House No. X existed on the estate, I hope no one would advise its being altered or modernised as it is called by adding Grecian Ornaments; but it seems a bold thing to suggest a new house in a stile which some may call the worst species of Gothic, yet I know no other kind of Gothic that is perfectly applicable to a house.

The Castle Gothic consists of large thick masses of wall, with very small apertures or windows, and is rather calculated for a prison, than the residence of modern elegance and cheerfulness. The Church or Abbey Gothic, consists of large apertures or windows betwixt small piers, and is only applicable to the Halls or Chapels of Colleges; but can hardly be adapted to any other purpose of modern habitation, than the Conservatory which is sometimes attached to the house. We are therefore in Gothic Architecture driven to the Date of Queen Elizabeth, which has been often abused as incongruous, because in many houses of that date, some bad Grecian ornaments have been introduced; but notwithstanding all objections, it is impossible to look at the Palaces of Burleigh, or Hatfield, without confessing their Grandeur: it may perhaps be urged the introduction of modern sash windows is a departure from the true character, but with the same reason we may object to a sash window with Grecian Porticos, since there are no examples in the models of antiquity from which these are copied, but whether in Grecian or Gothic buildings, it is sufficient, if the general character be preserved, and good taste which ought to be good sense, will make allowance for those deviations from Antiquity, which are founded on the superior comfort and accommodation of modern times.

6th: Of the Numerous objects of Comfort &c.

The various appendages which belong to a large house, form the last though not the least consideration in the choice of its Site, amongst these the Stable and Kitchen Garden and the Farm are not to be forgotten; in this respect it will be found that the situation at E has many advantages. The flat ground on the top of the hill may all be converted into Arable Land as far as the High Road after it is removed to its proper distance. The old premises at Panshanger with part of the present house will be at a convenient distance for stables and farm buildings, and the Kitchen garden may perhaps ultimately be removed from Cole-Green to a more convenient distance in the field F which will be near the stables for dung, near the back road for Coals and Tan,[34] and surrounded by the plantation which may be increased by adding an orchard or fruit trees within this Inclosure.

This would bring all the several objects of Comfort, Convenience, Utility, and Magnificence, into their proper situations, and make Panshanger one of the most perfect places in this Country.

65   Red Book: illustration X,
view of 'Gothic' house.

N.º XI.

A General View of the grounds near Panshanger from the opposite side of the valley shewing the sites D and E – with certain boards in the latter spot to ascertain the space for a House.

66   Red Book:
illustration XI, view of
the grounds from south
side of the valley, 'before'.

N.º XI.

67 Red Book:
illustration XI, view of
the grounds from south
side of the valley, 'after'.

Letter from H. Repton, 9 September 1800[35]

Harestreet near Romford
September 9 1800

My Lord

Being just returned from the North of England & about to make some engagements beyond Bristol I am unwilling to do so without again visiting Panshanger before I go into the West, because ~~it will be~~ <I shall not return till> late in October – & I suppose the ground for planting the opposite bank should be prepared before my return. – If therefore it is convenient to your Lordship I will <either> spend a day or two at Panshanger after the 16th or 17th Instant: or defer my visit till the end of October as your Lordship shall have the goodness to direct – I beg leave to present my Compliments to Mr Spencer Cowper & have the honour to be My Lord
Your Lordships
most obedient humble Servant
H. Repton

Piece of Water in the Park begun in July 1799, extract from the ledger of Thomas Pallett[36]

1799	Cash advanced to Willcox & Co – weekly on acct	£ s d	Mat^w Willcox & Co Bill for Diging and wheeling out by the cube yard	£ s d
July 20	By Draft **About 60 hands at work**	£55	1156 cu yds one stage of moory soil	£ s d
August 3	By ditto	£100	15 yards @ 3d	£14 9s 0d
			1245 gravel soil @ 4d	£20 15s 0d
10	By ditto **80 men**	£80	2510 two stages @ 5d	£52 5s 10d
			4755 three ditto @ 6d	£118 17s 6d
17	By ditto	£30	3846 four ditto @ 7d	£110 10s 2d
			1995 five ditto @ 7½d	£62 6s 10d
31	By ditto	£90	984 six ditto @ 8d	£32 16s 0d
			16,491 yards cost	£412 0s 4d

Sept[r] 16	By ditto **110 men**	£80	4200 yards to widen the south side of the piece of water, makeing a bank, wheeling & spreading earth @ 6d	£105
30		£75		
Oct[r] 12	By ditto	£65	12,029 yds wheeld part as far as five stages avaragd @ 6½d	£325 15s 8d
26	By ditto	£60	526 yds widening on north sides altering & slopeing wheeling	
Nov[r] 9	By ditto	£40	Ditto four stages @ 7d	£15 6s 10d
23	By ditto	£70	154 yds run @ 6d from Knaves Acre to Willow Tree	£30 16s
28	By ditto	£25		
Decem[r] 7	By ditto	£40	5750 yds south side of upper island from Knaves Acre to Willow Tree and alterations below ditto @ 7d	£167 14s 2d
			22,659 total of diging above Engine House	£1056 13s 0d
			5605 [&] 3866 below Caskade @ 6d	£236 15s 0d
			2109 yds straightning & widening the River below @ 3d	£26 7s 6d
	Carr[d] forward	£810	**Total of diging carried forward**	£1319 15s 6d
1800	Cash advancd bro[t] forw[d]	£810		
March 22	Per draft to Willcox & Co	£70	To removing Earth on the south side of the water, altering and widening ditto, wheeling & spreading about the meadow and men attending Mr Repton	£68 4s 3d

	27	Ditto	£20		
April 7		Ditto	£20		
12		Ditto	£35		
				To 833 roods (viz [blank] sqr yd to a rood)	
25		Ditto	£60	Leveling on the south side the water @ 4s	£166 12s 0d
May 3		Draft Hankin £53 6s 6d			
		Cash Hankin £11 13s 6d	£65	196 ditto on north side @ 3/6	£34 6s 0d
				302 ditto on the Island @ 3/9	£56 12s 6d
10		Draft	£50	437½ ditto north side @ 3/9	£82 0s 7d
17		Draft	£30	232 ditto below Caskade 3/9	£43 10s 0d
24		Draft	£21 1s		£383 1s 1d
31		Draft	£40		
				Total of wheeling & Leveling	£451 5s 4d
June 5		Draft	£106 1s		
14		Draft	£60		
21		Draft	£50		
28		Draft	£35		
				Total of alterations &c as per measurement	£169 5s 8d
July 5		Draft	£50		
12		Draft	£20		
18		Draft	£40	Day bill in 1799	£31 12s 6d
29		Draft	£110	Day bill in 1800	£58 3s 1d
August 4		Draft	£90		
9		Draft	£35		
Septʳ 6		Draft	£20		
20		Draft	£50		

Date	Item	Amount	Item	Amount
27	Draft	£20	Leveling alterations & day bills carried up	£710 6s 7d
Octr 4	Draft	£30		
11	Draft	£61 16s		
26	Draft	£21 2s	Diging &c brot forward	**£1,319 15s 6d**
		£2,020 0s 0d		
	By balance paid	£10 2s 1d		
	& settled all this water acct up to this time	£2,030 2s 1d		£2,030 2s 1d
			Total of diging brot forward	£1,319 15s 6d
	Brought forward cash reced Carried to folio 249	£850 0s 0d	Brought up	£710 6s 7d
	Balance due to the accountant	£1,180 2s 1d		
	Settled hereafter in 1802	£2,030 2s 1d	Total expence of a piece of water below Panshanger at Mich^s 1800 carried to folio 249	**£2,030 2s 1d**

Notes

1   G. Treasure, 'Cowper, William, first Earl Cowper (1665–1723)', *Oxford Dictionary of National Biography*, Oxford University Press, 2004, <http://www.oxforddnb.com/view/article/6511>, accessed 17 December 2016.

2   HALS: DE/P/T3312–13, lease and release of Panshanger, 1719.

3   HALS: DE/P/P4, 'A map of a particular estate of William Cowper', 1703–4.

4   HALS: DE/P/T3299, lease by John Elwes of Panshanger to George Willcocks, 1712.

5   HALS: DE/P/E146/5, letter to Earl Cowper, 1719.

6   HALS: DE/P/T3324, map of the manor of Panshanger by James Mouse, 1719.

7   HALS: DE/P/T3319–21, surveys of timber at Panshanger by William Lowen with outline plan of woods, 1719.

8   J.G. Alger, 'Seymour, Henry (1729–1805)', rev. H. Shore, *Oxford Dictionary of National Biography*, Oxford University Press, 2004 <http://www.oxforddnb.com/view/article/25173>, accessed 17 December 2016.

9   HALS: DE/Of/3/496, painting of Panshanger by H.G. Oldfield, *c.*1800.

10 G. Sheldrick, *The Accounts of Thomas Green 1742–1790*, Hertfordshire Record Society, vol. VIII (Hertford, 1992). In 1777 Thomas Green tuned the harpsichord for Lady Caroline Montague.

11 The accounts include 'men attending Mr. Repton'.

12 HALS: DE/P/EA23/2, ledger of Thomas Pallett, 1798–1811, fols 180–81.

13 HALS: DE/P/E6/1, Earl Cowper's Notes on 'dates of plantations' at Panshanger between 1799 and 1822.

14 HALS: DE/P/E2/1, letter from Repton to Earl Cowper, 1800.

15 HALS: DE/P/F471/5, diary of Edward Spencer Cowper, 1800. He confused their names, writing 'Mr Repton & his son Humphry came to Pansanger'.

16 HALS: DE/P/E6/1, Earl Cowper's Notes on 'dates of plantations'.

17 H. Prince, 'The changing landscape of Panshanger', *East Herts Archaeological Society Transactions*, 15/1 (1955–7), pp. 42–58, at p. 50.

18 HALS: DE/P/P33, map of the estates of Earl Cowper by Edward Johnson, 1809; HALS: DE/P/P38 map of Panshanger estate by Thomas Pallett, 1810.

19 HALS: DE/P/F471/5, diary of Edward Spencer Cowper, 1800. The jury comprised 14 landowners: William Baker of Bayfordbury, The Honourable Peniston Lamb of Brocket Hall, William Hale of King's Walden, Samuel Robert Gaussen of Brookmans, John Calvert of Albury, Baron Nathaniel Dimsdale of Hertford, Nicholson Calvert of Hunsdon, Thomas Hope Byde of Ware, John Baron Dickinson of Ware, John Chesshyre of Benington, Charles Fuller of Datchworth, Robert Mackey of Marden, Cornelius Cuyler of Welwyn and Henry Cowper of Tewin Water.

20 HALS: QS Highway Diversion orders 201–206, diversion of roads and footpaths in Hertford St Andrew, Tewin and Hertingfordbury parishes, November 1800. HALS: DE/P/EA23/2, ledger of Thomas Pallett, 1798–1811, fol. 176.

21 Repton, *Observations*, p. 137.

22 S. Flood (ed.), *John Carrington, Farmer of Bramfield, His Diary, 1798–1810, Volume I, 1798–1804*, Hertfordshire Record Society, vol. XXVI (Hertford, 2015), pp. 61 and 66.

23 HALS: DE/P/EA23/2, ledger of Thomas Pallett, 1798–1811, fol. 176.

24 HALS: DE/P/F471/9, diary of Edward Spencer Cowper, 1804; HALS: DE/P/E6/1, Earl Cowper's Notes on 'dates of plantations'.

25 Repton lists Panshanger as a site where he was assisted by his son 'in the architectural department': Repton, *Observations*, p. 186.

26 The one building which may have been built according to Repton's specifications is the boathouse shown between the small island and the north bank of the Broadwater on the 1809 estate map. Repton lists 'Plan for boathouse' among outstanding payments in his letter to Earl Cowper of January 1802, but the plan does not survive and the Earl's reference to planting trees at 'The island by the Boat House' over a year earlier casts some doubt over this theory, unless the Earl was referring to a boat house that had yet to be built.

27 HALS: DE/P/E2/2, letter from Repton to Earl Cowper, 1802.

28 Repton, *Observations*, p. 143.

29 HALS: DE/P/F471/9, diary of Edward Spencer Cowper, 1804; HALS: DE/P/EA23/2, ledger of Thomas Pallett, 1798–1811, 1805–6. The octagonal Keeper's House is annotated on the 1809 estate map and is now extended and called Riverside Cottage.

30 HALS: DE/P/A83, Bank pass-book, Hoares Bank, Jul 1797–Aug 1812.

31 HALS: DE/X3/9, diaries of John Carrington senior, 1806.

32 HALS: DE/X3/11, diaries of John Carrington senior, Jan 1808–Mar 1809.

33 HALS: DE/P/P21.

34 'Tan' refers to the bark used in hot beds, its gradual decomposition raising the ground temperature. It was referred to as 'tan' because the bark was first used in the leather tanning process before being sold on for use in gardens.

35 HALS: DE/P/E2/1.

36 HALS: DE/P/EA23/2, ledger of Thomas Pallett, 1798–1811, fols 180–81.

Tewin Water, Tewin and Digswell

TL 256146

THE HOUSE CALLED TEWIN WATER stands on the north bank of the river Mimram two miles (*c.*3.2 kilometres) upstream from Panshanger and the basic framework of the landscape that Repton saw when he visited in April 1799 had been laid out at the beginning of the eighteenth century by James Fleet, son of a Lord Mayor of London, who had bought the estate in 1713. The gardens were in the formal, geometric style of the time, and their principal feature was an ornamental canal that extended eastwards from the house.[1] At its eastern end Fleet built a 'very fine dove house' as an eye-catcher, and along its northern side he planted a double avenue of elm trees leading towards the church at Tewin.[2] Beyond the gardens was a park of around 40 acres (*c.* 16 hectares), bounded to the north by rectangular groves of trees planted in four or five straight rows; another grove of at least seven rows ascended the valley side north of the house. The park was depicted, as parkland, on the county map by Dury and Andrews, published in 1766, but it was usually referred to in estate documents as the 'warren'.[3]

The third Earl Cowper purchased the reversion of the Tewin Water estate but the widow of James Fleet, Lady Cathcart, held a life interest and it became the property of the Cowper family only after she died in 1789, in her ninety-eighth year. Her old house was then demolished and replaced by a new mansion, before the property was leased to Lord Townsend. When the fourth Earl Cowper came of age in 1797 he gave Tewin Water to his distant cousin and former guardian, Henry Cowper, for life.[4]

Henry did not like the new house and so, only seven years after it had been built, it was demolished and another 'more nobler house' was erected in its place.[5] He also set about improving its setting: permission was obtained to reroute a 'road and footpaths which used to go by the house' and the park was extended eastwards.[6] Cowper began to modernise Fleet's now rather old-fashioned design for the landscape in March 1798, 'turning the course of the river to make

68 Tewin Water, as illustrated in Peacock's *Polite Repository* for 1801.

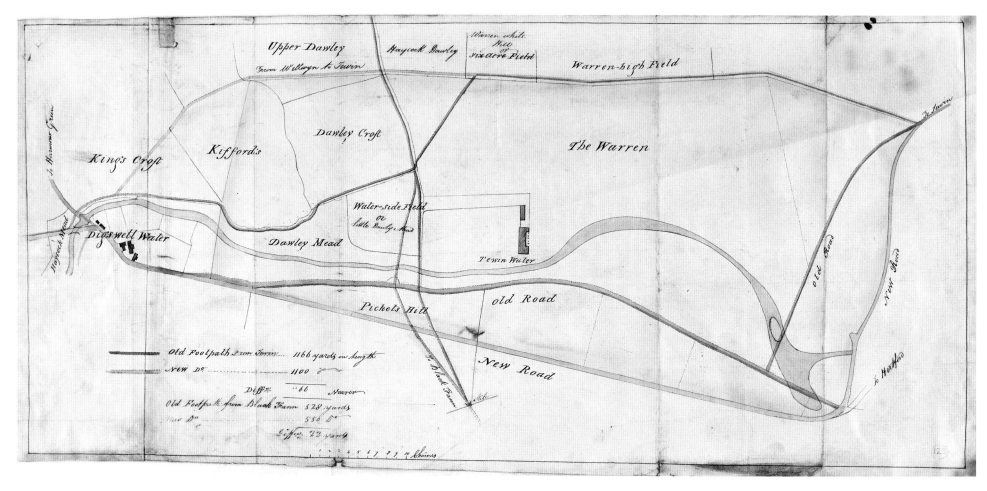

69   Map showing proposed diversion of footpaths at Tewin Water by a Quarter Sessions Highway Diversion Order of 1800.

a more famous water fronting the house' and converting the formal rectangular canal into a semi-circle of water.[7] But the result was evidently not a complete success and in 1799 he invited Repton to come and make proposals for further improvements.

Repton visited on 18 May and presented his ideas to Henry Cowper in a Red Book in July 1799, by which time he had also visited the fifth earl at Panshanger.[8] Repton also engraved a view of the house from the east, which was published in Peacock's *Polite Repository* for 1801 (Figure 68). Aware of the earl's properties along the beautiful Mimram valley between Welwyn and Hertford, Repton's expressed intention was to unite the woods and lawns of Digswell, Tewin Water, Panshanger and Cole Green to 'give each … a degree of extent and consequence which it could not boast exclusive of the others' and thereby 'enrich the general face of the country'.[9]

Much of Repton's scheme to improve the landscape at Tewin Water was carried out, including his main proposals regarding the moving of the public road away from the house and the restoration of the river 'to its original level and character'. A highway diversion order was obtained in June 1800 and the public road was moved southwards, as he proposed, 'beyond the brow of the hill', allowing the park to expand south of the river as far as the replacement road (Figure 69).[10] A round grove on the north side of the new road, within the new parkland, was later augmented to create the curving grove of trees which Repton advised would enhance the skyline in the view from the house, although the distant temple he proposed was never built. His recommendation to restore the Mimram to a 'rattling trout steam … fretting over its bed of gravel' appears to have been carried out, improving the

drainage of the surrounding land, enhancing the water flow and presumably enabling the north bank to become a 'fine meadow' rather than the 'swampy bed of rushes' he had observed in 1799. The wet ground at the southern end of the park was turned into a lake and allowed to flood across the course of the old road, just as Repton had envisaged.[11]

The park was also extended north-westwards, further, in fact, than Repton had suggested, thus absorbing some of the fields that he had recommended laying to grass so that, once the hedges were removed, the land would 'appear to be park'. As these fields actually became part of the park, Repton's proposed 'sunk fence' was not required. As per his instructions, new carriage drives were constructed through the park – one from Hertford and London and one from Welwyn – but neither seems to have followed the exact route shown on Repton's plan: the one from Hertford took a wider sweep to the north and that from Welwyn extended further to the north-west. Curiously, the latter crossed the public road at an oblique angle and continued westwards towards Digswell House, the next Cowper property in the valley.

A major concern for Repton was how to deal with the old-fashioned straight rows of trees in the park and, in particular, with the elm avenue leading to the east front of the house. His proposal to fell many of the trees close to the house in order to break up the lines of the avenue when viewed from the 'portico' or 'eating room' was evidently acted upon: an estate plan of 1808 indicates where the lines of trees had been – or were to be – removed (Figure 70).[12] Repton's proposals for the view from the west front were less dramatic than those to the south and east, but they too were implemented. The 'fence and plantation on the terrace' in the middle distance were removed to extend the vista but the distant 'Architectural seat' that he proposed as a termination to the view was not built.[13] The kitchen garden appears to have been laid out according to Repton's plan on either side of a long wall aligned west-north-west to east-south-east, with the stable adjoining to the east. But the wall itself had probably been built in the early eighteenth century, as it is labelled 'The Garden Wall' on a plan of *c.*1785–9, with 'Brick Wall field' lying on its north side.[14] A single row of trees appears to have been planted to screen the kitchen garden from the carriage drive and from the pleasure ground to the south, instead of the more generous plantations shown on Repton's plan.

Repton's landscape was maintained by successive owners for the next century and a half and a series of fashionable gardens was laid out on the banks of the Mimram. The river itself was enlivened from 1898 with the creation of 'several linns or small water falls' for Mr H. Tower.[15] After the death of Lady Beit in 1946 the mansion and 12 acres of the grounds were acquired by Hertfordshire County Council and converted into a school for the deaf. The remainder of the park became farmland and many of the old trees were felled.[16] In the late twentieth century the mansion was converted into apartments and a small residential estate was built on the site of the former kitchen gardens, incorporating the old garden wall. Much of the parkland landscape envisaged by Repton can still be traced today, however, and the river Mimram and the lake still exist in the form he proposed. Recent plans for the farmland at the eastern end of the former park included an intention to restore parts of the parkland landscape, which now lies close to the edge of Welwyn Garden City.

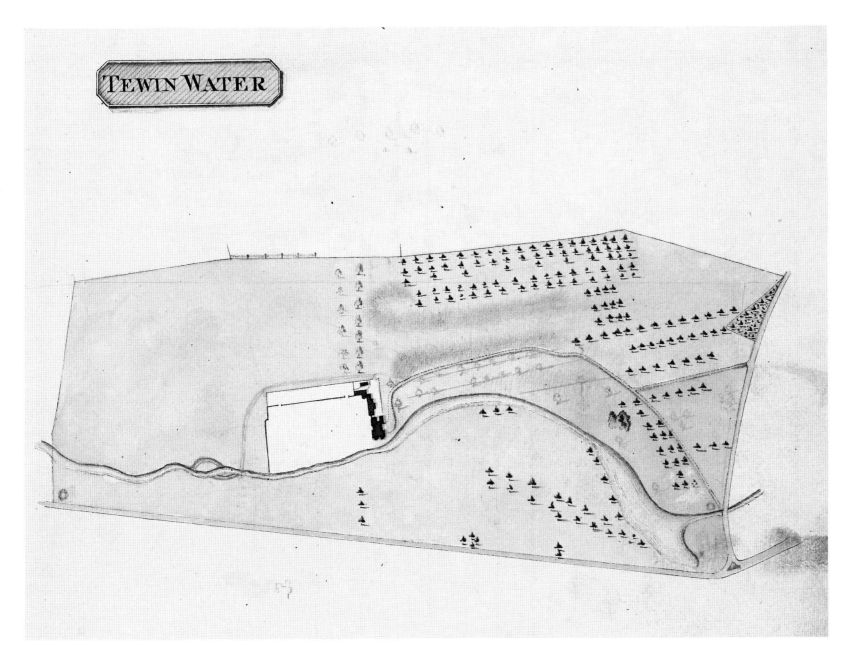

70   The grounds of Tewin Water, as shown on an estate map of 1808.

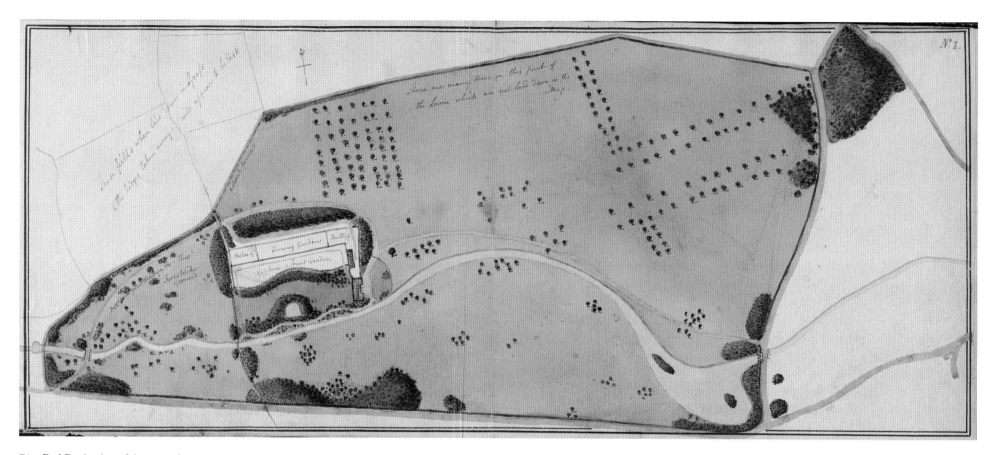

71   Red Book: plan of the grounds.

Tewin Water in Hertfordshire
a Seat of Henry Cowper Esq

Sir,

I have in my usual manner collected the several scattered hints I had the honour to suggest at Tewin water, and arranged them in this small volume, that no partial improvement may interfere with the general consideration of the whole subject; and altho' it may be necessary to alter in some measure a little of what has been already done with respect to the water, the roads, &c, yet I trust the reasons I shall give will evince, that the alterations are neither trivial, nor unnecessary.

The few sketches with which I have interspersed these remarks however deficient they may be as pictures, will I trust better serve to elucidate my opinion than mere words, which a reference to the map will farther serve to explain.

The whole of the beautiful valley from Welwin to Hertford, including Digswell, Tewin-water, Panshanger and Cole Green, belonging to the same noble Family, will give each of the places a degree of extent and consequence which it could not boast exclusive of the others, and while each possesses its independent privacy and seclusion, their united woods and lawns will by extending thro' the whole valley enrich the general face of the country; and therefore in what I have the honour to suggest with respect to Tewin Water, I do not lose sight of its relation to the adjoining Places.

I have the honour to be Sir
Your most obedient humble Servant
H Repton

At Tewin Water first visit May 18: 1799
At Harestreet by Romford Essex July. 1799

Situation.

The advantages of situation which Tewin Water possesses are great and various – it joins to a naturally fine gravel soil, a copious supply of beautifully coloured water, and such an extent of park without mixture of alien property that the boundary is no where obtrusive; to these may be added (by no means a small recommendation) its vicinity to the capital, which gives it all the convenience of a Villa, while the size and stile of the house, together with the extent and character of the place make it an adequate residence. And tho' at first sight the situation appears low and damp, since it is not so in reality, the first object of improvement will be to prevent unfavourable false impressions.

With respect to the house I must do Mr Grove the justice to say that I have seldom seen an instance of an Architect's being fettered in his plans by part of an old house, in which he has succeeded so well, by addition and alteration: for tho' it may almost be deemed an entire new building, yet he was confined by the old house to the present level of his floors. This makes me wish I had been consulted at an earlier stage of the business, or at least before the water had been penned up so high as to give his house the character of dampness: that nothing already done might have required alteration: this however will not I hope be attended with so much trouble, as to make it a serious inconvenience, when we consider the effect of the improvement both in point of beauty and convenience.

Character.

While the old house remained, the character of the place required that it should be surrounded by avenues pointing towards it in almost every direction: but these which were perfectly in harmony with the style of the old house, and the feelings of its inhabitants, would be incongruous in the view from a Grecian house, adapted to the purposes of modern habitation: the Character of Tewin Water will therefore be entirely changed by altering the old house and breaking some of its avenues.

Most of the fine trees at Tewin Water have been planted in rows or avenues and however false we may deem the taste of the last Century for planting trees in rows, the taste of the present times is equally false, if it condemns large trees because they stand in rows. A large tree in every situation is too respectable an object to be hastily sacrificed, and especially in compliance with the fashion of the day. A better reason than fashion must be adduced for cutting down large trees. Having in my printed work delivered my sentiments very fully on the subject of avenues, I cannot be understood to recommend them, but there is great difference betwixt planting a new avenue and cutting down an old one, which I never advise without ample consideration.

Principle of Improvement.

Few places would be worth possessing, if it were necessary to submit to the bad taste, the local attachment, or the caprice of former possessors. Thus altho' the late possessor of Tewin water might think a public road no less appropriate than cheerful immediately in front of the house; or a foot path with all its attendant inconveniences, cutting up the lawn in another direction, and after crossing the water, passing close under the windows, leaving the house on a kind of peninsula surrounded by carts, waggons, gypsies, poachers, &c. &c. who feel they have a right of intrusion; yet when the place with all its beauties and all its defects, shall pass under the correcting hand of good taste, the views from the house will be changed with the views of its possessor.

The Principle of Improvement consists first, in removing the road and its plantation from the south of the house, beyond the brow of the hill as marked on the ground, to fit into the other road as laid down on the map; making the lawn (which it will be necessary to break in parts by groups of single trees or masses of wood) flow beyond the brow of the hill, and have no apparent boundary. Secondly, the restoring the water to its original level and character, making it evidently the rattling trout stream of Hertfordshire, fretting over its bed of gravel, rather than appear an artificial canal in a clay soil, the natural river which drains the meadow instead of the penned up dike that poisons them and converts a fine meadow into a swampy bed of rushes; and where the ground is so wet as not easily to be drained, and the distance from the house will allow of it, an expanse of water may be formed to make decidedly good dry land, and water, of that which is at present neither one nor the other.

These first principles of improvement will then be considered as they affect the beauty of the scenery from various points, such as from the windows of the house, the roads, the walks, and various situations of the Grounds.

View to the East.

In looking from the Portico, or from the eating room, the two straight lines of trees are so evidently the remains of the Ancient stile of gardening, that we almost regret the straight line of water which formerly accompanied them, and are offended by a curved line because it mixes the styles of ancient and modern gardening, but as we ought not in this instance to hesitate which ought to prevail, it becomes necessary to break the lines of trees, which may be easily done as far as it relates to the view from the house, or any given point, tho' to break an avenue from every part is often impossible.

The sketch gives a rude hint of the scenery to the east, and shews two different modes of breaking the double avenue. In the distant part (near the man on horseback) it may perhaps be advisable to take down all the trees

N.º III.

72 Red Book: illustrations II and
III, view to the east, 'before'.

73   Red Book: illustrations II and III,
view to the east, 'after'.

and let the eye up to those on the summit of the hill, but if any are left it may be worth trying the experiment to remove some by drawing them in trenches from their linear position, to group the stems with those that are left; and as elms will sometimes bear to be transplanted at a very large size it is perfectly fair to try the experiment with those which are condemned. In two other places I have shewn the effect of planting thorns or brushwood to hide the equidistant stems of the trees, which is perhaps the most effectual mode of obliterating the formality of an avenue. In the <u>right</u> corner of this sketch No. II I have shewn the stumps of three trees, to point out how much of the distant lawn is hid by their tops; and in the opposite corner No. III I have given a hint of the distant water, and under the slide I have supposed a few thorns to mark the declivity of the opposite hill.

The Water.

In the double sketch No: II. & III. is attempted to be shewn an effect which painting cannot very well express, the difference between stagnant water and that which has a current, but it can only be distinguished by the reflection of objects on its banks, and the comparative degree of brilliancy.

It has been objected to my predecessor Brown and his school, with some reason, that he considered water wherever it could be obtained as a sufficient excuse for itself, however unnaturally placed; and that he was too much attached to the artificial mirror of a stagnant pool, to avail himself of those beauties which a small brook may present; forgetting that there can hardly be a greater contrast than is produced by Nature betwixt "The shallow brook, and river wide". The latter is only to be desired in those situations where the house stands above the low ground, and commands long reaches of a river, which may be supposed navigable; as will be that at Panshanger: but when the house stands low, the current of the stream adds to the salubrity, as well as the beauty of the scene, for the stagnant water near a house is always to be avoided, yet the current of a running water like the natural trout stream of Tewin-water refreshes the air and renders it peculiarly wholesome. The water at present wants character, it is neither a river nor a brook, it is too narrow for navigation, and too wide and deep to shew sufficient motion. I do not propose to reduce it ~~quite~~ to its natural size but to lower its surface, and slope the banks on each side that the ground may every where be higher than the water and drain into it.

View to the South.

In the sketch No: IV. is shewn the view to the south, with the effect of removing the road and the plantation, and of restoring the water to its natural character. This View has the advantage of fine trees in the old hedgerow, which will greatly contribute to break the opposite bank; it will however be necessary still farther to cloath and enrich its present naked appearance, which must be effected, not by an uniform belt on the summit of the hill, but by a wood, irregular in its outline, in one place flowing beyond the brow of the hill with a depth so great as totally to exclude the light, and in another suffering the lawn to sweep over the brow, leaving the imagination to extend the park to distant lines of hill and valley, commanding new scenes and abounding in fresh beauties. This bank will derive much of its cheerfulness from being fed by sheep and cattle; and the attention may be called to the opposite brow by the kind of seat I have described, in character with the style of the house which backed by trees already standing will be an interesting feature.

The hither bank when it falls more abruptly to the water than at present, will do away all appearance of dampness, and should be highly dressed garden scenery hanging to the water; this bank must be neatly mowed and beautifully varied with knots and groups of flowers, and flowering shrubs; because the water appears the natural barrier betwixt the fed lawn[18] and the ornamental shrubbery.

On the slide I have left a part of a large fir tree which is very unsightly and from its size depresses the house and contributes to make its situation lower than it is.

View to the West.

The improvement of the foregoing Views is much more obvious, and more easy to manage than of that to the West, where the ground is by nature flat and artificially rendered more so by the level of the water, which actually makes it wet and damp. The most simple, and least expensive way of raising the land, and of making it sound will be to lower the water as already proposed whose pernicious effects are here very evident. At first sight it appears necessary to fill the square pond, but as it would be difficult to procure earth to do this, without widening the river or destroying the terrace, neither of which are advisable; and as this small pond may be convenient for a stew pond,[19] I think it better to surround it with plantation which by projecting as forward as represented in the drawing, will contribute to break the uniform flat appearance of the ground. But we are most disgusted by the squareness of the view at present; this I propose to remedy by giving such an outline to the plantations as may leave an irregular intricate shape of grass, and to give it still greater extent, the fence and plantation on the terrace may be removed to let in a distant continuation of the lawn in that direction, separated from the mowed pleasure ground in reality, altho' united in appearance by a short sunk fence.

N.º IV.

74 Red Book:
illustration IV,
view to south,
'before'.

N.º IV.

75 Red Book:
illustration IV,
view to south,
'after'.

76   Red Book:
illustration V,
view to west,
'before'.

77 Red Book:
illustration V,
view to west,
'after'.

It is evident that this scene will derive great part of its cheerfulness from being interspersed with different kinds of objects, provided they are in their designs chaste and appropriate to the style of the house and to the character of flower garden scenery and not too numerous. Thus the Vase in the sketch, rising among and half concealed by its surrounding shrubs and flowers – the simple bench, – and even a few garden chairs carelessly scattered to command the most interesting points, or take advantage of the most desirable circumstances of sun or shade, – give the garden, which would otherwise be comparatively dull, the character of cheerfulness and appropriation, while the more distant Architectural seat, by leading the eye beyond the fence does away the idea of confinement, which at present so strongly prevails. The grass glade will acquire irregularity on the western side by the shape of the plantation to skreen the kitchen garden, as marked on the map, which recedes in the middle because the southern sun throws but little shadow, & projects at the two ends to allow for the lengthened shadows of morning & evening. I have supposed an open grove of beech or Spanish chesnut as a foreground to the picture & what is far more material as a skreen to mitigate the glare of the setting sun whose effulgence not Claude de Lorrain himself could represent, while in reality it will appear in all its dazzling brightness, divested of even the thin veil of clouds to which Painting has recourse to disguise the imperfection of Art.

Approach from Welwyn.

The consequence of making one line of road serve as the approach both from Hertford and from Welwin must be, that it would serve effectually for neither; while by approaching the house in two ways each road has its separate advantages and its seperate beauties. The approach from Welwin should enter the meadow to the west, which tho' neglected and overgrown with weeds may easily be drained, and made sound; while the masses of brushwood and trees scattered here and there, sometimes fringing the water which silently glides along in its deep worn channel, and sometimes overhanging and partially concealing it, as it rattles along its pebbled bed, will give this part of the ground the interesting character of natural forest scenery.

The temporary bridge was necessary for the conveyance of materials while the house was building, but may be removed to the place where the road will cross the water when the reason for its remaining ceases; after passing the bridge, the road instead of running parallel to the fence of the kitchen garden in the line of the foot path, should skirt along the outside of a plantation to conceal the pale, leaving a sufficient depth between the plantation and the pale for back road to the offices, while the approach-road sweeps round the skreen with views into a delightful valley beyond the pale, which by a sunk fence might seem to be actually a part of the park, and after passing a corner of the open grove which consists of several rows of large trees, it bursts upon the house, the water, and the opposite bank in an interesting point of view.

The Lake.

There is so much beauty and so much pleasure to be derived from a large expanse of glassy surface, that altho' I may have condemned Mr Brown's practice in too often introducing it, yet wherever it can be easily obtained I think it constitutes an essential part of a place, and as the low Ground is very rushy and bad, it will be easier to make an irregular shaped lake with islands to disguise its outline, than to dig a deep channel for the river and drain the land into it; of this the map will give some idea tho' subject to those variations which the natural levels of the ground may point out on the spot.

The brook will gradually expand itself into a small lake, and the mouth will be partly concealed by one of those islands which are generally formed by Nature in those situations where a river expands into a broad water. When the present highroad is turned, the water will very easily spread itself across the present road into a bay, which is now wet ground and the general effect of this lake cannot be better shewn than from the spot which I have chosen in sketch No. VII in a ploughed field, to exhibit the difference between the present and proposed landscape, for this reason it will be necessary in turning the road, to allow such a depth for planting between the water and the new road, that a walk or drive may pass round this bay to shew the ground to advantage.

Approach from Hertford.

It seems by the map of the County, that the nearest road from London to Tewin water is by Essendin and Cole Green, and should that be <the> case it would fit into the approach from Hertford and of course this will become the principal approach from London.

From the new high road the approach will enter the park in a plantation that extends along the proposed head of the lake. This road will be the most natural as well as the most interesting, because it is the nearest and because it passes within view of the water, which from its colour and shape will be far more attractive than the high ground of the park, and from various parts of this road the house will appear to advantage. One of these I have chosen for the sketch No. VII. to shew the effect of the water and also of opening the line of trees to let in a view of the stables, which contribute to elevate the house and yet being partly hid by the plantation before them, they will add to the importance of the mansion altho' of equal or greater length. The small cupola on the

N.º VII.

78 Red Book:
illustration VII,
view towards
the house from
the east, 'before'
(there is no
illustration VI).

79 Red Book:
illustration VII,
view towards the
house from the
east, 'after'.

80   Red Book:
illustration VIII,
view of the
house from the
south-east.

roof gives a play of outline which will be more conspicuous when backed by the plantation which I suppose to be grown up to the north of the garden.

Perhaps it may be objected to this sketch, that one drawing is enriched by sheep and cattle, while the other is more naked, but I consider this as a very essential part of the improvement suggested, since the banks of the water will be rendered sound by the same operation which produces the lake and that which is now rushy meadow will be converted into dry feeding pasture.

Conclusion.

Having described the general outline of improvement it may be proper to observe, that no plan on paper can be so accurate as to preclude the necessity of actually marking on the spot, those circumstances of detail which a plan cannot describe. Of this kind are the several lines of road and walks and the particular shape of the water, with the outlines of plantations &c which will sometimes depend on a few yards for a good or bad effect.

The walks near the house and from thence to the foot-path-bridge will require very little alteration, but when the road is turned, it will be advisable to get an easy and short line of communication (perhaps by a ferry boat) across the water to the opposite bank, from whence the place looks very advantageously; because the house is backed by a considerable mass of wood, and being seen across the water it appears more elevated. This will be particularly obvious when the road and pale and young plantation are removed, and the feeding lawn brought down to the water's edge.

I shall conclude these remarks with the sketch No. VIII taken from a spot where the house is seen under the branches of some very respectable trees now growing in the present hedgerow.

Pencil note, probably in Repton's hand, on page facing last illustration of house:

No roof seen

Chimneys stand the other way

No bow to the Atticks

No recess between the Bows

Side windows in the bows narrower than the middle

Notes

1 HALS: DE/P/T2345, deeds Tewin Water House, 1713; HALS: DE/P/T2400B, 'An Eye draft of a Plan of several parcels of land situate in the Parishes of Tewin and Digswell, the estate of the Rt. Hon'ble Lady Cathcart', *c.*1785–9.

2 TNA: PROB 11/659/148, will of James Fleet, 1733; HALS: DE/P/T2400B, plan of Lady Cathcart's lands; John Carrington, diary entries March 1798. The Carrington diaries are an important source for the landscaping carried out at Tewin Water in the decade preceding Repton's involvement. They have been published in S. Flood (ed.), *John Carrington, Farmer of Bramfield, His Diary, 1798–1810, Volume 1, 1798–1804*, Hertfordshire Record Society, vol. XXVI (Hertford, 2015).

3 HALS: DE/P/T2345, deeds, 1713; HALS DE/P/T2400B, plan of *c.*1785–9; Flood, *Carrington Diary*, 11 August 1798, p. 7.

4 Flood, *Carrington Diary*, 26 July 1798, p. 6.

5 Flood, *Carrington Diary*, 26 April 1798, pp. 1–2.

6 HALS: DE/P/T2400B; W. le Hardy, *Calendar to the Sessions Books 1752 to 1799*, Vol. VIII, Hertfordshire County Records (Hertford, 1935), p. 405: footpath diversion 1791 and p. 476, footpath diversion 1798.

7 Flood, *Carrington Diary*, entries March and April 1798.

8 HALS: DE/Z42/Z1.

9 HALS: DE/Z42/Z1, Repton's letter to Henry Cowper at the front of the Red Book, July 1799.

10 HALS: QS Highway Diversion orders 119–123, diversion of roads and footpaths in Tewin and Digswell, June 1800.

11 HALS: QS Highway Diversion, order 123, plan showing diversion of roads and footpaths in Tewin and Digswell, June 1800.

12 HALS: DE/P/P31, plan by T. Pallett, 1808.

13 The 'terrace' marked the western end of the seven-acre garden enclosure during the eighteenth century and probably also carried the footpath between Black Fan and Burnham Green before it was diverted in 1798.

14 HALS: DE/P/T2400B.

15 *The Gardening World*, 15, 29 July 1899, p. 755. The rocks may have been 'Pulhamite', a term used for various forms of artificial stone developed by James Pulham of Broxbourne in Hertfordshire from the late 1830s and widely used in Victorian gardens.

16 G.H. Moodey, *East Hertfordshire Archaeological Society Newsletter*, 8 (1957), p. 3.

17 HALS: DE/Z42/Z1.

18 By 'fed lawn' Repton is referring to that part of the grassland near the house that was grazed by sheep and cattle, rather than mown: that is, the park as opposed to the garden.

19 A 'stew' or 'stew pond', from the Latin *servatoria*, was a narrow pond located near the mansion in which freshwater fish were kept prior to being used in the kitchen.

Wall Hall, St Stephen (St Albans) and Aldenham

TQ 1352098794

HUMPHRY REPTON PREPARED A RED Book for Wall Hall in April 1803, following a visit at the end of 1802, and it survives in private ownership. The house is also illustrated in an engraving, based on a drawing by Repton, which appeared in Peacock's *Polite Repository* for April 1804; and is referred to briefly in a passage in Repton's *Observations on the Theory and Practice of Landscape Gardening*. Interestingly, the final image in the Red Book – 'The first View of the House from the new Approach' – is simply the engraving from the *Polite Repository*, pasted onto the page. This suggests that in some cases these published illustrations must have been prepared and engraved at an early stage of Repton's involvement with a particular place – even before the production of the Red Book – and may thus on occasions show proposed improvements which, at the time the *Repository* went to press, had not yet been implemented, and in some cases may never have been.[1]

Wall Hall house is a striking early nineteenth-century gothic building that stands on an undulating plateau to the south of the river Colne (Figure 81). To the east the land rises gently towards the hamlet of Kemp Row, and to the north and west it slopes more steeply towards the river, which here flows in a gentle bend and in a broad floodplain. The local soils comprise, for the most part, well-drained flinty coarse loams of the Sonning 1 Association. In 1799 the estate was bought by George Woodford Thellusson from Thomas Neate for £24,000.[2] Wall Hall was a manor, documented from the thirteenth century, but although the house appears to have been a gentleman's residence in the eighteenth century – occupied by a merchant named Thomas Vanderell from 1754 – no park or extensive pleasure grounds appear to be associated with it on Dury and Andrews' county map of 1766 (on which it is labelled 'Wars Hall'). Henry George Oldfield, writing shortly after 1800, thought that it had been 'only a large farm' before Thelluson purchased it.[3] Dury and Andrews' map shows that it was surrounded by fields: the nearest buildings were at a place labelled 'Anchor Pond', half a mile (*c*.800 metres) to the south; and at Otterspool, beside the Colne, a slightly greater distance to the south-west.

Thellusson was a merchant who had served as MP for Southwark in London.[4] He inherited a substantial sum on the death of his father, the immensely wealthy merchant Peter Thellusson of Brodsworth Hall, Yorkshire, in 1797, but a complicated will meant that he and his two brothers did not receive the bulk of the family wealth, which was instead to be managed for the benefit of the grandchildren. The government, who envisaged that no less than £20,000,000 would eventually accrue to the invested fund, passed the Thellusson Act in 1808 limiting the arrangement to 21 years, to prevent the vast sum from destabilising the economy. In the event, due to family litigation and poor management, only £600,000, roughly the original amount invested, remained after this period of time.[5]

81   Wall Hall as it is today, divided into apartments.

George Thellusson himself was a director of the East India Company from 1796 to 1809, which included the period during which the East India College at Haileybury was being built and Repton was advising on the grounds there. It is thought that 'Tellson's' in Charles Dickens' novel *A Tale of Two Cities*, depicted as the most respected bank in England, is a reference to the family firm in general and to George, its most active member, in particular. Nevertheless, the company was not free from financial problems, and in 1803 Joseph Farington commented in his diary that: 'The Thelusson's might have been of more consideration, but they have been losers by speculation & have not conducted themselves as to be esteemed: Their Bond is looked upon to be of more value than their Word.'[6] Given that Thellusson himself was also found guilty of 'treating' – illegally influencing electors by providing them with food, drink and entertainment – leading to his election (for Southwark in 1796) being declared void, Dickens' characterisation is perhaps somewhat inaccurate.

Soon after he acquired Wall Hall, Thelluson remodelled and updated the house. A survey, and plan and elevation showing proposed changes, by Sir John Soane and dated November 1800, survive in the Soane Museum in London. The elevation shows a two-storey house in simple Neo-Classical style, but an undated drawing by Henry George Oldfield shows a slightly different house – less rigorously classical and with attic windows, which has an identical tetrastyle (four-columned) portico to that proposed by Soane.[7] It was thus at a later date that the house was further altered, to give it its present gothic appearance. This had certainly happened by the time of Thellusson's death in 1811, for the sale

82 Wall Hall, as illustrated in Peacock's *Polite Repository* of 1804. This is how the house appeared at the time the Red Book was drawn up.

particulars drawn up in the following year described the house as Aldenham Abbey and noted its 'Castellated Fronts'.[8] The gothic style of the new house bears a striking resemblance to that of Port Eliot in Cornwall, designed by Soane and with grounds landscaped by Repton, so it is possible that Soane was himself called in by Thellusson to further alter the mansion. Either way, there is no doubt that the Red Book was drawn up to improve the landscape around the earlier classical house, which is indeed that illustrated in the *Polite Repository* (Figure 82) and thus in the small vignette included towards the end of the Red Book. Repton must have been consulted soon after Soane's alterations had been completed: the latter's plans were made in November 1800 and Repton's first visit occurred only two years later. It is noteworthy that in his *Observations on the Theory and Practice of Landscape Architecture* Repton mentions Wall Hall as an example

83 The area later occupied by the southern section of Wall Hall's park, as shown on the enclosure map for Aldenham, 1803.

of a house where architectural changes made it 'necessary to make alterations to the grounds also'.[9]

Soon after Thelluson purchased Wall Hall, in 1803, 575 acres (c. 240 hectares) of common land and residual patches of open field were enclosed in Aldenham by a parliamentary act passed in 1801.[10] Most of the parish was unaffected, having been anciently enclosed, but the act provided an opportunity for a number of wealthy residents, including Thellusson, to close or divert public roads on or near their properties, the roads often surviving in whole or part as estate drives. The enclosure map of 1803 shows that much of what was to become the main drive to Wall Hall, from Aldenham church, was one of these (Figure 83).[11] It shows 'Wall Hall Farm' on the site later occupied by the home farm: the site of Wall Hall itself lay across the parish boundary, in St Stephen's parish, and is not shown, but the map provides a useful impression of the agricultural landscape that Repton was dealing with, and can be compared with one attached to the sale particulars drawn up in 1812, when the property was put on the market following Thellusson's death in 1811, by which time an extensive pleasure ground and small park had been laid out around the house (Figure 84).[12] Much of this had apparently been completed by 1806, when the draft Ordnance Survey drawings were made.

Repton's Red Book makes no reference to the pleasure grounds at Wall Hall, his advice being almost entirely concerned with a new approach to the house and with the design of buildings placed along it. Unfortunately, it contains no plan (the approach had been staked out on the ground and were shown on 'the large map', since lost). The sale map shows that the hall was, by 1812, approached from Aldenham along a drive that left the public road near the parish church, at a point a little to the north of where the old public road (closed at the enclosure) had done, but which then followed its line, running north-westward and then north and entering the park by crossing a sunk fence, itself adapted from an earlier field boundary. As it curved northwards, it was joined by another drive, approaching from Watford via Otterspool. This also followed – in part – the line of an earlier lane, shown on the enclosure map. Passing through an earlier spinney (shown on the 1803 map), it terminated at a turning circle below the west, or entrance front, of the mansion. A secondary drive branched off the main approach shortly after it began, passing to the west of home farm, crossing the main drive and then curving west to follow the line of an earlier road running north-eastwards along the valley of the Colne.

Repton suggested building a lodge at the 'four cross ways', apparently the junction of the main drive with the public road near Aldenham church: a lodge had certainly been built here by 1812. A little further along the approach was to be ornamented with a 'rustic hovel' or thatched seat, erected on the edge of a dell; another watercolour shows how a cottage, probably that at Anchor Road, was to be altered to form a 'keeper's lodge'. Repton suggested that a rough wooden bench might be erected near this point, placed under a venerable tree, to give good views across the landscape and towards Aldenham church. Repton's proposals thus appear to relate entirely to the approach to Wall Hall, leading from Aldenham church to the entrance to the park, although the description of how the drive was to pass by means of a bridge under 'the high road' is admittedly hard to square with this interpretation.

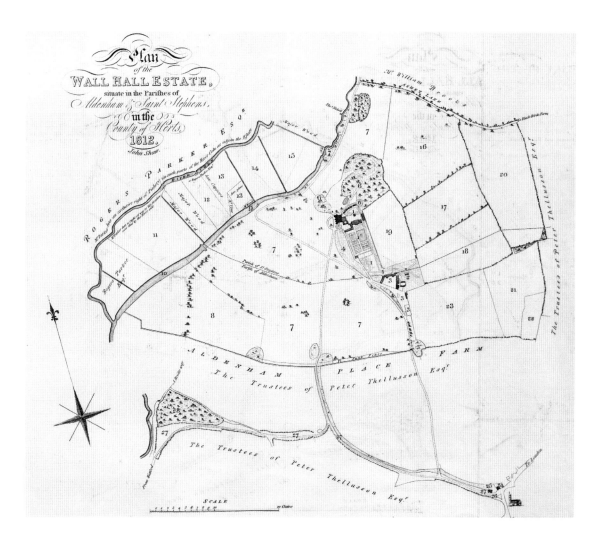

In addition, Repton also suggested improvements to Otterspool House, which stood beside the other drive (from Watford), near the river Colne, and which had formed part of the estate since 1798.[13] The building, described as 'new-built' in 1766, had served as an inn with a grotto, providing a salubrious

84 Wall Hall, as shown on the sale map of 1812. Many of the features of the grounds, although not mentioned in the Red Book, have a very 'Reptonian' appearance.

place to drink the waters, which were said to be beneficial. Repton thought it 'a very ugly house [which] may be transformed into a Cottage with a room near the water, which will always be a powerful source of attraction and one of the most valuable appendages to the scenery of Wall Hall'. His sketch shows how it was to be reduced from three storeys to one and provided with a canted bay window and recessed windows. He proposed whitewashing it and adding trellising and ornamental planting. A striking feature of the Wall Hall Red Book is the low-key, inexpensive nature of the improvements suggested. Repton thus shows a simple wooden bridge taking the highway over the drive but suggests that 'a much more beautiful, but more costly design might be made for the same purpose in Masonry: and perhaps on the whole it would be more advisable because more durable'.

While the line of the approach to Wall Hall from Aldenham as shown on the 1812 sale map may well have been decided by Repton, there is no evidence that the 'rustic hovel' on the edge of the dell was ever constructed, and the proposed alterations to Otterspool House were certainly not carried out. We should, however, also note that a number of features that do not appear in the Red Book, but which are described in the 1812 sale particulars (or shown on the accompanying map) have a rather 'Reptonian' feel, so it is possible that the Red Book charts only part of Repton's involvement with the place, as it does at Panshanger, and that he also contributed to the design of the park and pleasure grounds, presumably after the house had been remodelled in gothic form. Near the hall, the 1812 map shows a lawn, shrubbery and both a 'flower garden' and a 'circular flower garden', while the particulars

describe 'dry gravel walks, leading through beautiful Shrubberies, Flower Gardens &c … and through beautiful Rustic Virandas, entwined by Honeysuckles' to 'an extensive range of Pheasantries, Aviaries, Bowers, &c.'. They also led to 'Gothic ruins' and a 'spacious Rustic Dairy'.[14] Given Repton's involvement at the Thelluson family's principal residence at Rendlesham in Suffolk from 1799, and at Haileybury between 1808 and 1810, a continuing engagement would not be surprising. The flower gardens and pheasantries seem very much in his style. In the wider landscape, the manner in which the southern boundary of the park is defined on the 1812 map not by a belt but by a sunken fence linking a series of 'clumps' formed from pre-existing spinnies also seems very 'Reptonian'. We should also note that a narrow, sinuous water body on the northern edge of the park (converted from a formed channel of the river Colne, and retained by a dam at its eastern end) was, intriguingly, attributed to Repton by a governess to J. Pierrepoint Morgan's children in the late nineteenth century.[15] It is described on the 1812 map as 'The Water'; it was also known as the 'Lily Pond' and is shown on the Ordnance Survey first edition 6-inch map as 'Fish Pond'. The 1812 particulars describe it as 'A Fine Stream of clear running Water, made at considerable Expence, [which] presents a pleasing Object from the House'. It is crossed by a bridge that almost certainly dates from Thelluson's time. Attention might also be drawn to the two gothic ruins, in close proximity, to the south of the house, which are mentioned in the 1812 particulars. One is a tall structure of cement-rendered brick with an arched doorway to the north featuring a window – incorporating genuine medieval tracery, possibly from Aldenham church – above it. The other, lying some 90 yards (c.80 metres) to the south-east and reached by a path, is a gothic façade of brick, part rendered, with a turret and gothic arch: it stands just to the north of the home farm.

The Red Book for Wall Hall is, in summary, hard to interpret but few of its proposals appear to have been implemented. Yet, at the same time, some of the features of the grounds that *were* created during Thellusson's time appear to have a rather 'Reptonian' feel, raising the possibility that the Red Book records only some of Repton's activities here. Either way, little that dates from the early nineteenth century survives in the landscape today. In 1812 the property was purchased by Sir Charles Maurice Pole, who extended the walks and the shrubberies screening the kitchen garden and added to the planting in other ways: an undated memorandum on a scrap of torn paper in the Wall Hall archive states '*Mem. The Cedar tree on Front Lawn was planted in March 1814, being then about 3½ ft in height*'.[16] On the death of his widow in 1842 the estate was inherited by her daughter Henrietta Maria, and her husband, William Stuart. In 1860 the house was extended[17] and the conservatory and southern terrace built, and by the time of Stuart's death in 1874 many other changes and additions had been made. By 1883 the park had been extended to the south-east, beyond the sunk fence.[18] In the 1890s Charles and Florence van Raalte further extended the pattern of paths in the pleasure grounds, edging them with bricks of tufa. A croquet lawn, tennis lawn and nine-hole golf course were laid out and a grotto with ferns installed at the southern end of the terrace. On the 'Lily Pond' a boathouse was built, remains of which existed until recently. Still further changes

were made by the banker John Pierrepoint Morgan, who leased the estate from 1901 and purchased it outright in 1910, enlarging it to *c.*1,000 acres (*c.* 400 hectares) and changing its name back from Aldenham Abbey to Wall Hall.

On Morgan's death in 1942 Hertfordshire County Council acquired the property and in 1949 converted it into a teacher training college. New buildings were erected and further added to when the college became part of Hatfield Polytechnic (later the University of Hertfordshire). The house and park were divorced and the golf course enlarged to 18 holes, effectively destroying the park. The immediate grounds of the house were maintained until the 1980s, when budgets were cut: little of the historic planting now survives. In the first years of the present century a small group of houses was built within the park to the south-east of the farm, and more within and around the kitchen garden, while the hall itself was converted into flats. The pleasure grounds to the north and east are very overgrown and have lost definition.

Only a few fragments of Thellusson's (and Repton's) landscape thus now survive. The secondary approach, via the farm, still remains, although the main drive has largely disappeared, only the final section, near the house, remaining. The 'sunk fence' still exists in the form of a substantial ditch and 'The Water' survives, although now silted up, and is still crossed by the bridge, which was probably erected in Thelluson's time. The Gothic ruins still stand, although now in an even more ruinous state, and the walls of the kitchen garden survive, although the interior, as noted, is now filled with houses.

Wall Hall in Hertfordshire
A Seat of George Woodford Thellusson Esq[r]

Introduction.

Sir,

Having generally delivered my opinion in writing on such subjects as I considered of importance you will not I trust be displeased to see the following remarks concerning the improvement of Wall-hall: especially as the sketches to explain my intentions will thus be better preserved.

Altho' many Gentlemen have acquired great proficiency in the Architecture, yet few are able to carry their designs into execution without the aim of professional Artists, and nothing is more fatal to good taste than the confidence placed in ignorant Workmen. Had the great Lords Burlington and Leicester employed Carpenters and Mechanics instead of such Architect as Kent and Brettingham, their designs would not have been quoted as standards of applause. A proper knowledge in the detail of any Art requires the study of a man's life, it therefore casts no reflection on a Gentleman's taste to suppose he is not a perfect Architect but on the Professor attaches all the shame of ignorance if the common rules of proportion are violated. I have therefore frequently been hurt by having incorrect designs unjustly attributed to me which had been executed without my knowledge or consent, in places where I have been consulted.

For this reason I have subjoined a few hints for such buildings as may be applicable to their respective situations and circumstances, since it is by the adaptation of the works of Art that the Scenery of <u>Nature</u> is most frequently either adorned or disfigured.

I have the honour to be Sir
Your most obedient Humble Servant
H Repton

First visit to Wall Hall November 1802
Plans finished at Harestreet near Romford April 1803

Character and Situation.

There are few Counties in England which possess more natural beauties than Hartfordshire, yet there is none in which these beauties require to be more brought into notice by the assistance of Art, since however contradictory it may appear, almost every part of Hartfordshire altho' uneven, appears flat; and the wooded, appears naked. This seeming paradox I shall thus explain – The whole County like the environs of Wall hall, is intersected by valleys, but there are few hills, because the summits of the eminences are broad and flat, or what is called table land; and therefore unless the Spectator be placed near the brow which slopes into the valley, he will only look across a plain, and as these flat surfaces are generally arable land and less wooded than the sides of the vallies, both the richness of cloathing and the inequality of the ground will be in a great measure lost, this is evidently the case in many parts of the present Approach.

Beside the variety which may be produced in this Approach by these different objects and by shewing the Scenery to advantage, it may still further be varied by giving more breadth to those parts where two branches diverge, and in these places many large and handsome trees (now lost in hedgerows) will be brought into notice. This will be particularly the case where the Approaches from London and from Watford join each other. And as the remarkable spring near the river is one of those striking features which demand peculiar attention I shall conclude these remarks with the Sketch No. VI to describe the manner in which a very ugly house may be transformed into a Cottage with a room near the water, which will always be a powerful source of attraction and one of the most valuable appendages to the scenery of Wall Hall.

New Approach

The principal advantages proposed by the new line of approach are 1st. To shew the natural beauties of the Situation. 2nd. To pass by a nearer road thro' the grounds than along the present high road, and thirdly to give importance to a place, which from the command of surrounding property and the general style of elegance prevailing around the Mansion requires greater attention than was necessary for a mere farm house.

The whole of this line having been accurately marked on the ground and described on the large map, it will only be necessary to mention those spots which may be changed or improved, of which the first is the four cross ways represented in the annexed Sketch No. 1.

Here a cottage will be useful and without aiming at any architectural ornaments too rich for the Style of the house, or affecting any rude picturesque or pseudo Gothic building I have supposed a Cottage such as may

85   Red Book:
illustration I,
improvements to
the 'four cross ways',
'before'.

86 Red Book:
illustration I,
improvements to
the 'four cross ways',
'after', with cottage.

87   Red Book:
illustration II,
the thatched seat
near the dell,
'before'.

88   Red Book:
illustration II,
the thatched seat
near the dell,
'after'.

89 Red Book:
illustration
III, the drive,
'before'.

N.º III.

90 Red Book:
illustration III,
the drive, 'after',
with bridge
carrying the
'high road'.

91　Red Book: illustration
IV, proposed conversion of a
cottage to a 'keeper's lodge',
'before'.

92 Red Book: illustration IV,
proposed conversion of a cottage
to a 'keeper's lodge', 'after'.

appear to belong rather to the place than to the person who inhabits the Cottage. The general effect will be seen by comparing this portrait of the spot both with and without such a building.

The Sketch No. II in like manner describes the situation of a small thatched hovel or seat near the little dell, thro which I suppose the Approach to pass, and as this road will become a favorite walk, such a covered Seat commanding a View of the valley and town of Watford, will not be less useful than ornamental.

The Sketch No. III represents the manner in which the Approach may pass under the high road by means of a wooden bridge, altho' a much more beautiful, but more costly design might be made for the same purpose The next object of attention in this Approach is the cottage proposed to be altered for a keepers lodge and this by only changing its colour and planting around it may be converted into a pleasing object as shewn in Sketch No. IV.

Near this spot the view of Aldenham church furnishes a subject for the Sketch No. V.

During the whole course of this Drive, the grass borders on each side of the road may be kept fine by occasionally driving a flock of sheep from the entrance of the Approach to the entrance of the Park or Lawn.

The first View of the House from the new Approach is represented in the annexed Vignette.

[The illustration is not reproduced here – it is the same as the Peacock's *Polite Repository* engraving, see Figure 82]

93   Red Book: illustration V, the entrance drive, with Aldenham church in the distance.

Overleaf Left
94   Red Book: illustration VI, proposed changes to Otterspool House, 'before'.

Right
95   Red Book: illustration VI, proposed changes to Otterspool House, 'after'.

Notes

1   Repton, *Observations*, p.186.
2   HALS: DE/Wh/T1, title deeds of the Aldenham estate, 1754–1805.
3   HALS: DE/Of/8/326–7, drawing by Henry George Oldfield and associated notes.
4   <http://www.historyofparliamentonline.org/research/members/members-1790-1820>, accessed 15 July 2017. This account draws extensively on Elizabeth Banks, 'Wall Hall: Historic Landscape Assessment Appendices' (for Octagon Developments Ltd, 2000).
5   P. Polden, *Peter Thellusson's Will of 1797 and its Consequences on Chancery Law* (Lampeter, 2002).
6   K. Garlick and A. MacIntyre (eds), *The Diary of Joseph Farington, Volume VI April 1803–December 1804* (New Haven and London, 1979).
7   JSM: 4/4/9–11, architectural drawings, Wall Hall, Hertfordshire: new entrance front and rooms for G.W. Thellusson, 1800.
8   HALS: DP/3/29/9A and B, sale particulars and map, Aldenham Abbey, 1812.
9   'The operations of landscape gardening have often been classed under the general term of *improvement*; but there are three distinct *species*. ... the *second* to those where the houses by additions, having changed their original character, or aspect, renders it necessary to make alterations in the grounds also; ... Among the second may be mentioned those, in which the entrance of the house being changed, new rooms added, or barns, stables and kitchen-gardens removed, new arrangements have taken place as at ARLINGTON HALL, CLAYBERRY, WALLHALL, WEST-COKER, BETCHWORTH, HIGHLANDS, BRANDSBURY, HOLWOOD, &c', H. Repton, *Observations*, p. 186.
10 HALS: DP/3/26/1, private Act of Parliament, 41 Geo 3 c.75.
11 HALS: QS/E/2 and 3, Aldenham enclosure award and map, 1803.
12 HALS: DP/3/29/9A, sale particulars 1812.
13 HALS: DE/Wh/T6, title deeds Otterspool estate, 1798–1906.
14 HALS: DP/3/29/9A, sale particulars 1812.
15 Hertfordshire College of Higher Education, *Wall Hall in Times Past: Reflections on a nineteenth-century country estate* (Aldenham, 1981), p. 22.
16 'Plan of Aldenham Abbey The Property of Sir Charles Morice Pole Bt.', 1826 (T. Godman and Sons, Surveyors). Map formerly at Wall Hall, current whereabouts unknown.
17 Engraving by Rock & Co., 1860.
18 Ordnance Survey first edition 6-inch map, 1883, sheet Hertfordshire XXXIX.
19 Private collection; photographic copy held at HALS.

Woodhill, Essendon

TL 266058

UNTIL THE MIDDLE OF THE eighteenth century the area now known as Woodhill formed part of an estate belonging to the Church family, which extended over a large tract of land to the south-east of Hatfield Park. From the later eighteenth century they sold off portions of their property to various bankers, merchants and others seeking to build a fashionable residence within easy distance of London. Woodhill, then known as Ballancebury and comprising two cottages or small farms, was acquired by the apothecary William Roberts. He built a new house of modest proportions on the site of one of the houses, which in 1753 he sold to Samuel Read, a scalemaker.[1] The house is clearly shown on Dury and Andrews' county map of 1766. The property had a number of subsequent owners before George Stainforth, a banker, bought it from General Lascelles in 1784.[2] He also acquired the neighbouring house and its land, creating a property covering, in all, some 42 acres (*c.*17 hectares). Over the next 15 years he purchased further land around Woodhill from various owners and, by 1803, when Repton drew up his proposals, the estate comprised around 100 acres (*c.*40 hectares). George Stainforth died in 1815 and Woodhill was sold in 1820.[3] The conveyance document for the sale includes a very detailed map of the estate (Figure 96), which is immensely useful in assessing how far Repton's proposals, made only 12 years earlier, were implemented. The Ordnance Survey draft drawings in the British Library are also helpful in this respect, having been surveyed closer to the time of Repton's involvement (in 1805/6), although they are rather less detailed in character.[4] These maps show that the property was bisected by a public road, Kentish Lane, running roughly north–south: the hall and a diminutive park stood to the west, and a number of fields bounded by strips of woodland (and thus with a marked *ferme ornée* appearance) to the east.

There is no evidence that any member of the Stainforth family resided in Hertfordshire before George and his brother Richard, a merchant and financier with connections to the South Sea Company, moved here at the end of the eighteenth century: George to Woodhill, and Richard to the Woodhall estate, Watton at Stone, in 1786.[5] The Stainforth family were well connected in the financial world. Richard was married to Maria, the eldest child of Sir Francis Baring (1st Baronet), the founder of the company that became Baring's Bank. His son, Sir Thomas Baring (2nd Baronet), was closely linked with the Stainforths in various financial transactions, including the eventual sale of Woodhill in 1820, and was an executor of Richard's will. Richard's association with Sir Thomas Rumbold, the owner of Watton Woodhall, was probably not a wise one, as Rumbold died insolvent in 1791.[6] Richard gave his address as Woodhall as late as 1820, but by 1822 was living in London, and he died in 1824 on a property in Walthamstow on the edge of Epping Forest.[7]

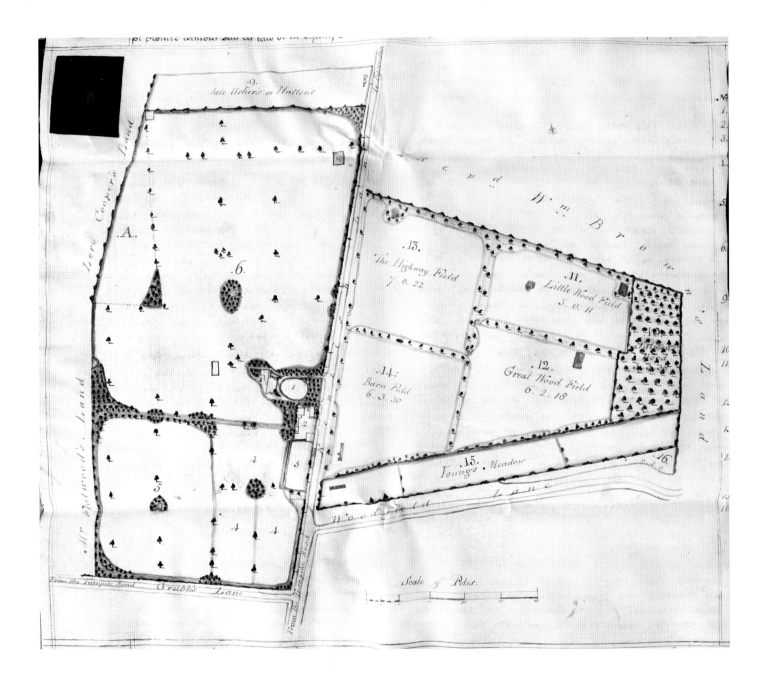

96 The Woodhill
estate, as shown on an
estate map of 1820.

George Stainforth was already married to Fanny Francescutti when he bought Woodhill. Little is known about his career, but he appears on lists of bankers trying to 'preserve public credit' at the time of a financial panic in 1797 caused by the collapse of a land speculation 'bubble' in the United States. The Bank Restriction Act (1797) allowed the Bank of England to refuse to convert banknotes into gold, its directors fearing insolvency if too many English account holders wished so to do, a move which caused considerable alarm at a time when the government had overprinted paper currency in order to help fund the war with France. Stainforth was among a number of bankers who assured the public that they would continue to accept banknotes, and notices to that effect were published in the newspapers, his name appearing in advertisements placed in the *Star* by the Sheriff and Grand Jury of Hertfordshire and by 'The Bank' (the Bank of England) at Mansion House in London in the *Oracle and Public Advertiser*.[8]

The Red Book contains eight pages of text, an overall plan and five sketches, of which four have flaps. The original is held in the Sir John Soane Museum in London but it has been rarely consulted, which means that the sketches are very bright and Repton's artistry is evident.[9] Indeed, although André Rogger and Stephen Daniels include it in their lists of Red Books they do not provide any details, in spite of the fact that it provides some valuable insights into how Repton treated small 'villa' properties.[10] The text is particularly concerned with issues of 'character', Repton's phraseology on this matter (especially in the opening paragraph) seeming at times to verge on the tactless; and more specifically with how the relatively small Woodhill should be marked out in

97   Woodhill, as illustrated in Peacock's *Polite Repository* of 1806.

the landscape as a gentleman's residence and distinguished from a mere farm. His proposals thus include masking the stables from view of the public road with a row of trees; erecting similar fences on both sides of Kentish Lane so that the latter would clearly appear to run *through* a continuous property; and making various changes to the field lying to the south of the house, including the addition of a covered seat, in order to 'change its Character from a common green field to the Lawn of a Gentleman's Place'. He proposed alterations to the main entrance, replacing one gate with two and providing a turning circle for carriages; removing vegetation to open up views into the wider landscape; adding trelliswork to the house; and, as he often suggested, hiding the wall of the kitchen garden with additional planting. He also thought that the fields to the east of the lane, lined with strips of woodland, might be improved by selective planting and removal of trees, but suggested that this would be best explained on the ground, in conversation – presumably an attempt to obtain a further paid consultation.

It is unclear how much of this advice was acted upon. The house was also illustrated by Repton for the *Polite Repository* and the engraving, published in 1806, shows the proposed trelliswork added to the house, although this does not necessarily mean that this had been done (Figure 97). The plan drawn up when the property was sold in 1820 shows that the entrance remained unaltered and suggests that the line of trees intended to screen the stables had not been planted (see Figure 96). The clumps of firs in the field to the south of the house, which Repton recommended should be removed, was still in place at the time and no attempt had been made to screen the wall of the kitchen garden. Some of the minor aspects of Repton's proposals may have been adopted – and some of the suggested planting might not appear on the 1820 map because it was not yet sufficiently mature – but on the whole it seems likely that little in the Red Book was actually executed.

At the sale in 1820 the property was acquired by William Franks, a barrister and member of an influential legal and financial family. He demolished Stainforth's house, retaining only a small section, and erected a new residence. He diverted Kentish Lane to the east, away from the house; extended the park; undertook much planting; and built an ice house and two lodges, thus leaving no doubt that Woodhill was indeed a 'gentleman's place'. It is this landscape, rather than that visited (and possibly improved) by Repton, that still survives in part. The house itself is now divided into flats and the grounds shared between neighbouring properties.

Wood Hill in Hertfordshire
A Seat of George Stainforth Esq[r].

Introduction.

Sir,

The improvements hinted in the following pages being in themselves so obvious tho' inconsiderable, it is only in compliance with your wishes that I have committed my thoughts to writing. I might plead in justification of my opinion a thousand wise sayings such as that the man in health needs no Physician – that it is better to let <u>well</u> alone than mar by mending &c. &c. And therefore I do not hesitate to pronounce Woodhill so cheerful, so pleasing, and so Gentleman like a place, that my art can derive little credit from my late visit. I shall however as a professional man describe what may be done, and as a friend, what may be left undone. At the same time I rejoice in the honour and the opportunity of thus recording myself.

Dear Sir Very respectfully and sincerely Yours

H Repton

Harestreet near Romford April 25, 1803.

Character and Situation.

After the volume of Observations on Landscape Gardening so lately published, little more can be said (by me at least) on the general principles of the Art. Yet the situation of Woodhill suggests an observation that may not be deemed irrelevant. Every rational improvement of a place must depend on its Character, and the Character must depend on its Uses. If a Nobleman letts a palace to a Farmer, it will cease to be a palace; and if a Gentleman visibly lives in the midst of barns and dung yards, his house will no longer be a mansion but a farm house. A Villa, a Shooting box and every Rural retreat of elegance, require the removal or the concealment of all that is dirty and offensive. For this reason I was surprized in my approach to Woodhill, when I found an elegant house attached to a farmer's premises, or rather when I saw so much of the latter, and so little of the former. A hasty observer would say 'those barns and yards should all be removed' while Prudence would rather suggest some expedient to conceal them.

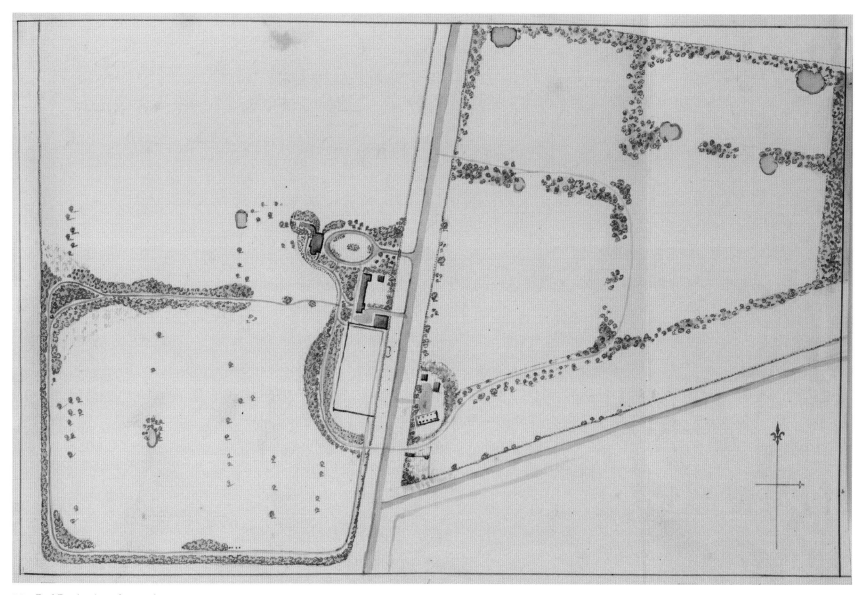

98   Red Book: plan of grounds.

The Road.

The singular neatness and beauty of the Road gives it more the appearance of a gravel walk across a lawn than of a public highway; and Woodhill can hardly be described as "standing near or by the side of this road", it ought rather to be said that "the road passes thro' the premises". This idea will be strongly enforced by a similarity of fence on each side of the road, at least in front of the house: this alone will perhaps be sufficient, but without such attention from the appearance of barns near the house, while some barns remain on the East side of the road, that land will appear to belong to a different proprietor because it is natural to suppose that a farm yard should be all brought together in one place. At present the lofty roof of the Stables plainly shows that it was a barn, and the adjoining yards surrounded by such buildings detract from the elegance of the house; Yet I must allow that with certain establishments there may be great convenience in the proximity of such premises, it is not therefore the situation, but the display of them that offends; and if there were sufficient depth to hide them from the road, there would be less necessity for removing them to the opposite side.

I shall now surprize the advocates for irregularity, by daring to advise a row of trees on the outside as the best means of hiding these premises; for which I hope leave might be obtained: but if it were possible to inclose so much of the waste as would give space for a close plantation, I should not recommend it; because the singular effect of this road would be injured by such an encroachment.

It now remains to justify my opinion that these trees should be planted in a row and at equal distances. The straight line of road is a work of Art, the pale and clipped hedge are also straight and parallel to this road, and evidently the work of Art, in such a situation Art is avowed and the affectation of Nature becomes a ridiculous attempt. It is like a waving line of walk in a kitchen garden or a meandering path along an Avenue. Such a row of trees will not entirely hide the buildings, but they will draw the attention from them and direct the eye to the opposite side of the road which will be opened by a light pale and thus the first impression of the place will be improved.

99 Red Book:
the public road
and barns,
'before'.

100 Red Book:
the public road
and barns, 'after'.

Overleaf
Left
101 Red Book:
the entrance
front, 'before'.

Right
102 Red Book:
the entrance
front, 'after'.

103   Red Book: garden front
and view to south, 'before'.

104   Red Book: the garden
front and view to south, 'after'.

The Fore Court.

The present Entrance is by two gates so near to each other that I think one placed in the centre would answer both purposes, and beside the advantage on the score of simplicity in having one gate instead of two left open, I will enumerate the following reasons for my opinion.

1st The present road shews only the angle of a house which being symmetrical may better be viewed in front.

2nd Carriages waiting for Company cannot be driven round as they would otherwise be to exercise the horses; without going every time into the high road leaving both gates open.

3rd This road being in the midst of flowering shrubs may occasionally be used as a Walk within the premises; and then the skreen towards the North West being partially opened under the trees, by removing the firs and evergreens a View may be introduced which is no where else so well displayed. Of this the annexed sketch gives some idea.

And thus the improvement in points of beauty will be found to have some merit from its utility.

Views from the House.

Few Situations can boast such variety of Landscapes as those from Woodhill house. That towards the <u>North</u> neither admits nor requires improvement. Towards the <u>South</u> the View is less perfect for this reason I was tempted to open a View into more distant scenery, but it can only be done partially and with the sacrifice of certain trees and more valuable bushes. We must therefore attempt improvement by simpler means. At present the View is a plain grass field bounded by a meagre and ragged outline and badly broken by a clump of firs surrounded with a hedge. The latter may be removed and the boundary may be improved either by planting in the lane beyond or in the front of the present hedge. This View wants features and the appearance of a covered seat at a distance, or a bench round a tree near the house will change its Character from a common grass field to the Lawn of a Gentleman's Place.

The View towards the <u>West</u> is extensive but wants shade and foreground; these will both be produced by the Trellis covering suggested in the annexed sketch, and thus internal convenience may promote external ornament.

The Walks.

In the preceding sketch [see Figures 105 and 106] a hint is also given that the red Garden wall should be hid by a plantation. This will furnish a sheltered Walk instead of passing thro' the kitchen garden in the return from a Walk which now forms the pleasing circuit of part of the place but from whence this Garden wall is an unsightly object.

It may perhaps be objected that such a plantation to the South West of a Garden would shade the wall fruit but I should recommend it be brought forward boldly into the field in the manner described on the map, leaving room for an orchard and a potatoe ground within the inclosure. Thus the Sun's rays would not be obstructed while such plantation would act as a screen from the sweeping horisontal winds so fatal to our early blossoms.

Conclusion.

The irregular but simple Front of the House towards the South and West will admit of such additions as are suggested in the drawing No V. taken from a tree round which I proposed a bench to be placed. In this sketch I have introduced a few young trees to break the appearance of the Offices, at the same time that they form a foreground to the West View from the house and shade the library from the setting Sun; thus again, here also, the useful becomes ornamental.

The beautiful and interesting fields on the East side of the road, are so surrounded by wood that they may be greatly improved: but the particular manner in which some trees may be removed and others grouped into natural masses, can only be described on the spot, or executed at leisure, by a painter's eye with a master's hand, feeling for its effects; and tho' I dare not on the map suggest how this may be effected, yet considering to whom these hints are addressed I think in conversation I can explain the principles which should direct the process.

105   Red Book: the
walks and kitchen
garden wall, 'before'.

106 Red Book: the walks and kitchen garden wall, 'after'.

107 Red Book: sketch at the end of the Red Book, labelled 'Hint for a Cottage by the Farm Yard' but not apparently referred to in the text. It probably shows the buildings on the opposite (eastern) side of the road to Woodhill, with a proposal for modifying or replacing the structure shown beside the entrance here on Repton's plan (Figure 98).

Notes

1   HALS: DE/X9/75168, title deeds and correspondence of the Church family 1634–1861, Articles of Agreement between William Roberts and Samuel Read, 3 Nov. 1753.

2   HALS: DE/X9/75216–7, memoranda of title to the Woodhill Estate 1753–1820, compiled by Mr Humphreys of Smith and Lawford, solicitors 2 Oct. 1820.

3   *Cambridge Chronicle and Journal*, Friday 29 September 1815, announcement of George Stainforth's death at Woodhill; HALS: DE/X9/T4, conveyance document for the sale of Woodhill in 1820.

4   BL: OSD 149.

5   HALS: DE/AS/4328–9, mortgage by demise for 500 years, Sir Thomas Rumbold to Richard Stainforth and others, 8 December 1786.

6   H. Prince, *Parks in Hertfordshire since 1500* (Hatfield, 2008), pp. 142–3.

7   TNA: PROB 11/1687, Richard Stainforth's will, 1824.

8   Declaration to preserve public credit by the Sheriff, Grand Jury of Herts and others, *Star* (London), Friday, 10 March 1797; issue 2672. Also by 'The Bank' (Bank of England), *Oracle and Public Advertiser* (London), Monday, 6 March 1797; issue 19,563.

9   JSM Vol. 30: H. Repton, Red Book for Woodhill, 1803. A photographic copy is held at HALS: Acc 5388.

10 Rogger, *Landscapes of Taste*, p. 207, and Daniels, *Humphry Repton*, p. 261.

11 JSM: Vol. 30.

Part II: The Minor Sites

THE FOLLOWING ELEVEN COMMISSIONS ARE 'minor' only in the sense that relatively little is known about them. Some are places mentioned in Repton's account book, which spans the first two years of his career and is held in Norfolk Record Office; some are referred to in one of his published works or in his correspondence; a few are associated with Repton only because he provided sketches of them that were engraved for publication in Peacock's *Polite Repository*. Although poorly documented, some – perhaps most – of these places originally had Red Books, and Wyddial in particular was clearly considered by Repton as a seminal commission.

Bedwell Park, Essendon and Little Berkhampstead[1]

TL 276076

BEDWELL PARK LIES IN THE parishes of Essendon and Little Berkhampstead, three miles (around two kilometres) east of Hatfield and five miles (around three kilometres) south-west of Hertford. A small stream, the boundary between the two parishes, runs through the eastern part of the park. The soils are formed in pebble gravel over London clay. The principal documentary evidence connecting Repton to Bedwell is a letter that he wrote to his son William, dated 25 February 1808, which mentions a proposed visit to 'Hartfordshire to earn 20 Guineas' and suggesting that William should contact him at Bedwell Park, the seat of Sir Culling Smith, Bart.[2] This amount of money would imply several days' work, and almost certainly the production of a Red Book.[3] In addition, there is a small engraving, dated 1810, mounted in the King's Topographical Collection volume for Hertfordshire, which – because of its style and size, and almanac details on the reverse – was almost certainly extracted from a copy of Peacock's *Polite Repository* for 1810 (Figure 108).[4] This shows a rather 'Reptonian' scene, especially in terms of the pergola attached to the house, although by 1810 Repton's connections with the *Polite Repository* were probably limited.[5]

Sir Culling Smith, first baronet, was born in 1731, the son of a merchant possibly of Huguenot extraction and his wife, Culling, a sister and co-heiress of John Horne, governor of Bombay.[6] In 1802 he was made baronet of Hadley, Middlesex, where he had family connections, his own wife being the sister of John Burrows, rector of Hadley.[7] In 1807 Sir Culling bought Bedwell Park from Samuel Whitbread II and in 1809 he acquired some additional neighbouring land.[8] He was in his late seventies when he commissioned Repton to suggest improvements, and he died four years afterwards, in 1812, and was buried at St Mary the Virgin, Monken Hadley.[9] The estate subsequently passed to the second, third and fourth baronets until 1875, when the title became extinct, though the property remained in the family until 1946. Extensive alterations were made to the house by the third baronet in the 1860s.

Bedwell Park was a long-established seat. In the early fifteenth century a park was created here, and from 1539 to 1547 the manor was in the hands of the Crown, and was used on several occasions as a residence for the children of Henry VIII.[10] An engraving by Drapentier in Chauncy's *Historical Antiquities of Hertfordshire* (1700) shows the house surrounded by a series of walled gardens, with a short avenue leading to a building in the park.[11] Chauncy adds that the then owner, Thomas Atkins, had 'much adorned and beautified this Seat with pleasant gardens'. However, only two years later, after the death of Thomas Atkins in 1701, William Cowper described in a letter to his wife how the gardens had 'mightily gone to ruine'.[12] In the course of the

108 Illustration of Bedwell Park, 1810, probably from the *Polite Repository*.

Ordnance Survey six-inch sheet of the 1880s, seem to show a more wooded park, with thicker belts and a screen around the kitchen garden, but whether any of this was due to Repton's influence remains unclear. While both the chronology and style of the probable *Polite Repository* engraving in the King's Topographical Collection certainly fit in well with the surviving letter written by Repton to his son, there is tantalisingly little definitive evidence of any plans made by him for Bedwell Park.

In 1946 the estate became the base for the Royal Victoria Patriotic School and remained so until 1972, when it became a golf club. In 2006 the house was converted to executive housing, flats and maisonettes, and extra housing was built in the grounds.

seventeenth century most of the former park was converted to farmland, but was subsequently reinstated, and Dury and Andrews' county map of 1766 shows a deer park and gardens covering, in all, some 180 acres (*c.*70 hectares). The landscape was still at this time essentially formal in character, with avenues of trees and geometric groves; these features are also shown in more detail on an estate map of 1765.[13] The Ordnance Survey drawings made in 1805, however, show that the overall design had been deformalised, the parkland extended and narrow perimeter belts established by Samuel Whitbread or his son.[14]

Quite what Repton added to the landscape is unclear. There is evidence that between 1808 and 1812 the roads in the surrounding area were realigned, but the park does not appear to have been extended further.[15] Bryant's map of 1822 (Figure 109), and subsequent maps, such as the tithe award of 1838[16] and the

Letter from Humphry Repton to William Repton[17]
London 25 February 1808

Dear William

You are a shabby fellow not to be decided when You come – an event of too much consequence to be left uncertain – George wont come to Harestreet till Brother William comes – Mary must got back to meet Brother William – (for she is at Mrs Heatons) – I dont know how to make my engagements – not to miss of you – but know – that on Sunday next I cross over to Hartfordshire – to earn 20 Guineas & will be in London on Friday night if you write & say when you shall be in Town – & we will all go to Harestreet together – so write to me there on Monday – or after that day to me at Sir Culling Smith, Bart, Bedwell Park <(Hatfield)> Herts.

Notes

1   Late nineteenth-century ecclesiastical parishes.
2   Huntington Library, San Marino, California: HM 40849.
3   Daniels, *Humphry Repton*, p. 261.
4   BL: The King's Topographical Collection, maps K Top XV 60 3.
5   Temple, 'Humphry Repton, illustrator', p. 169.
6   Debrett's, *Baronetage of England* (London, 1832), p. 548.
7   London Gazette No. 15536, 30 November 1802.
8   HALS: DE/F443–6 and DE/F463.
9   LMA: DRO/017/A/01/002, Burial Register of St Mary the Virgin, Monken Hadley, 26 October 1812.
10 A. Rowe, *Medieval Parks of Hertfordshire* (Hatfield, 2009), pp. 90–93.
11 H. Chauncy, *Historical Antiquities of Hertfordshire* (London, 1700), between pp. 276 and 277.
12 HALS: DE/P/F81.
13 HALS: 64333, survey of Bedwell Park by James Crow, 1765.
14 S. Spooner, 'The Diversity of Designed Landscapes: a regional approach *c*.1660–1830', unpublished PhD thesis (University of East Anglia, 2010), pp. 88–90.
15 HALS: H838, undated sketch showing highway diversion, Essendon.
16 HALS: DSA4/37/2.
17 Huntington Library, San Marino, California: HM 40849.

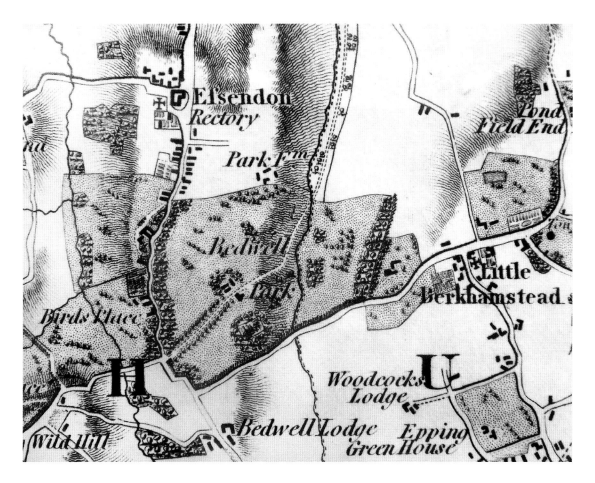

109   Bedwell Park, as shown on Andrew Bryant's county map of 1822.

Brookmans Park, North Mimms

TL253 047

ANDREW FOUNTAINE BUILT A NEW house at Brookmans in the late seventeenth century, which was acquired – together with its associated estate of 400 acres (*c.* 160 hectares) – by Lord John Somers in 1701. On his death in 1716 the property passed to his sister and her descendants, her son Sir Charles Cocks becoming the second Lord Somers.[1] The house is shown with gardens, but no park, on Dury and Andrews' county map of 1766. By the time that Mimms Common was enclosed in 1778, however, a park of 240 acres (*c.* 97 hectares) had been laid out, to judge from the enclosure

110   Brookman's Park, as illustrated in Peacock's Polite Repository for 1798.

map.[2] The estate was sold in 1784 to Alexander Higginson, a lawyer, who sold it the following year to Humphrey Sibthorpe of nearby Skimpans. He in turn sold it in 1786 to Peter Gaussen for £16,000.[3] The Gaussen family were to remain at Brookmans until 1923.

It was Peter Gaussen's son Samuel who engaged Humphry Repton to advise on the landscape some time before 1794.[4] Brookman's Park was illustrated in Peacock's *Polite Repository* for 1798 (Figure 110) and, while no Red Book is known to survive, one was certainly made by Repton and is referred to in his *Sketches and Hints on Landscape Gardening* of 1794. In this he describes how he broke up the line of an avenue there, presumably framing the view towards and away from the house. Other proposals must have been made, but later maps – such as the Ordnance Survey draft drawing of 1805[5] or Bryant's county map of 1822 (Figure 111) – appear to show a landscape park of normal eighteenth- or early nineteenth-century form, with a number of clumps and a small double lake, and bounded on the north side by a narrow belt of trees. In the 1810s there were elaborate flower gardens at Brookmans, but there is no evidence to connect them with Repton.[6]

Samuel Gaussen and his son, also Samuel, systematically expanded the estate and in 1838 the latter's son, Robert William Gaussen, purchased the 328 acres of the neighbouring Gobions

110   Brookman's Park, as illustrated in Peacock's Polite Repository for 1798.

estate from the trustees of T.N. Kemble for £23,000.[7] The park was greatly expanded and a new entrance drive laid out, leading off Swanley Bar road through the great castellated arch originally constructed in the early eighteenth century (to designs by James Gibbs) as part of Charles Bridgeman's complex gardens at Gobions.[8] In 1891 Brookmans burnt to the ground but the family continued to reside in the converted stables until the estate was broken up in 1923. Part of the park was then built over and most of the remainder converted into a golf course. Some of the parkland planting, especially the larger areas of woodland, survives, but whether this includes any of Repton's work is unknown.

Extract from *Sketches and Hints on Landscape Gardening* (1794)

...*and at* Brookmans, I elucidate the necessity of fixing on proper trees to form the outline in breaking an avenue; or, if the trees have stood so long near each other that no good outline can be formed, then the tops of some neighbouring trees may be so introduced as in some degree to supply the defect.[9]

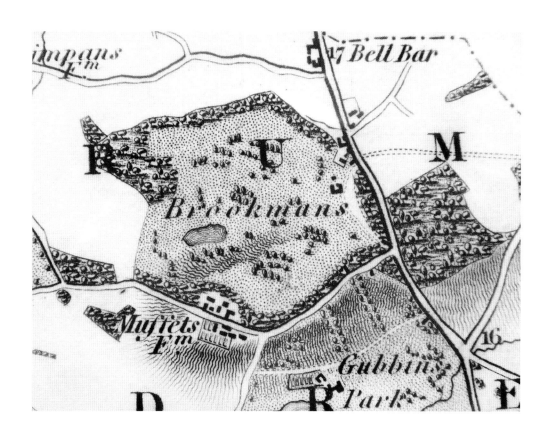

111   Brookman's Park, as shown on Andrew Bryant's county map of 1822.

Notes

1   P. Kingsford, *A Modern History of Brookman's Park 1700–1950* (Potters Bar, 1983), p. 10.

2   HALS: PC267a, Act of Parliament for the enclosure of North Mimms Common, 1778 (18 Geo 3 c.49) and PC267b, copy map inrolled in the Court of Common Pleas by the North Mimms Enclosure Commissioners, 15 May 1782.

3   R. Clutterbuck, *History and Antiquities of the County of Hertfordshire* (London, 1815–27), vol. I, p. 453; HALS: 34024, sale agreement between Dr Sibthorpe & Peter Gaussen, May 1786; and 34028–9, conveyancing documents, August 1786.

4   Daniels, *Humphry Repton*, p. 260.

5   BL: OSD 149.

6   HALS: 34150, account book of expenses for the flower garden, 1817–18.

7   HALS: 23704 and 34198; P. Kingsford, *The Gobions Estate, North Mymms* (Potters Bar, 1993), p. 11.

8   A. Rowe and T. Williamson, 'New light on Gobions', *Garden History*, 40/1 (2012), pp. 82–97.

9   H. Repton, *Sketches and Hints on Landscape Gardening* (London, 1794), p. 24.

Cashiobury Park, Watford

TQ 095972

CASHIOBURY (OR CASSIOBURY) HOUSE STOOD just north of the town of Watford, on a low plateau overlooking, to the west, the river Gade and, from 1795, the Grand Junction Canal. Unlike most of Repton's commissions in south Hertfordshire, Cashiobury was the centre of an extensive and long-established estate and the house and its park already had a long and complex history. The noted forester Moses Cook was gardener in the late seventeenth century; the landscape was illustrated by Kip and Knyff in their *Britannia Illustrata* of 1707; Charles Bridgeman

112 Cashiobury Park, as illustrated in Peacock's *Polite Repository* for 1802.

worked here in the 1720s and probably Thomas Wright in the early 1740s.[1]

George Capel Coningsby, fifth earl of Essex and owner of Cashiobury from 1799 to 1839, remodelled the house in extravagant Gothic fashion between *c.*1800 and 1805 to designs by James Wyatt, with the work – as at Ashridge – being completed by his nephew Jeffry Wyatt.[2] In a remarkable parallel with Ashridge, Repton appears to have been involved at around the same time in making alterations to the grounds. His *Memoirs* contains some rather waspish comments on the text of a letter written in August 1801 by the earl of Essex (reproduced below, p. 238) concerning his designs for an unnamed place, very probably Cashiobury,[3] while his work at Cashiobury is briefly referred to in *Observations on the Theory and Practice of Landscape Gardening*, published in 1803.[4] In addition, an engraving based on a drawing by Repton appeared in the 1802 edition of Peacock's *Polite Repository* (Figure 112). All this suggests that Repton was working at Cashiobury around 1801, but a longer involvement with the place is also probable. Repton described in his *Memoirs* how the fifth earl took exception to how his 'late predecessor' had been included by Repton in a list of his creditors, suggesting that work had been undertaken for the fourth earl, who had died in 1799 (Repton may have worked at the adjacent estate of The Grove (q.v.) in the late 1790s, and could well have offered some advice on the grounds of Cashiobury at the same time). But there are also drawings of an orangery, now in Watford Museum, that appear to be by Repton's son, John Adey Repton (Figures 113 and 114), together with a design for a 'hermitage' (Figure 115): these are undated, but pasted into an album entitled 'Plans & Sketches Cottages &c &c &c Cashiobury 1812'. This contains other notes and sketches, at least one of which may possibly be in Humphry Repton's hand, so it is quite possible that Repton (and his son) continued to be involved at Cashiobury over an extended period of time.

Dorothy Stroud has suggested that Repton advised on alterations to the Home Park, that part of Cashiobury's extensive grounds lying to the east of the Gade, and that he may in particular have been responsible for altering the course of the river, widening it and making it run in a pronounced bend so that it was more visible from the house. This change is not shown on a detailed estate map of 1798[5] but had probably been carried out by 1806, to judge from the draft Ordnance Survey drawings, although this may not be entirely reliable as a source as the surveyor responsible for this particular sheet is known to have made errors in other contexts (Figure 116).[6] Bryant's map of 1822, by contrast, displays a much more pronounced curve in the Gade at this point, leaving open the question of the precise timing of works to the river, and whether they were carried out in one or more stages. Either way, there is no direct evidence to connect this change with Repton. William Sawrey Gilpin, who later undertook some work at Cashiobury, wrote that someone he called 'the improver' – quite possibly Repton – had in fact concealed the 'cheerfulness' of the scene created by the river and canal, and by the wooded bank beyond, by poorly judged planting, which he himself had remedied by the judicious removal of trees.[7]

113   One of several designs for an orangery at Cashiobury, probably by John Adey Repton.

114   Another of the designs for an orangery at Cashiobury, probably by John Adey Repton. This may be the 'Chinese Conservatory' noted by Loudon in 1825.

115   Design for a hermitage at Cashiobury, possibly by John Adey Repton.

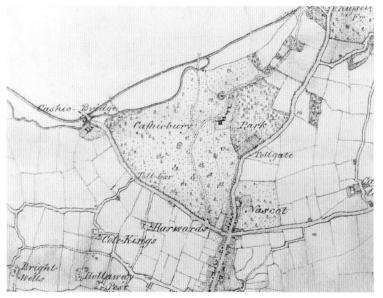

116   Cashiobury Park, as shown on the draft Ordnance Survey drawings of 1806.

While Repton may thus have advised on the parkland, the somewhat meagre evidence suggests that he was more concerned with the pleasure grounds and gardens near the house. The 1798 estate map shows that, to the east of the house, the old-fashioned woodland garden or wilderness designed by Moses Cook still survived, with radiating straight walks focused on a building called the Temple Cottage. In *Observations* Repton describes how he advised that the trees within this area should be drastically thinned in order to create a 'spacious internal lawn of intricate shape and irregular surface' – something which he noted had been carried out to his satisfaction,[8] a statement confirmed by later maps, such as the Watford tithe map of 1842 (Figure 117).[9] In addition, both the letter from the fifth earl quoted in the *Memoirs* and a reference in Repton's Red Book for Montreal in Kent in 1811 refer to a straight walk or 'mall' at Cashiobury that had been created under his direction.[10] This may be the 'broad walk' immediately below the house on which William Gilpin commented favourably in 1832.[11]

It is possible that Repton (and his son) contributed rather more to the immediate setting of the house. In the 1810s and 1820s various visitors commented on the complexity and sophistication of the pleasure grounds at Cashiobury. They were characterised by a range of distinct, but connected, gardens. In 1816 Frances Calvert described Lady Essex's flower gardens as 'the most complete in England',[12] while in 1820 Thomas Creevey lamented that he had not seen the flower garden 'which is the great lion of the place'.[13] Robert Havell in 1823 described how there was a Chinese garden, 'with analogous buildings, inscriptions, rocks, and plants'; an 'American nursery'; a garden invoking the 'frozen regions of the North'; and another devoted to tropical plants.

The whole may be said to consist of devious walks, avenues, arches, lawns, alcoves, groves, orangeries, &c., which on a cursory view present an endless variety and intricacy, although by a closer examination we discover order, science, and taste to pervade the whole …

There were rich and varied plantings featuring 'almost every species of deciduous and exotic trees, plants, and shrubs that will live in the English climate', as well as hot houses and green houses 'to rear and preserve the more delicate and tender shrubs and fruits'.[14]

Loudon in 1825 noted a 'Turkish pavilion' and a 'series of different sorts of flower-gardens', as well as a 'Chinese conservatory' and displays of American plants, 'grouped together in dug masses, surrounded by turf'. There were massed displays of roses, some 'encircled by basket-work'; complex rockeries displaying a wide range of minerals; a 'picturesque acquarium'; and elaborate conservatories.[15] Most of this was still in place in the 1830s, when Prince Herman Pückler-Muskau visited and Britton wrote his history of Cashiobury.[16]

The similarity with the complex and interconnected series of gardens created by Repton at Ashridge is notable. It is true that 1801 seems rather early in the development of Repton's style for such a design, but here the possibility of a longer, ongoing involvement with Cashiobury should be noted: the Chinese conservatory described by Loudon as a 'sort of low pagoda' sounds remarkably like the design for a conservatory, probably by John Adey Repton, held by Watford Museum (see Figure 114). Indeed, James Main specifically described in 1828 how the grounds of Cashiobury had been remodelled 'under the immediate directions of Mr. Repton, then in the zenith of his fame'.[17] On the other hand, no other early

117 Cashiobury Park house and pleasure grounds, as shown on the Watford tithe map of 1842.

nineteenth-century commentators refer to the gardens as having been designed by Repton – a particularly surprising omission, perhaps, in the case of Loudon and Pückler-Muskau, noted admirers of his work. Other designers were certainly patronised by the fifth earl. A range of lodges and *cottages ornées* in and around the park were the work of Jeffry Wyatt and Samuel Wyatt, while Uvedale Price, who had known the earl since at least 1801,[18] was at Cashiobury for two days in 1824, clearing excess undergrowth from an area known as the 'Horse-shoe dell' but also – to judge from letters sent to his friends Sir George Beaumont and Samuel Rogers

– undertaking other work.[19] In addition, as already noted, the designer William Sawrey Gilpin made alterations to the planting in the park in the 1820s, most notably to open up views towards the river and canal that had only recently been closed off.[20] The earl himself, a man of wide aesthetic tastes, was also actively involved in the gardens, to judge from comments by Repton and Price, while Loudon reported that a lodge at the south-eastern entrance to the park had been built to 'the proprietor's own designs.'[21]

Whatever Repton may have contributed to the landscape of Cashiobury, little survives on the ground today. The house was demolished in 1927 and much of the park was built on; the rest became a golf course and a public park. A solitary cedar of Lebanon growing within the latter may have been established by Repton. The gardens so admired by nineteenth-century visitors now lie under residential streets, but some of the trees growing in the suburban gardens may have been planted by him.[22]

Extract from Repton's *Memoirs*

But if my ways were (generally) ways of pleasantness, still it was not always that my paths were paths of peace – of which I will give one instance without a name, for altho' I have never envied any man for his riches or title, I have sometimes felt it hard that those who possessed both should wish to deprive me of my fair share of the only merit I did possess. And if this should ever reach the eye of Noble Lord ... Essex who boasts that everything that was done at his place was his taste and design let him recollect that after writing fifty letters with the most trifling queries about a line of fence, or a gravel walk, and after denying that he had ever taken my opinion, and referring to me as a common tradesman to put in my claim among his late father's creditors, he would surely blush to read that he himself wrote the following letter –

August 7th 1801

Sir, I was last night favour'd with your letter and will lose no time in assuring you that its contents were most satisfactory. Everything that you suggested evidently proves that you neither regard the absurd criticisms or follow the plan of the abominable tastemongers, who for the sake of alteration wish to strike out new ideas which they themselves do not understand. I admire your strait gravel walk which will perfectly accord with that side of the house which requires a proportional degree of formal grandeur. I have no other observation to make of the rest of the sketches, except that they are all executed with taste and judgment and I shall have great pleasure in meeting you at [his place] in October.

Oh fie my Lord! How can you tell everybody that Mr. Repton never did anything for you?[23]

Extract from *Observations on the Theory and Practice of Landscape Gardening*, pp. 78–9

In some places belonging to ancient noble families, it is not uncommon to see woods of vast extent intersected by vistas and glades in many directions; this particularly the case at BURLEY, and at CASHIOBURY. It is the property of a straight glade or vista to lead the eye to the extremity of a wood, without attracting the attention to its depth.

I have occasionally been required to fell great quantities of timber, from other motives than merely to improve the landscape; and in some instances this work of necessity has produced the most fortunate improvements. I do not hesitate to say, that some woods might be increased five-fold in apparent quantity, by taking away a prodigious number of trees, which are really lost to view; but unless such necessity existed, there is more difficulty and temerity in suggesting improvement by cutting down, however profitable, and however suddenly the effect is produced, than by planting, though the latter be tedious and expensive.

I have seldom found great opposition to my hints for planting, but to cutting down trees innumerable obstacles present themselves; as if, unmindful of their value, and heedless of their slow growth, I should advise a *military abatis*, or one general sweep, denuding the face of a whole country. What I should advise both at BURLEY and CASHIOBURY,* would be to open some large areas within the woods, to produce a spacious internal lawn of intricate shape and irregular surface, preserving a sufficient number of detached trees or groups, to continue the general effect of one great mass of wood.

*   This advice has been followed at Cashiobury since the above pages were written, and the effect is all that I had promised to myself.

The *Observations* contains two other references to Cashiobury. On page 171 Repton describes open quadrangles at Cobham Hall and Cashiobury, 'to both which have been judiciously added square courts of offices, under the direction of Mr. James Wyatt'; on page 201 he refers to the octagonal kitchen 'introduced at CASHIOBURY, with admirable effect, by Mr. James Wyatt, under whose direction that ancient abbey has been lately altered with such good taste and contrivance, that I shall beg leave to refer to it as a specimen of adapting ancient buildings to modern purposes'; while on page 212 he complemented the 'cheerfulness and magnificence of plate glass in the large Gothic windows' at Cashiobury and Cobham.

Notes

1 S.K. Priestley and P. Rabbitts, *Cassiobury, Ancient Seat of the Earls of Essex* (Stroud, 2014), pp. 60 and 73.

2 Priestley and Rabbitts, *Cassiobury*, pp. 60 and 73.

3 Gore and Carter, *Humphry Repton's Memoirs*, pp. 116–17.

4 Repton, *Observations*, pp. 78–9, 171, 201, 212.

5 HALS: DE/X736/E2, survey and valuation, 1798.

6 BL: OSD 151. The surveyor, William Hyett, was later strongly criticised by his employer, the Board of Ordnance: see Macnair *et al.*, *Dury & Andrews' Map of Hertfordshire*, p. 62.

7 W.S. Gilpin, *Practical Hints Upon Landscape Gardening* (Edinburgh, 1832), pp. 117–18, 187–8.

8 Repton, *Observations*, p. 79, note b.

9 HALS: DSA4/111/2.

10 H. Repton, *Report concerning Montreal in Kent, seat of the Right Honourable Lord Amherst*, 1812: Microfilm of Exported MSS, RP142, from J. Phibbs, 'A Documented History of Cassiobury Park' (2001), vol. 2.

11 Gilpin, *Practical Hints*, p. 47.

12 A.E. Blake (ed.), *An Irish Beauty of the Regency, compiled from "Mes Souvenirs," The unpublished journals of Mrs. Calvert 1789–1822* (London, 1911), pp. 269–70.

13 Sir H. Maxwell (ed.), *The Creevey Papers: A Selection from the Correspondence & Diaries of the Late Thomas Creevey, M.P.* (London, 1912), p. 296.

14 R. Havell, *A Series of Picturesque views of Noblemen's and Gentlemen's Seats with Historical and Descriptive Accounts of each Subject* (London, 1823), p. 110.

15 J.C. Loudon, 'Notes made during a tour to Cashiobury, Ashridge Park, Woburn Abbey, and Hatfield House, in October, 1825', *The Gardener's Magazine*, 12 (1836), pp. 279–87.

16 Prince Herman Pückler-Muskau, *A Tour of England, Ireland, and France in the Years 1826, 1827, 1828, and 1829 with remarks on the manners and customs of the inhabitants, and anecdotes of distinguished Public Characters, by a German Prince* (London, 1833), pp. 65–7; J. Britton, *The History and Description of Cassiobury Park* (London, 1837), pp. 26–7 and 29–30.

17 J. Main, 'Reviews', *The Gardener's Magazine*, 4 (1828), p. 116.

18 C. Watkins and B. Cowell, *Uvedale Price: Decoding the Picturesque* (Woodbridge, 2012), p. 145.

19 Letters dated 26 July 1824, Uvedale Price to Samuel Rogers, Foxley, in P.W. Clayden, *Rogers and his Contemporaries* (London, 1889), vol. 1, pp. 379–81; and 2 September 1824, Uvedale Price to Sir George Beaumont, in C. Watkins and B. Cowell (eds), *The Letters of Uvedale Price* (London, 2006), p. 310.

20 Gilpin, *Practical Hints*, pp. 117–18, 187–8.

21 Loudon, 'Notes made during a tour', pp. 280 and 287.

22 Land Use Consultants, 'Cassiobury Park Conservation Management Plan' (2014), p. 42.

23 Gore and Carter, *Humphry Repton's Memoirs*, pp. 116–17.

Digswell House, Digswell

TL 237148

The evidence for associating Repton with Digswell is entirely circumstantial, but nevertheless intriguing. The Digswell estate was purchased by the third Earl Cowper in 1786 following the death of the previous owner, Richard Willis, who had employed Capability Brown to make improvements around 1770. From 1800 estate records show the fifth earl taking an active interest in the landscape, cutting rides through Sherrardspark Wood, building a brick arch at the end of one of them and replanting the avenue in Monks Walk with beech trees. Digswell House was to become the home of the earl's younger brother, Edward Spencer Cowper, and in 1804 work started on the building of a new house, designed by the architect Samuel Wyatt. Edward Spencer Cowper had taken an active interest in laying out the landscape at his brother's estate at nearby Panshanger, designed by Repton, and had spent time with him there in 1800.[1] He also spent much time at the home of his guardian Henry Cowper at Tewin Water in 1804, making frequent visits thereafter, and must also have been familiar with Repton's work at that place.[2]

There is no hard evidence that Repton was commissioned to make proposals for the grounds of Digswell House, or indeed that he ever visited Digswell. Cowper's diaries show that he himself had a keen and practical interest in gardening and landscape design and was not above getting his hands dirty in his own garden and park.[3] Work on laying out the gardens started in earnest in 1808.

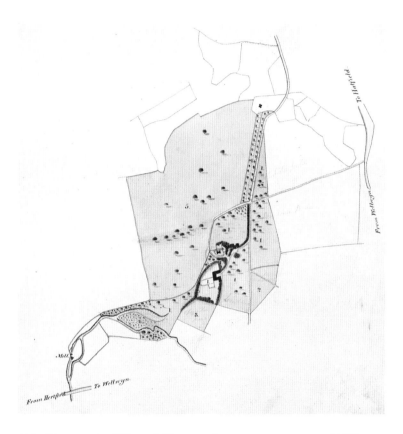

118   The grounds of Digswell House, as shown on an estate map of 1833.

In March of that year Cowper took on a new gardener – Samuel Marshall – and expenditure of £6 7s 6d is recorded in the estate accounts in September 1808.[4] On 3 November Cowper visited Munn's Nursery at Hertford 'to choose american plants &c' and the next day he 'Rode to Digswell & planted the american shrubs &c in the bog earth border'.[5] A year later Cowper's attention had turned to improving his park. On 30 November he 'mark'd out plantations by the entrance from the high road, single trees &c' and the next day 'marked out the line of the new piece of Water'.[6] This was to be a narrow lake beside the river Mimram and it was completed the following summer. His diary entry on 21 June 1810 notes 'the piece of water quite finish'd today. Flood gate put down about one o'clock.'[7] Two days later he wrote, 'The water quite full & running over the head at seven this morning.' The earliest map to show the lake is an estate map of 1833 (Figure 118).

There is thus no indication in the diaries, or in any other source, that Repton was directly involved in laying out the grounds of Digswell, but his influence, at the very least, can be detected in an undated illustration of the newly built house, which includes treillage on the east wing and Hardenberg baskets on the lawn, both of which are distinctly 'Reptonian' in character (Figure 119). Very similar features can be seen in Repton's Red Book illustrations for Tewin Water (see Figure 77) and Woodhill (see Figures 104 and 105). It is possible that he advised not only on the layout of the pleasure grounds near the house but also on the wider landscape, including the lake.

119 An undated painting of Digswell House by J. Trower.

Notes

1 HALS: DE/P/F471/5, Edward Spencer Cowper's diary, 1800 records the visit of Repton and his son to Panshanger 19–21 September, and how on Sunday 20 September he 'Walked about the grounds the whole day marking plantations'.
2 HALS: DE/P/F471/9–11, diaries of Edward Spencer Cowper, 1804–6.
3 He wrote lists of plants (now barely legible) in his diaries for 1811, 1820 and 1821.
4 HALS: DE/P/F471/13, diary of Edward Spencer Cowper, 1808. HALS: DE/P/EA23/2, ledger by Thomas Pallett, 1798–1811, fol. 46 (rev).
5 HALS: DE/P/F471/13, diary of Edward Spencer Cowper, 1808.
6 HALS: DE/P/F471/14, diary of Edward Spencer Cowper, 1809.
7 HALS: DE/P/F471/15, diary of Edward Spencer Cowper, 1810.

The Grove, Watford

TL 08209877

THE GROVE STANDS ON HIGH ground overlooking the river Gade to the east. The geology comprises Gerrards Cross gravels, with a chalky till containing flints on the valley slopes and alluvium in the valley bottom.[1] The Grand Union (originally Junction) Canal and the river Gade flow southwards through the eastern side of the grounds, into Cashiobury Park (see above, pp. 234–40). Repton's involvement at The Grove is suggested by two pieces of evidence. He supplied an engraving of the house for the 1798 issue of Peacock's *Polite Repository* (Figure 120) and he included 'The Grove' in a list of what he called 'creations' – that is, places where a new house had been erected on a site where no building had previously existed – in a discussion in his *Observations on the Theory and Practice of Landscape Gardening* of 1803.[2] This is a slightly mysterious allusion. The Grove had been built in the early eighteenth century, altered subsequently, and provided with elaborate grounds containing a large number of ornamental buildings including an 'Egyptian Pyramid, with Sphinxes'.[3] The nearby Dower House had also long been in existence:[4] both are clearly shown on Dury and Andrews' county map of 1766. It is thus probable that the reference to 'The Grove' in *Observations* is, in fact, to 'The Grove, Southgate', which is mentioned elsewhere in that work, and identifiable with the present Grovelands in Southgate, Middlesex, whose landscape Repton certainly did design.[5]

If Repton did indeed work at The Grove his client must have been Thomas Villiers Hyde, second earl of Clarendon from 1786 until 1824. The Villiers family was connected with the Capels of Cashiobury by the marriage of the first earl of Clarendon to Charlotte Capel, daughter of William Capel, third earl of Essex and Jane Hyde, a descendant of an earlier line of Clarendons. It is possible that Repton was responsible for altering the straight stretch of water in the park shown on the Ordnance Survey drawings of 1806, and apparently created under the terms of an

120   The Grove, Watford, as illustrated in Peacock's *Polite Repository* for 1798.

Act of Parliament in 1795 to maintain a flow of water to the house and gardens following the building of the canal through the park.[6] By 1812 Daniel Carless Webb noted the presence of a statue of Neptune on an island in an extensive stretch of water, and the Watford tithe map shows that by 1842 the present, more irregular water body had certainly come into existence (Figure 121).[7] More probably, Repton may have advised on the pleasure grounds and gardens of the Grove and/or the Dower House. Writing under her married name of Mrs Earle, Maria Theresa Villiers (1836–1925) described how, when she was a child, the 'old-fashioned' flower garden at the Dower House had been maintained by the same gardener for over 30 years, a time span which could have taken its history back to the late 1790s, and thus to the period of the *Polite Repository* illustration.[8]

Today the mansion and park are used as a hotel and golf course, and the Dower House and surrounding land are a private residence and preserved within a conservation area. In the absence of a Red Book, the attribution of particular surviving features to Repton is very uncertain.

121   The grounds of The Grove, Watford, as shown on the Watford tithe map of 1842.

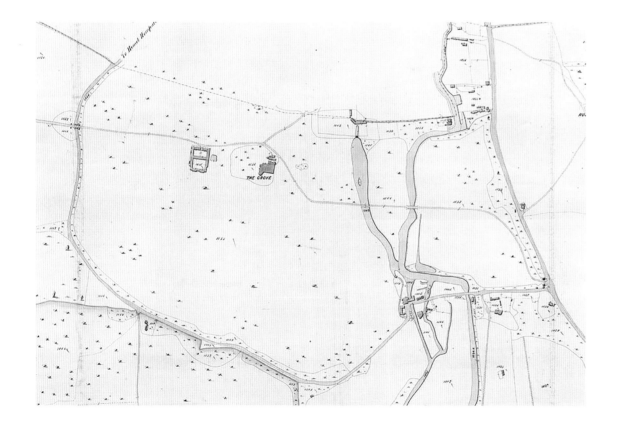

Notes

1   British Geological Survey, Geology of Britain Viewer, bgs.ac.uk.
2   Repton, *Observations*, p. 186.
3   D.C. Webb, *Observations and Remarks during Four Excursions made to Various Parts of Great Britain in … 1810 and 1811* (London, 1812), p. 162; Hertfordshire Gardens Trust and T. Williamson, *The Parks and Gardens of West Hertfordshire* (Letchworth, 2000), pp. 45–7.
4   Historic England List Entry Number 1101132.
5   Stroud, *Humphry Repton*, p. 98.
6   BL: OSD 151; HALS: DE/Ls/Q18, 'An Act for authorizing the Company of Proprietors of the Grand Junction Canal', 5 March 1795, 35 Geo 3 c.8.
7   Webb, *Observations and Remarks*, p. 162; HALS: DSA4/111/2, tithe map for Watford, 1842.
8   C.W. Earle, *Pot-Pourri from a Surrey Garden* (London, 1897), pp. 4–5.

Hilfield House, Aldenham

TQ 152962

HILFIELD HOUSE (OR LODGE) STANDS in the south-western portion of the parish of Aldenham, close to the boundary with Bushey. It was built for the Hon. George Villiers (1759–1827) soon after his marriage to Theresa Parker (the only daughter of Lord Boringdon) in April 1798.[1] It replaced his earlier home at Delrow House, around a mile (1.6 kilometres) to the north-west, as a secondary country retreat from the family's main house in Grosvenor Square in London.[2] Villiers was an intimate of the royal family, and especially of Princess Amelia, something that brought him a number of significant sinecures in the royal household. His father was Thomas Villiers, second earl of Clarendon, who had probably commissioned Repton to improve the grounds at The Grove in nearby Watford a year or so earlier (see above, pp. 243–4). Villiers had, to judge from the surviving land tax returns, been steadily acquiring land in the parish since 1795, including the site for his new house.[3]

This replaced an earlier building on the site – 'Sly's Hill' – which had probably been no more than a modest farm, as it is shown, but not named, on Dury and Andrews' county map of 1766. Villiers consulted Samuel Lapidge, an associate of Capability Brown and usually thought of as a landscape gardener, about its design, and although his plans were rejected his proposals for laying out the grounds were apparently acted upon (although Theresa Villiers described in a letter how she was appalled – and amused – by Lapidge's drunken and vulgar behaviour). Next, John Nash (who had already made improvements to the Villiers' London residence) was asked to supply plans, but these too were set aside and the house was eventually built to designs by Jeffry Wyatt. Construction began in 1798 and was completed in 1801.[4] Like Cashiobury and Ashridge, also by Wyatt and built a few years later, Hilfield is a gothic building, of rendered brick under a slate roof and featuring a mass of turrets, crenellations and a four-storey central tower. Its medieval style is reflected in its alternative names: 'Sly's Castle', 'Sly's Hill Castle', and 'Hill Field Castle' (Figure 122).

Repton was consulted about the landscape for the new house in 1799. The commission may have come via his work at the Grove a year or so before; through Nash, with whom Repton was in effective partnership until 1799; or, more probably, through Wyatt, with whom Repton had worked on several occasions. The only surviving evidence for his involvement is a letter written by Theresa Villiers in November 1799 in which she describes how her husband begrudged paying Repton's bill for 10 guineas, presumably because it appeared excessive, but settled the account, although the payment was accompanied by a strongly worded letter. She recounted Repton's reply that: 'if he could forget his own character as a Gentleman, he could retaliate by answering Mr V's letter in the same stile but that he should content himself with saying that, however, disagreeable Mr V might think it to pay

Overleaf
122 Hilfield House, Aldenham ('Sly's Hill Castle') as sketched by H.G. Oldfield shortly after its completion around 1801.

the 10gns, it was a much greater hardship to him to receive them accompanied by such a letter.'[5]

It is uncertain how much Repton contributed to the grounds of Hilfield. On the one hand, the 10 guineas charged suggests a major involvement, perhaps the production of a Red Book, but, on the other, the apparent quarrel with Villiers may imply that his advice was not fully taken up. It is clear that the landscape appears to have developed rapidly in the years around 1800, and that much of its basic form was apparently decided *before* Repton was consulted. The pleasure grounds were thus begun in late 1798 and were apparently laid out to designs by Lapidge, as interpreted by Theresa Villiers and her gardener.[6] The 1803 enclosure map for Aldenham shows that their boundary featured several curious bastion-shaped projections, more in the style of the 1730s than the 1790s, and most unlike anything that Repton is known to have designed (Figure 123).[7] In late 1798 the house was screened from the nearby public road – Hilfield Lane – with trees, further augmented in 1799 with specimens sent by Theresa Villiers' aunt Ann Robinson.[8] In 1803, however, Villiers took advantage of the parliamentary enclosure of the parish to divert the lane rather further to the south-west, away from the house, along its present line (in the words of the award, 'across old inclosed lands belonging to the Honourable George Villiers at Slyes Hill') and the grounds were extended in this direction.[9] The enclosure map shows the line of the new road and also – in dotted outline – that of the old. It also shows that the park was already in place, although at this stage covering only *c.*57 acres (*c.*23 hectares). It lay mainly to the south of the house, and had a small lake lying roughly east–west across its centre (Figure 123). The enclosure award also records, however, the exchanges of land that Villiers was making with neighbouring proprietors – principally the Worshipful Company of Brewers – and by the time a survey of Villiers' properties was made in 1804 the park had been extended to around 124 acres (*c.*50 hectares), and the lake enlarged.[10]

Through mismanagement of his post as Paymaster of the Marines Villiers fell into debt with the Crown and was forced to surrender all his property, including his lands in Aldenham, which were then sold in lots. In 1809 Hilfield and its immediate grounds were purchased by Captain John Fam Timins of the East India Company, whose family continued to own the estate until the early twentieth century. Hilfield House still exists but most of the park was destroyed when Hill Field Park Reservoir was constructed in the early 1950s, while its northern portion now lies under Elstree airfield. The pleasure grounds survive around the house, but have largely expanded beyond their original bastioned boundaries and, while some trees of probable early nineteenth-century date remain, there is nothing in the landscape today that seems particularly 'Reptonian'.

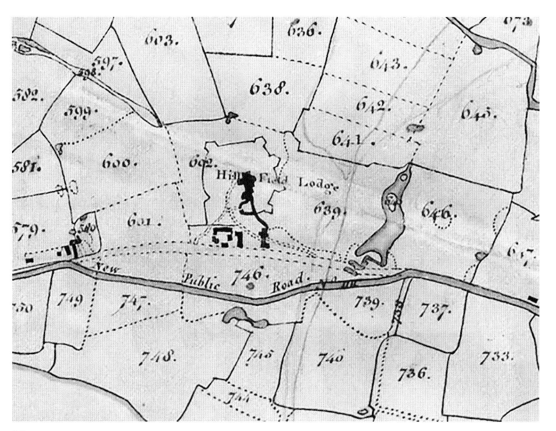

123 The grounds of Hilfield House, as shown on the Aldenham enclosure map of 1803.

Notes

1 Plymouth and West Devon Record Office: 69/M/3/87, marriage settlement, 16 April 1798.
2 Much of what follows is derived from Anida Rayfield's research on the letters of Theresa Villiers (née Parker), based in particular on Plymouth and West Devon Record Office: 1259/2, family correspondence.
3 HALS: Aldenham land tax returns, 1795–1816; DE/Tm/24132–24854, title deeds of the Hilfield Lodge estate, 1647–1821.
4 Plymouth and West Devon RO: 1259/2/409 and 419; D. Linstrum, *Sir Jeffry Wyatville, Architect to the King* (Oxford, 1972), pp. 73–4.
5 Plymouth and West Devon RO: 1259/2/475–9.
6 Again, as suggested by Anida Rayfield's important research on the letters of Theresa Villiers.
7 HALS: QS/E/3.
8 Plymouth and West Devon RO: 1259/2/476–9.
9 HALS: QS/E/2.
10 HALS: DP/3/29/9A, plan of 'Hill Field Lodge Estate property of Hon George Villiers', 1804.

Little Court, Buntingford (Layston)

TL 364297

HUMPHRY REPTON WAS INVOLVED WITH Little Court in 1790, when it was owned by Richard Spurrier, a local solicitor. Two one-day visits are recorded in Repton's account book in August and October of that year.[1] A note on the page, 'See page 27 of new ledger', suggests that further work was carried out at a later date. No record has been found of a Red Book for the site, but it is quite possible, given the time that was spent on the project, that one was produced. Richard Spurrier died in 1792, and this may have put a stop to any work on the grounds.[2]

Relatively little is known of the history of Little Court, a house apparently built in 1598 and illustrated by Drapentier for Chauncy's *Historical Antiquities* of 1700.[3] A map of 1744 shows that it was then owned by Lucius Charles Cary, 7th Viscount Falkland (1707–85).[4] The property came into the hands of the Spurrier family around 1785, but they had sold it by 1805, indicating a relatively brief association. The house was sold again in 1818 and the map drawn up at the time suggests that it stood in grounds of *c.*18 acres (around seven hectares), including the park and kitchen garden.[5] It provides no details of the landscape, beyond showing that the house was approached, as today, by a drive leading in from the south-west corner – presumably across the brick bridge spanning the river Rib that still survives, and which is apparently of late eighteenth-century date.

In the year following the sale the old house was demolished and the present building erected; the garden appears to have been completely remodelled at the same time. The house survives, in a small park and with a walled kitchen garden to the south, but it is now unclear what, if anything, designed by Repton remains.

Notes
1   NRO: MS10.
2   Prince, *Parks in Hertfordshire since 1500*, p. 119.
3   W. Page (ed.), *VCH Hertfordshire* vol. 4 (London, 1914), p. 80.
4   HALS: 54835, 'A Survey of the Demesne Land of the Manour of Corney Bury' in the parishes of Layston and Wyddial, 1744.
5   HALS: DE/Ry/P12, auction sale map, 20 May 1818.

Marchmont House, Hemel Hempstead

TL 0529 0681

MARCHMONT HOUSE IS A SMALL late eighteenth-century 'villa' located between the hamlet of Picott's End and Hemel Hempstead Old Town, on the eastern side of the river Gade. It was built for Hugh Hume-Campbell, third earl of Marchmont (1708–94), a prominent Scottish politician and an acquaintance of Alexander Pope, as a convenient base for his London activities.[1] It is named after the family seat of Marchmont House in the (former) County of Berwick in Scotland. Following the earl's death the property passed to his daughter in-law, Amabel Grey, first countess de

Grey. She probably sold it to Thomas Green, who was the owner at the time of Repton's possible involvement, the only evidence for which is an engraving he prepared for the 1804 issue of Peacock's *Polite Repository* (Figure 124). In this the house, described as the residence of Thomas Green, appears different in a number of details from today: several additions have been made since the early nineteenth century, to both the north and the east, including a full-height bow on the eastern end of the south elevation. These have considerably enlarged what was originally a house of modest size. The veranda on the western elevation, however, was already in place when Repton prepared his illustration. Repton's illustration shows the house standing in simple parkland, with the river Gade in the foreground.

There are no surviving archives relating to the property from this period other than a map of 1805, showing an 'estate at Picotts End belonging to Thomas Abbot Green' (Figure 125).[2] This shows the house placed close to the main road leading north from Hemel Hempstead, with a diminutive park, covering just under 20 acres (eight hectares) and of fairly standard late eighteenth-century form, extending west down to the Gade. Drives or walks are shown running through narrow belts along the southern and western perimeters and across the northern section of the park. The parkland planting appears to stand in straight lines, suggesting it was derived, in the customary fashion, from earlier

124 Marchmont House, Hemel Hempstead, as illustrated in Peacock's *Polite Repository* for 1804.

hedgerows. The house is flanked by small areas of pleasure ground and a detached walled kitchen garden lies some 150 metres to the north. The carriage drive approaching from the south led smoothly off the public road in the approved Repton fashion; the veranda on the western side of the house is also characteristic of his style, as are the narrow belts and walks. Nevertheless, the full extent of Repton's work at Marchmont remains unknown. The house is now a public house and restaurant (The Marchmont Arms) and part of the former pleasure grounds is used for car parking. The A4147 Link Road now cuts east–west through the southern section of the park.

Notes

1   Spooner, 'Diversity of Designed Landscapes', p. 74. Stone and Fawtier-Stone, *An Open Elite?* p. 133.
2   HALS: DE/X134/P2.

125   The grounds of Marchmont House, as shown on a map of 1805.

Offley Place, Great Offley

TL 14532699

OFFLEY PLACE STANDS A SHORT distance to the south-east of Offley village, within a park that has been in existence since the seventeenth century and is first depicted on Seller's county map of 1676. The house was illustrated by Drapentier for Chauncy's *Historical Antiquities* of 1700, but was largely rebuilt (to designs by Robert Smirke) in 1806–10.[1] The evidence for Repton's involvement at Offley rests solely on the fact that he provided an illustration of the house and its immediate surroundings for Peacock's *Polite Repository* for 1795, showing it before Smirke's rebuilding, although already apparently much altered from the house depicted by Drapentier in 1700 (Figure 126). Although, as we have noted, inclusion in the *Polite Repository* is not in itself firm evidence that Repton actually worked at a particular place, the fact that he had already been paid by the owner, Lady Salusbury, for advising on improvements at her other house – Brandsbury in Middlesex – in 1789 (producing one of his first Red Books for the property) makes an association probable.[2] Nevertheless, neither the scale nor character of his work at Offley are known. Nothing in the *Polite Repository* view looks particularly 'Reptonian', no contemporary estate accounts have survived and the enclosure map of 1807 does not provide any details of the park or gardens.[3] There were further significant changes to the landscape around the time that the house was rebuilt, involving the expansion of the park northwards following the closure of a public road.[4] Nothing obviously in Repton's style appears on Bryant's county map of 1822 or on a sale map of 1841 (Figure 127), although both show narrow perimeter belts and clumps, some of which could conceivably have been his work.[5]

126 Offley Place, as illustrated in Peacock's *Polite Repository* for 1795.

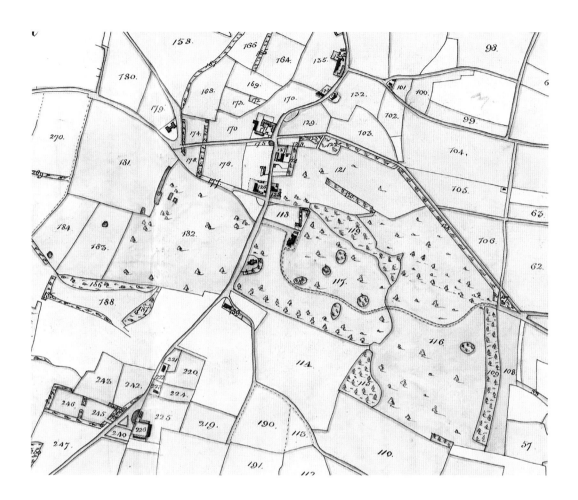

127 The grounds of
Offley Place, as shown
on a sale map of 1841.

Notes

1 N. Pevsner and B. Cherry, *The Buildings of England: Hertfordshire* (London, 1977), p. 265; HALS: H 942.581, unpublished 'History of Offley Place' (photocopy: no date or author, but probably by Herbert G. Salusbury Hughes); Chauncy, *Historical Antiquities of Hertfordshire*, between pp. 404 and 405.

2 NRO: MS10.

3 HALS: QS/55 and 56, Offley enclosure map and award, 1807.

4 HALS: QS Highway Diversion orders Nos 308–311, highway from Hitchin to Luton, 1807–10.

5 HALS: DE/Lg/T24, map with agreement between Lady Salusbury & the Marquess of Winchester, 1841.

Organ Hall, Aldenham

TQ 167997

THERE ARE THREE PIECES OF evidence linking Humphry Repton with Organ Hall. An engraving of the house, based on a sketch by him, appeared in Peacock's *Polite Repository* for 1804 (Figure 128). Repton refers to the property in *Observations on the Theory and Practice of Landscape Gardening* (1803) as one of the places where he 'gave general plans for the whole, with the assistance of my Son only in the architectural department', clearly implying the production of a Red Book.[1] Lastly, in his final book, *Fragments*

128 Organ Hall, Aldenham, as illustrated in Peacock's *Polite Repository* for 1804.

of the Theory and Practice of Landscape Gardening (1816), he uses Organ Hall to illustrate the importance of aspect:

> At Organ Hall, in Hertfordshire, a seat of William Towgood, Esq., the living-room was towards the south-west and, during a heavy storm of wind and rain, we accidentally went into the butler's pantry, which looked towards the south-east, where we found the storm abated, and the view from the windows perfectly clear and free from wet; but on returning into the other room, the storm appeared as violent as ever; and the windows were entirely covered with drops which obscured all view.[2]

The Organ Hall estate originally straddled Theobald Street, the ancient road that now links Radlett to Borehamwood, along the Tykeswater stream, a tributary of the river Colne. The first (later 'Old') Organ Hall was built close to Theobald Street, on low-lying land near the Tykeswater. The property's history is intimately linked to that of the Newberries estate, which lay just over a mile to the north-west, close to Shenley Hill and Shenley Road. In the seventeenth century these properties were owned as a single unit by Edward Briscoe,[3] but during the eighteenth century they seem to have become separated. Old Organ Hall functioned as a farm and was surrounded by fields; Newberries House and its extensive outbuildings, on the higher ground of Shenley Hill, became a separate estate, while another house, known as 'New' Organ Hall, was built close by, on the same hill but a little to the south-west. On Dury and Andrews' county map of 1766 a 'Mr Risrow' is named as the occupier of New Organ Hall and 'Admiral Durell' (correctly, Durcell) as that of Newberries. All three houses – Old Organ Hall, New Organ Hall and Newberries (together with its stable block) – were illustrated by Henry George Oldfield some time around 1802.[4]

In 1801 William Towgood bought New Organ Hall and its 130-acre (*c.*53-hectare) estate, having previously rented it from the Schribier or Schreiber family of Tewin House, Tewin.[5] Towgood, a partner in a sugar-refining company, was from a wealthy London-based merchant-banking family and was an elder brother of Matthew Towgood, who had recently purchased the New Barnes estate, a few miles to the north (see above, pp. 103–19).[6] In the following year the Newberries estate, comprising about 100 acres (*c.*40 hectares) of fields and woodland, came on the market, and this was also bought by William. Over the next 18 years he laid out the grounds of New Organ Hall/Newberries as one entity, apparently demolishing the old Newberries house in the process, although continuing to use its outbuildings, and closing at least one public right of way through the grounds.[7]

Repton was presumably involved soon after the two estates were united in 1802. The character and scale of his contribution is unknown, but it is possible to see some of the more general changes made to the local landscape by Towgood by comparing Dury and Andrews' county map of 1766 with the Ordnance Survey drawings of 1805 and Bryant's map of 1822 (Figures

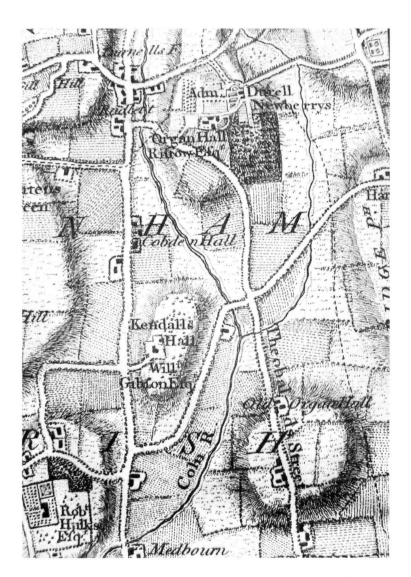

129 The locations of Old Organ Hall, Organ Hall, and Newberries House as shown on Dury and Andrews' county map of 1766.

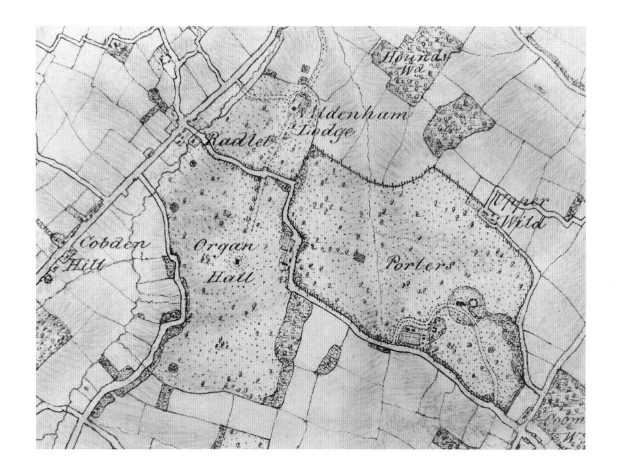

130 The grounds of Organ Hall, as shown on the draft Ordnance Survey drawings of 1805.

Hall, which appears to have been from Theobald Street to the south-west. It is possible, therefore, that this was a new driveway made after discussion with Repton, who, as noted elsewhere, had a particular interest in approaches. It ran along the ridge of the hill and would certainly have provided striking views for visitors to the estate.[8]

Repton's influence on other aspects of the landscape is perhaps suggested by a description of the grounds contained in the advertisement drawn up in 1823, when the estate was put up for sale. The house is described as:

> Seated in the centre of its admired grounds, which include Ten Acres of Plantation, Lawn and Shrubbery, disposed in the best possible manner, and adorned with a profusion of rare and valuable shrubs. Encircling the whole, are Two Hundred and Twenty-five Acres of Park-like Grounds. The land is of the best description, and is surrounded by the thriving plantations, with its full-grown timber scattered in pleasing negligence.[9]

129, 130 and 131). The most obvious change is the disappearance of Newberries as a separate entity and the conversion of the immediate surroundings of New Organ Hall from arable fields and orchard to a substantial area of parkland with decorative tree planting. There seems to have been one main approach to the house, leaving Shenley Hill to the north-west, but not at the place where the entrance to the Newberries House had left that road in 1766, nor on the line of the old approach to New Organ

A plan of the estate accompanying sale particulars of 1884, although made 60 years later, gives some idea of the layout. It shows areas of planting, particularly along the roads and around the house, plus clumps of trees elsewhere in the park, many hiding old gravel and chalk pits and screening two estate cottages on Shenley Hill.[10] Some of this, likewise, has a vaguely 'Reptonian' feel.

In March 1820 Towgood moved to Cardiff, soon became partner in the bank of Towgood, Yerbury and Towgood and died, aged 76, in 1835.[11] The new Organ Hall estate that he had created was sold to Peter Hunter of Tyttenhanger.[12] Three years later, in August 1823, it was on the market again, confusingly now referred to as 'That Distinguished and Greatly-admired VILLA called Newberries', the name by which the estate has been known ever since.[13] At this point about 230 acres (c.93 hectares) of land were attached to the house. The landscape continued to develop during the nineteenth century – by 1884 a second entrance drive had been laid out, leading in from Theobald Street to the south-west. By this time both entrances were provided with gate lodges.[14] The North Lodge, on what is now Williams Way in Radlett, may have been part of Repton's plan for the new driveway, but South Lodge, on what is now Craigweil Avenue, is known to date from the 1860s, because when the Midland Railway was built along the western edge of the estate, part of the agreement was that the entrance to the property be moved further up Theobald Street.[15] A bridge across the Tykeswater that may have served the older entrance still survives, now located within a car park near the junction between Theobald Street and the main road, Watling Street. The house was demolished in 1957 and its site and grounds acquired by the developers William Old & Co. Today the area occupied by the grounds is largely built over: the rest comprises an area of modern plantation and paddocks without significant tree planting.[16]

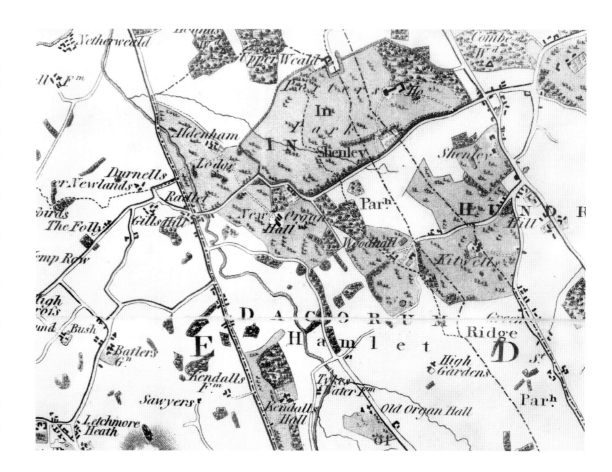

131   The grounds of Organ Hall, as shown on Andrew Bryant's county map of 1822.

Notes

1 Repton, *Observations*, p. 186.
2 Repton, *Fragments*, pp. 107–8.
3 Cussans, *History of Hertfordshire*, vol. 3, p. 310.
4 HALS: DE/Of/1/151–7.
5 HALS: Pamphlets Aldenham 3, A. Tibbits, 'History of Newberries in the Parish of Aldenham and the County of Hertford and of the Title of Mr Henry James Lubbock thereto' (copy of handwritten document *c.*1890), p. 9.
6 LMA: MS11936/399/639 418, Sun Fire Office Insurance 1795, for William Towgood, John Danvers Esq and Co, 21 Bread Street Hill, London, sugar refiners.
7 HALS: Highway diversion orders Nos 8–11, Michaelmas Sessions, 1806 (although the associated map was drawn by Thomas Godman, in 1803).
8 BL: OSD 151.
9 Sales by Auction, *County Chronicle*, 26 August 1823.
10 HALS: 37316, Messrs Humbert and Sons, sale particulars for the 'Freehold Residential Estate known as Newberries', 1884.
11 *The Times*, 4 March 1835; TNA: PROB 11/1848/407, will of William Towgood of Cardiff, 27 June 1835.
12 Tibbits, 'History of Newberries', pp. 7–11.
13 Sales by Auction, *County Chronicle*, 26 August 1823.
14 HALS: pamphlet file H 796.358, 'Radlett Cricket Club', p. 6; D. Wratten, *Book of Radlett and Aldenham* (Buckingham, 1990), p. 44.
15 Tibbits, 'History of Newberries', pp. 17–18.
16 Wratten, *Book of Radlett and Aldenham*, p. 34.

Wyddial Hall

TL 374319

WYDDIAL HALL STANDS IN THE parish of Wyddial, north-east of Buntingford on the watershed between the rivers Rib and Quin. The geology comprises chalk with a covering of boulder clay:[1] the soils within the park are slow-draining loams of the Hanslope Association.[2] Unlike many of the places where Repton worked in Hertfordshire, Wyddial had a long previous history. Although no park is shown on either Saxton's county map of 1577 or Norden's of 1598, a list of parks suitable for breeding horses in the county, drawn up in 1583, includes a reference to 'Widiall Parke' owned by a Mr J. Gill.[3] However, this park may have lapsed, as Chauncy in 1700 described how the owner of Wyddial in the late seventeenth century, the London lawyer Richard Goulston, 'made a Park to his house, and died … 2d of September, 1686'.[4] This park appears on John Oliver's county map of 1695 and a marriage settlement of 1700, between Richard Go(u)lston (Richard's grandson) and Margaret Turner, refers to 'all that Parke or impaled Ground now stored with Deer called Wyddial Park', including a rabbit warren of nine acres.[5] These features are all shown on an engraving of the hall, drawn from the east, by Drapentier and published in Chauncy's *Historical Antiquities* of 1700. The hall burnt down in 1733 but was rebuilt using as much of the original structure as possible.[6] A survey of the manor of Corney Bury, made in 1744, shows the new hall in elevation, with sash windows symmetrically placed around

a central door in correct Georgian fashion, and describes the adjacent land as the property of Francis Goulston;[7] and Dury and Andrew's county map of 1766 shows a park of around 300 acres (*c*.120 hectares), containing avenues extending north, east and west from the hall, which is marked as the residence of a third Richard G(o)ulston (born in 1726). A mortgage dated July 1766 refers to a 'park or impaled ground now or lately stocked or stored with deer called Wyddial Park'.[8] Also mentioned are 'All those parcels of ground adjoining or lying near to the said Manor House called the Homestall containing … nine acres part therof

132 Wyddial Hall, as illustrated in Peacock's *Polite Repository* for 1791.

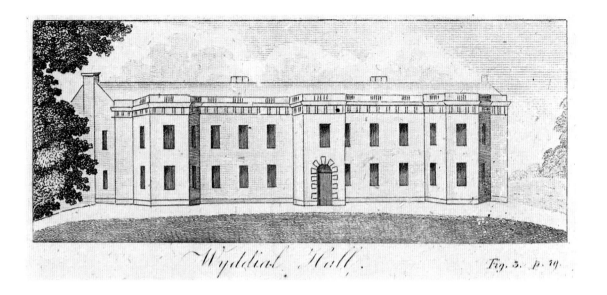

Wyddial Hall.

Fig. 3. p. 19.

133 H.G. Oldfield's 'Descriptive sketch' of Wyddial Hall, drawn in 1789 and published in the *Gentleman's Magazine* of January 1793.

was formerly used as a Warren', suggesting little change in the landscape since the start of the century. A map of 1768, surveyed by Owen Swan, shows the park, but provides no details of the features within it.[9]

Stephen Comyn, a barrister and Bencher of the Inner Temple, purchased Wyddial from Richard and Francis Goulston in 1772.[10] He died the following year and Comyn's heirs sold the property to Brabazon Ellis; by 1780 his son, John Thomas Ellis (1756–1836), had inherited. He was educated at Lincoln's Inn, was appointed Sheriff of Hertfordshire in 1784 and in 1786 was elected MP for Lostwithiel,[11] and married Mary Ann (Marianne) Heaton. It was John Thomas Ellis who employed Repton to make alterations to the property. The park at Wyddial had by this time contracted to 140 acres (*c.*57 hectares) from the estimated 300 acres in 1766.[12]

Repton's account book records how he spent four days at Wyddial in March 1790, a further five days preparing the drawings and another day and a half on the project: payments were also made to William Wilkins for a drawing of a lodge. The balance was carried over to the subsequent (lost) ledger, moreover, suggesting that the work was still ongoing.[13] Repton prepared a Red Book for the site and, although this is now lost, his own transcription of part of its contents still survives in the 1792 Red Books for Stoke Park and Hanslope in Buckinghamshire (see below). In addition, Repton made a drawing of the house that was published in Peacock's *Polite Repository* for 1791 (Figure 132). There is also a reference to Wyddial in Repton's *Sketches and Hints on Landscape Gardening* of 1803, as a place where he had 'ornamented water'.[14]

Repton often suggested making changes to the mansion as well as to its landscape, but the evidence for this happening at Wyddial is questionable. An article written in 1913[15] quotes *The Topographer* from April 1789, which mentions a 'Descriptive Sketch' of Wyddial Hall, noting that the present possessor had covered the outside with stucco. The sketch is probably the drawing (Figure 133) that Henry George Oldfield refers to in a letter of 4 January 1793.[16] Since this illustration is not in colour it is impossible to tell whether the stucco was painted white, but it certainly appears so in a later view that Oldfield prepared (Figure 134).[17] This is important because at a number of places Repton proposed covering houses with stucco and painting them white. In the case of Wyddial the timing seems wrong for adding the stucco – he would have had to have made this recommendation in late 1788/early 1789 for it to be reported by April 1789, a year

134 Wyddial
Hall, undated
sketch by
H.G. Oldfield.

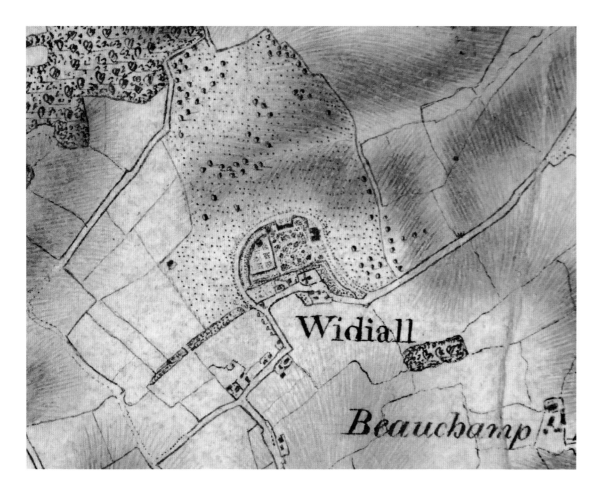

Topographer notes the 'handsome park surrounding the house' and comments that the 'landscape was very prettily developed', it seems that Ellis wanted it updated.

This was clearly an important commission for Repton, and one perhaps critical in the development of his ideas on unity, composition and colour. Indeed, Wyddial is cited in no fewer than six of Repton's Red Books – more than any other place except Cobham in Kent.[19] In the lost Red Book, to judge from the extracts from it contained in the Red Books for Stoke Park and Hanslope, Repton emphasised the need for outlying parts of a property to be visible from the park, not in close proximity: 'farmland, subdivided by hedges, should be seen at one remove, beyond a perimeter belt, rather than directly juxtaposed with the open parkland'. The same sentiments, although worded slightly differently, are repeated in the Red Books for Honing (May 1792), Courteenhall (March 1793) and Warley (March 1795).[20] In the Glemham Red Book (April 1791) Repton also stresses the need for the maintenance of overall harmony of colour in the view from a house, advising that a visible field should not be 'in Corn', and refers the owner to his remarks on Wyddial.[21]

The way in which Repton's ideas were implemented at Wyddial can perhaps be discerned on the draft Ordnance Survey drawings of 1800 (Figure 135), made soon after his involvement there.[22] These show that the hall and its immediate grounds were divided from the wider parkland by an encircling driveway. This would have provided extensive views across the park towards College Wood (now part of Capons Wood) in the distance. The hedge marking the boundary of the park to the east was disguised by trees planted, in front and behind it, presumably to

135 The grounds of Wyddial Hall, as shown on the draft Ordnance Survey drawings of 1800.

before his commission. However, Oldfield's second drawing must post-date 1796, since the notes on the following page (p. 399) mention that the property was let to Thomas Calvert, and we know that this occurred on 26 December 1796.[18] It thus remains possible that the colour, at least, may have owed something to Repton's influence. Repton's main efforts were, however, clearly directed towards the setting of the house. Although *The*

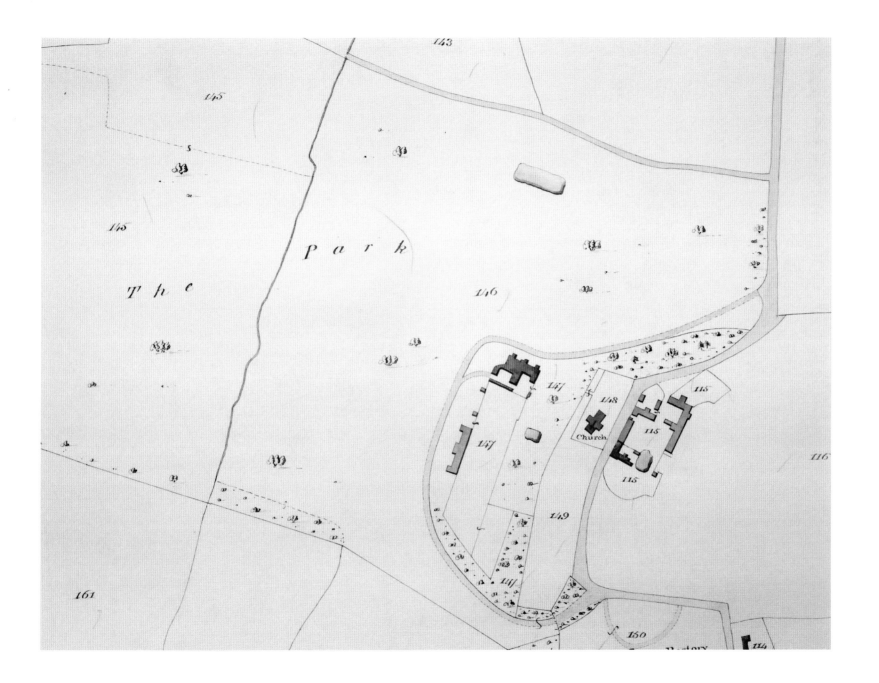

136   The grounds
of Wyddial Hall, as
shown on the tithe
map of 1840 (north is
roughly to the left).

limit views of the fields beyond. The engraving of Wyddial in the *Polite Repository* (see Figure 132) shows the house with a distant backdrop of woodland on the northern side of the park, which is itself scattered with specimen trees and clumps, some of which survive today.

The bulk of the garden lay to the south and west of the house and on the Ordnance Survey drawings there is a hint of a formal layout, possibly a kitchen garden, enclosed by a curved wall to the west. The garden near the house appears informally scattered with what could be shrubberies interspersed with trees. The location of the 'artifical piece of water' that Repton refers to in *Sketches and Hints* is not clear. It might have been the formal water body lying to the south-west of the hall (and north-west of the parish church) or the larger example located to the east, both of which are shown on the tithe map of 1840 (Figure 136) and the Ordnance Survey 6-inch map surveyed in 1877.[23]

John Thomas Ellis did not enjoy his new landscape for long, for in 1796 the property was leased for ten years to Thomas Calvert of Berkeley Square. John Thomas and Mary Ann had four sons, of whom three died before their father. In 1836 their third son, Charles Arthur Hill Heaton Ellis, succeeded and he made some adjustments to the garden.[24] In the course of the nineteenth century the park appears to have been extended to the east and west, but in the later twentieth century it contracted once again. The northern part of the eighteenth-century park was ploughed up and to the east the boundary retracted to that which had existed in Repton's time. Here, Repton's scattered trees were augmented to form a more continuous belt. The property now has separate dwellings in the Coach House and Wyddial Parva, which are served by the western arm of the drive. The park remains under grass and in good condition, but it is uncertain what surviving features can be attributed to Repton.

Extract from the Red Book for Stoke Park, Buckinghamshire, 1792 (a section written as if in response to comments from the estate's owner)

'The Viscount then proceeds thus, "As to the colour of the open parts, if it is a corn-country you cannot possibly connect it with your ground unless you make part of your ground of the same colour with the surrounding fields, and give the appearance of cultivation." In answer to this I shall transcribe the following page from my remarks on Wyddiall Hall, a seat of J. T. Ellis Esqr.

"Every piece of Land within such a distance of a house as the magnitude of that house seems to require in park or paddock, should appear to belong to it not only to give the importance of undivided property, but because without Unity no 'composition' can be pleasing; this makes the [sight] of a hedge or pale so disgusting, we see two distinct objects, a park, and a farm, and we see the line which divides them from each other; consequently the ideas excited by one being blended with the other, that Unity is destroyed which is a great source of pleasure in the human mind. A Park is a whole consisting of Lawn, Wood, and Water; and A Farm is not less a whole tho' divided into a thousand different inclosures, but the two can never be considered with unity in the same point of view. If the park be divided from the farm only by a hedge, we know the breadth of the hedge and its proximity is as offensive as if a pale made the line of separation, but if instead of a pale or hedge as a boundary, we substitute a wood of sufficient depth to act as a skreen, the imagination gives still greater extent to that wood than it really has, and when we see a distant arable country over the tops of this mass of trees, it becomes so much softened by the aerial perspective that instead of offending, it is a pleasing appendage to the Landscape, because it is subordinate."

"Quant à la couleur des terrasses, si le pays extérieur est en terres labourables, il est absolument necessaire pour vous y bien lier, d'introduire intérieurement dans vos terrasses les couleurs des champs, & l'aspect de la culture." &c'[25]

Extract from the Red Book for Hanslope Park, Buckinghamshire, 1792

The Wyddial extract quoted by Repton in his Red Book for Hanslope Park is the same as that given above from the Stoke Park Red Book, except that, instead of using the phrase 'divided into a thousand different inclosures, but the two can never be considered with unity in the same point of view', he there says 'subdivided into fifty different inclosures; but these two objects can never', and so on. It is now, of course, impossible to say which most closely copies the original.

In *Sketches and Hints on Landscape Gardening*, Chapter 4, p. 29

'Concerning water, I must therefore for the present only mention a few places where artificial pieces of water have been ornamented under my direction [...]. The subject has already been mentioned in the following Red Book viz. Ferry Hall, Rudding, Widdial Hall ... '.

With this consideration of Wyddial – one of many places in Hertfordshire at which the extent and character of Repton's activities remain obscure – we come to the end of this short volume. Its primary purpose has been to present the principal documentary evidence for Humphry Repton's work in the county of Hertfordshire, rather than to discuss or analyse it. We hope that by adopting such an approach we will have provided material which other students of garden history, landscape history and local history can use in their own investigations. This said, the research carried out by members of the Hertfordshire Gardens Trust, in order to provide a framework and a context for understanding this corpus of evidence, has unquestionably served to cast some important new light on Repton and his art. By examining the landscapes that Repton created within a relatively restricted geographical compass – that of a county still rural, but already being drawn closer and closer into the orbit of London – we can understand better the character of his style, and what it meant to contemporaries.

Notes

1   Macnair *et al.*, *Dury and Andrews' Map of Hertfordshire*, p. 70.

2   Cranfield University, 'The Soils Guide, Land Information System', 2016 <www.landis.org.uk>, accessed 27 August 2016.

3   TNA: SP12/163/14, 'Certificate of the horsemen within the county of Hertford; and of the parks and commons for the breed of horses, with the names of the owners or occupiers', 1583.

4   Chauncy, *Historical Antiquities of Hertfordshire*, p. 112.

5   HALS: DE/Wy/39542.

6   Stroud, *Humphry Repton*, p. 49 and Historic England List Number 1307579.

7   HALS: 54835, 'A Survey of the Demesne Land of the Manour of Corney Bury, in the Hundred of Edwinstree, and County of Hertford, by Philip Jackson', 1744.

8   HALS: DE/Wy/39601 and 39607.

9   HALS: 54027.

10   Cussans, *History of Hertfordshire*, Vol. 1, p. 120.

11   <http://www.historyofparliamentonline.org/research/members/members-1754-1790>, accessed 15 May 2016.

12   Prince, *Parks in Hertfordshire since 1500*, p. 139.

13   NRO: MS10.

14   Repton, *Sketches and Hints*, p. 29.

15   'Hertfordshire Archaeological Notes and Queries', *Hertfordshire Mercury*, 4 October 1913, p. 2.

16   Letter to Mr Urban reproduced in the *Gentleman's Magazine* of January 1793, vol. lxiii, p. 19.

17   HALS: DE/Of/7/398–9.

18   HALS: DE/Wy/39636.

19   Many thanks to John Phibbs for this information.

20   Many thanks to John Phibbs for these transcriptions, and for his unpublished report of 20 February 1988 for English Heritage.

21   S. Daniels (ed.), *Humphry Repton: The Red Books for Brandsbury and Glemham Hall* (Washington, 1994).

22   BL: OSD 142.

23   HALS: DSA4/121/2, Wyddial tithe map, 1840.

24   Page, *VCH Hertfordshire*, Vol. 4, p. 116.

25   Repton is here quoting the words of the French landscape designer, R.C.Gérardin, in *De La Composition des Paysages*: 'As to the colour of the terraces, if the exterior country is arable land, it is absolutely necessary for you to be firmly connected to it, to introduce internally into your terraces the colours of the fields, and the appearance of cultivation'.

Bibliography

Primary sources

Manuscript sources

General

British Library (BL): Ordnance Survey drawings, 1800–1805.

Bodleian Library: Ms Eng. Misc d.571.f.224, letter, William Mason to William Gilpin, 26 December 1794.

Norfolk Record Office: MS10, Humphry Repton's Account Book, 1788–1790.

Peacock, W., *Peacock's Polite Repository* (London, *c*.1786–*c*.1870s).

University of Florida: SB471. R427, Red Book for Witton Hall, Norfolk, 1801.

Ashridge House

Ashridge House archives: plan of 'Ashridge mansion and pleasure grounds', n.d. [1857].

Getty Research Institute, Los Angeles, California: 850834, H. Repton, *Report Concerning the Gardens of Ashridge*, March 1813.

Hertfordshire Archives and Local Studies (HALS):

56482, Map of Ashridge Park, 1823.

DE/X230/Z1–3, diaries of William Buckingham, steward and agent to Francis, 3rd Duke of Bridgewater, 1813–14, 1822–27.

Bedwell Park

BL: The King's Topographical Collection, maps K Top XV 60 3, Peacock's *Polite Repository* for May 1810.

HALS:

64333, survey of Bedwell by James Crow, 1765.

DE/F441–2, valuation of timber, Bedwell Park, June 1807.

DE/F443–6, printed sale particulars of Bedwell Park estate with agreement signed by Culling Smith, July 1807.

DE/F463, particular of estate purchased by Sir Culling Smith from Mr Whitbread, January 1809.

DE/P/F81, letter William Cowper to his wife, 1701.

DSA4/37/2, tithe map of the parish of Essendon, 1838.

H838, undated map showing highway diversion.

Huntington Library, San Marino, California: HM 40849, Letter from Humphry Repton to his son, John Adey Repton, 25 February 1808.

London Metropolitan Archives: DRO/017/A/01/002, Burial Register of St Mary the Virgin, Monken Hadley, 26 October 1812.

Brookmans Park

HALS:

23704, Abstract of title to the Manor of Gobions, 1664–1837.

34024, sale agreement between Dr Sibthorpe & Peter Gaussen, May 1786.

34028–9, conveyancing documents, August 1786.

34150, account book of expenses of the flower garden, 1817–18.

34198, conveyance of Gobions estate to Robert William Gaussen, 1838, with endorsement dated 1840 concerning making new private entrance to the property.

34418, sale particulars of the Gobions Estate, October 1838.

PC267a, Act of Parliament for the enclosure of North Mimms Common, 1778.

PC267b, copy of the award of the Enclosure Commissioners inrolled in the Court of Common Pleas, 15 May 1782.

Cashiobury Park

HALS:

DE/X736/E2, survey and valuation (with plans) of Cashiobury estate, 1798.

DSA4/111/2, tithe map for the parish of Watford, 1842.

Watford Museum: Album labelled 'Plans & Sketches Cottages &c Cassiobury 1812' [No reference].

Digswell House

HALS:

DE/P/P48 survey (with plans) of Earl Cowper's Hertfordshire estates, 1833.

DE/P/EA23/2 Ledger by Thomas Pallett, 1798–1811.

DE/P/F471/5–15, diaries of Edward Spencer Cowper, 1800–1810.

The Grove
HALS:

> DE/Ls/Q18, An Act for authorizing the Company of Proprietors of the Grand Junction Canal …, 5th March 1795, 35 Geo 3 c.8.
> DSA4/111/2, Tithe map for the parish of Watford, 1842.

Haileybury
BL:

> IOR J/1/22–26 correspondence and papers addressed to the Committee of College, 1807–1811.
> IOR L/L/2/1351–1373, property records for East India College, Haileybury, 1806–1861.
> IOR J/2/1, Committee of College Minutes, Reports and Papers, 1804–1813.

HALS: DP/4/29/18, map of the parish of Great Amwell, 1836.

Hilfield
HALS:

> Aldenham parish land tax returns, 1795–1816.
> DE/Of/1/142, drawing by Henry George Oldfield, *c.*1801.
> DE/Tm/24132–25194, title deeds of Hill Field Lodge estate, 1647–1931.
> DP/3/29/9A, plan of Hill Field Lodge estate property of Hon. George Villiers, 1804.
> QS/E/2–3, Enclosure map and award for the parish of Aldenham, 1803.

Plymouth and West Devon Record Office:

> 1259/2/409, 419, 475–9 and 540, letters of Theresa Villiers (née Parker), 1798–1800.
> 69/M/3/87, marriage settlement, George Villiers and Theresa Parker, 16 April 1798.

Lamer House
HALS:

> 27362, undated 'particuler of the Mannor of Lamere'.
> 27424/1–10, Lamer account book, 1767–1786.
> 80232–38, Lamer estate rentals and accounts, 1787–1916.
> CP109/29/2, 'A Plan of the Manor of Whethampsted in the County of Hertford belonging to the Dean and Chapter of the Collegiate Church of St Peter Westminster'. Surveyed by D. Munford, 1799.
> D/EB2102/T20, deeds of house, orchard and land near Lamer Park gate, 1589–1676.
> DE/Bg/3/195, drawing of Lamer Park by John Buckler, 1834.
> DE/Gd(Add)/P1, maps of Lamer Park estate surveyed by E. Johnson, 1827.

> DE/Gd(Add)/P6, undated sketch of proposed improvement to old Library Front, Lamer House.
> DE/X269/B58, sale particulars, 1953.

Little Court
HALS:

> 54835, 'A Survey of the Demesne Land of the Manour of Corney Bury, in the Hundred of Edwinstree, and County of Hertford, by Philip Jackson', 1744.
> DE/Ry/P12, auction sale map, 20 May 1818.

New Barnes
Gorhambury Estates Company Ltd: Red Book of New Barnes, 1802.
HALS:

> DE/Hx/E740, Sale Particulars of New Barnes estate, 22 June 1886.
> DE/Of/8/546, drawing by Henry George Oldfield, *c.*1800.
> DP/93/1/3, St Peter St Albans baptism register, 1796–1812.
> XIII/30, map of the Manor of Sopwell, *c.*1660.

TNA: PROB 11/1202/74, will of Matthew Towgood, banker, Clements Lane, City of London, 1791.

Marchmont House
HALS: DE/X134/P2, map of 'estate at Picotts End belonging to Thomas Abbot Green', 1805.

Offley Place
HALS:

> DE/Lg/T24, map with agreement between Lady Salusbury & the Marquess of Winchester, 1841.
> H 942.581, unpublished 'History of Offley Place' (photocopy: no date or author, but probably by Herbert G. Salusbury Hughes).
> QS Highway Diversion orders Nos 308–311, highway from Hitchin to Luton, 1807–10.
> QS/55 and 56, Offley enclosure map and award, 1807.

Organ Hall
HALS:

> 37316, Messrs Humbert and Sons, sale particulars for the 'Freehold Residential Estate known as Newberries', 1884.
> DE/Of/1/151–7, drawing by Henry George Oldfield and associated notes, *c.*1802.
> Highway diversion orders Nos 8–11, Michaelmas Sessions, 1806 and associated map drawn, by Thomas Godman, 1803.

Pamphlet file H 796.358, 'Radlett Cricket Club'.

Pamphlets Aldenham 3, A. Tibbits, 'History of Newberries in the Parish of Aldenham and the County of Hertford and of the Title of Mr Henry James Lubbock thereto' (copy of handwritten document c.1890).

LMA: MS11936/399/639 418, Sun Fire Office Insurance 1795, for William Towgood, John Danvers Esq and Co, 21 Bread Street Hill, London, sugar refiners.

TNA: PROB 11/1848/407, will of William Towgood of Cardiff, 27 June 1835.

Panshanger

HALS:

DE/Of/3/496, drawing of Panshanger by Henry George Oldfield, *c*.1800.

DE/P/A83, Earl Cowper's Bank pass-book, account with Messrs Hoares, July 1797–August 1812.

DE/P/E146/5, letter to Earl Cowper, 1719.

DE/P/E2/1–2, letters from Repton to Earl Cowper 1800 and 1802.

DE/P/E6/1, Notes on 'dates of plantations' at Panshanger 1799–1822. Originally drawn up in May 1806, with additions to 1822; also includes references to building work at Panshanger Mansion.

DE/P/EA23/2, General Estate Account, Aug 1798–Oct 1811.

DE/P/F471/5, /9, diary of Edward Spencer Cowper, 1800, 1804.

DE/P/P21, 'Red Book' by Humphry Repton, 1799.

DE/P/P33, plan of the Cowper estates, 1809.

DE/P/P38, Panshanger estate survey, 1810.

DE/P/P4, a map of a particular estate of William Cowper, 1703–4.

DE/P/T3299, lease of Panshanger by John Elwes to George Willcocks, 1712.

DE/P/T3312–13, lease and release of Panshanger, 1719.

DE/P/T3319–21, surveys of timber at Panshanger by William Lowen, 1719.

DE/P/T3324, 'A Map of the Lands Belonging to the Manor of Panshanger in the Parish of St Andrew, Hertford in the Possession of the Right Hon'le Will'm Earl Cowper Barron Wingham Vizecount Fordwich' by James Mouse, 1719.

DE/X3/1–15, diaries of John Carrington, senior, 1798–1810.

QS/E32, Hertingfordbury enclosure act, 1801 and final award, 1813 (see also the pre-enclosure plans of 1801 drawn up for Earl Cowper by the same surveyor, DE/P/P24–25).

Quarter Sessions highway diversion orders Nos 201–206, diversion of roads and footpaths in Hertford St Andrew, Tewin and Hertingfordbury parishes, November 1800.

Tewin Water

HALS:

DE/P/P14, plan of the old and proposed new roads at Tewin Water *c*.1800.

DE/P/P31, plan by T Pallett, 1808.

DE/P/T2345, deeds Tewin Water House, 1713.

DE/P/T2400B, 'An Eye draft of a Plan of several parcels of land situate in the Parishes of Tewin and Digswell, the estate of the Rt. Hon'ble Lady Cathcart', *c*.1785–9.

DE/X3/1–15, diaries of John Carrington, senior, 1798–1810.

DE/Z42/Z1, Repton Red Book, 1799.

QS Highway Diversion orders 119–123, diversion of roads and footpaths in Tewin and Digswell, June 1800.

TNA: PROB 11/659/148, will of James Fleet, 1733.

Wall Hall

HALS:

DE/Of/8/326–7, drawing by Henry George Oldfield and associated notes.

DE/Wh/T1, title deeds of the Aldenham estate, 1754–1805.

DE/Wh/T6, title deeds Otterspool estate, 1798–1906.

DP/3/26/1, private Act of Parliament, 41 Geo 3 c.75.

DP/3/29/9A and B, sale particulars and map, Aldenham Abbey, 1812.

QS/E/2 and 3, Aldenham enclosure map and award, 1803.

John Soane Museum (JSM): 4/4/9–11, architectural drawings, Wall Hall, Hertfordshire: new entrance front and rooms for G.W. Thellusson, 1800.

Woodhill

JSM: Vol. 30, Repton Red Book, 1803.

HALS:

Acc 5388, photographs of Repton Red Book, 1803.

DE/AS/4328–9, mortgage by demise for 500 years, Sir Thomas Rumbold to Richard Stainforth and others, 8 December 1786.

DE/X9/75168, title deeds and correspondence of the Church family 1634–1861.

DE/X9/75216–7, memoranda of title to the Woodhill Estate 1753–1820, compiled by Mr Humphreys of Smith and Lawford, solicitors 2 Oct 1820.

DE/X9/T4, conveyance and map for the sale of Woodhill, 1820.

TNA: PROB 11/1687, Richard Stainforth's will, 1824.

Wyddial Hall

TNA: SP12/163/14, 'Certificate of the horsemen within the county of Hertford; and of the parks and commons for the breed of horses, with the names of the owners or occupiers', 1583.

HALS:

54027, 'A Survey of the Several Farms in the Parishes of Barkway and Widial in the County of Herts: Belonging to Richard Gulston Esqr. Taken by Owen Swan 1768'.

54835, 'A Survey of the Demesne Land of the Manour of Corney Bury, in the Hundred of Edwinstree, and County of Hertford, by Philip Jackson', 1744.

DE/Of/7/398–9, drawing by Henry George Oldfield and associated notes, post 1796.

DE/Wy/39542, marriage settlement, Richard Goulston and Margaret Turner, 11 April 1700.

DE/Wy/39601 and 39607, mortgage, July 1766.

DE/Wy/39636, lease to Thomas Calvert, 26 December 1796.

DSA4/121/2, tithe map for the parish of Wyddial, 1840.

Printed primary sources

Ashridge Management College, *The Gardens of Ashridge by Humphry Repton* (Ashridge, 2013).

Branch Johnson, W., *'Memorandums For …' The Diary between 1798 and 1810 of John Carrington Farmer, Chief Constable, Tax Assessor, Surveyor of Highways and Overseer of the Poor, of Bramfield in Hertfordshire* (Chichester, 1973).

Bryant's Map of Hertfordshire, 1822 (Hertfordshire Record Society, 2003).

Daniels, S., *Humphry Repton: The Red Books for Brandsbury and Glemham Hall* (Washington, 1994).

Dury & Andrews' Map of Hertfordshire, 1766 (Hertfordshire Record Society, 2004).

Flood, S. (ed.), *John Carrington, Farmer of Bramfield, His Diary, 1798–1810, Volume I, 1798–1804,* Hertfordshire Record Society, vol. XXVI (Hertford, 2015).

Gore, A. and Carter, G. (eds), *Humphry Repton's Memoirs* (London, 2005).

Le Hardy, W., *Calendar to the Sessions Books and other Sessions Records, 1752 to 1799,* Hertfordshire County Records, vol. VIII (Hertford, 1935).

Sheldrick, G. (ed.), *The Accounts of Thomas Green, 1742–1790,* Hertfordshire Record Society, vol. VIII (Hertford, 1992).

Todd, H.J., *The history of the College of Bonhommes, at Ashridge, in the county of Buckingham, founded in the year 1276, by Edmund, earl of Cornwall* (London, 1823).

Way, T. (ed.), *Humphry Repton's Red Books of Panshanger and Tewin Water, Hertfordshire, 1799–1800,* Hertfordshire Record Society, vol. XXVII (Hertford, 2011).

Secondary sources

Blake, W. (ed.), *An Irish Beauty of the Regency, compiled from "Mes Souvenirs," the unpublished journals of Mrs. Calvert 1789–1822* (London, 1911).

Britton, J., *The History and Description of Cassiobury Park* (London, 1837).

Broad, D., *The History of Little Paxton: The story of a Huntingdonshire village on the banks of the river Great Ouse* (Little Paxton, 1989).

Brown, D. 'Nathaniel Richmond (1724–1784): "One of the gentleman improvers"', unpublished PhD thesis (University of East Anglia, 2000).

Brown, D. and Williamson, T., *Lancelot Brown and the Capability Men: Landscape revolution in eighteenth-century England* (London, 2016).

Carter, G., Goode, P. and Laurie, K. (eds), *Humphry Repton, Landscape Gardener* (Norwich, 1973).

Chauncy, H., *Historical Antiquities of Hertfordshire* (London, 1700).

Clayden, P.W., *Rogers and his Contemporaries,* vol. 1 (London, 1889).

Clutterbuck, R., *The History and Antiquities of the County of Hertford,* 3 vols (London, 1815–27).

Cussans, J.E., *History of Hertfordshire,* 3 vols (London, 1870–78).

Daniels, S., *Humphry Repton: Landscape gardening and the geography of Georgian England* (London, 1999).

Daniels, S., 'The political landscape', in Carter *et al.* (eds), *Humphry Repton,* pp. 110–21.

Delille, J., *Les Jardins, en Quatre Chants* (Paris, 1780).

Desmond, R.G., *A Dictionary of British and Irish Horticulturalists* (London, 1994).

Desmond, R.G., 'A Repton garden at Haileybury', *Garden History,* 6 (1978), pp. 16–19.

Earle, C.W., *Pot-Pourri from a Surrey Garden* (London, 1897).

Farrington, A., *The Records of the East India College Haileybury & Other Institutions* (London, 1976).

Forster, E.M., *Howard's End* (London, 1910).

Garlick, K. and MacIntyre, A. (eds), *The Diary of Joseph Farington, Volume VI, April 1803–December 1804* (New Haven and London, 1979).

Gilpin, W.S., *Practical Hints Upon Landscape Gardening* (Edinburgh, 1832).

Goode, P., 'The Picturesque controversy', in Carter *et al.* (eds), *Humphry Repton,* pp. 33–9.

Harwood, K., 'Some Hertfordshire Nabobs', in Rowe (ed.), *Hertfordshire Garden History,* pp. 49–77.

Havell, R., *A Series of Picturesque Views of Noblemen's and Gentlemen's Seats with Historical and Descriptive Accounts of each Subject* (London, 1823).

Hertfordshire College of Higher Education, *Wall Hall in Times Past: Reflections on a nineteenth-century country estate* (Aldenham, 1981).

Hertfordshire Gardens Trust and Williamson, T., *The Parks and Gardens of West Hertfordshire* (Letchworth, 2003).

Kingsford, P., *The Gobions Estate, North Mymms, Hertfordshire* (Potters Bar, 1993).

Kingsford, P., *A Modern History of Brookman's Park, 1700–1950* (Potters Bar, 1983).

Laird, M., *The Flowering of the Landscape Garden: English pleasure grounds, 1720–1800* (Philadelphia, 1999).

Lamb, C., *Elia and the Last Essays of Elia* (London, 1903).

Linstrum, D., *Sir Jeffry Wyatville, Architect to the King* (Oxford, 1972).

Loudon, J.C., 'Notes made during a tour to Cashiobury, Ashridge Park, Woburn Abbey, and Hatfield House, in October, 1825', *The Gardener's Magazine*, 12 (1836), pp. 277–87.

MacNair, A., Rowe, A. and Williamson, T., *Dury and Andrews' Map of Hertfordshire: Society and landscape in the eighteenth century* (Oxford, 2015).

Maxwell, Sir H. (ed.), *The Creevey Papers: A selection from the correspondence and diaries of the late Thomas Creevey, M.P.* (London, 1912).

Mayer, L., *Humphry Repton* (Princes Risborough, 2014).

Norman, S., *Sopwell, a history and collection of memories* (St Albans, 2012).

Oman, C., *Ayot Rectory* (London, 1965).

Page, W. (ed.), The *Victoria History of the Counties of England: A History of Hertfordshire*, 4 vols (London, 1902–14).

Payne Knight, R., *The Landscape: A didactic poem in three books, addressed to Uvedale Price* (London, 1795).

Pevsner, N. and Cherry, B., *The Buildings of England: Hertfordshire* (London, 1977).

Phillips, H., *Flora Historica* (London, 1824).

Phillips, H., *Sylva Florifera* (London, 1823).

Polden, P., *Peter Thellusson's Will of 1797 and its Consequences on Chancery Law* (Lampeter, 2002).

Priestley, S.K. and Rabbitts, P., *Cassiobury, Ancient Seat of the Earls of Essex* (Stroud, 2014).

Prince, H., 'The changing landscape of Panshanger', *East Herts Archaeological Society Transactions*, 15/1 (1955), pp. 42–58.

Prince, H., *Parks in Hertfordshire since 1500* (Hatfield, 2008).

Pückler-Muskau, Prince H., *A Tour of England, Ireland, and France in the Years 1826, 1827, 1828, and 1829 with remarks on the manners and customs of the inhabitants, and anecdotes of distinguished Public Characters, by a German Prince* (London, 1833).

Rackham, O., 'Pre-existing trees and woods in country-house parks', *Landscapes*, 5/2 (2004), pp. 1–15.

Repton, H., *Fragments on the Theory and Practice of Landscape Gardening* (London, 1816).

Repton, H., *Observations on the Theory and Practice of Landscape Gardening* (London, 1803).

Repton, H., *Sketches and Hints on Landscape Gardening* (London, 1794).

Rogger, A., *Landscapes of Taste: the art of Humphry Repton's Red Books* (London, 2007).

Rowe, A. (ed.), *Hertfordshire Garden History: A miscellany* (Hatfield, 2007).

Rowe, A., *Medieval Parks of Hertfordshire* (Hatfield, 2009).

Rowe, A. and Williamson, T., 'New light on Gobions', *Garden History*, 40/1 (2012), pp. 82–97.

Smith, J.T., *Hertfordshire Houses: A selective inventory* (London, 1993).

Spooner, S., 'The Diversity of Designed Landscapes: A regional approach c.1660–1830', PhD thesis (University of East Anglia, 2010).

Spooner, S., *Regions and Designed Landscapes in Georgian England* (London, 2015).

Stern, D., *A Hertfordshire Demesne of Westminster Abbey* (Hatfield, 2000).

Stone, L. and Fawtier-Stone, J., *An Open Elite? England 1540–1880* (Oxford, 1984).

Stroud, D., *Humphry Repton* (London, 1962).

Stuart, D., *The Garden Triumphant: A Victorian legacy* (London, 1988).

Temple, N., 'Humphry Repton, illustrator, and William Peacock's "Polite Repository" 1790–1811', *Garden History*, 16/2 (1988), pp. 161–73.

The Gardening World, 15, 29 July 1899, p. 755 (copy of an anonymous article on Tewin Water).

Watkins, C. and Cowell, B. (eds), The *Letters of Uvedale Price* (London, 2006).

Watkins, C. and Cowell, B., *Uvedale Price: Decoding the Picturesque* (Woodbridge, 2012).

Webb, D.C., *Observations and Remarks during Four Excursions made to Various Parts of Great Britain in … 1810 and 1811* (London, 1812).

Williamson, T., 'The character of Hertfordshire's parks and gardens', in Rowe (ed.), *Hertfordshire Garden History*, pp. 1–25.

Wratten, D., *Book of Radlett and Aldenham* (Buckingham, 1990).

Young, A., *General View of the Agriculture of the County of Hertfordshire* (London, 1804).

Internet sources

Cranfield University, 'The Soils Guide, Land Information System' (2016) <www.landis.org.uk>, accessed 27 August 2016.

Oxford Dictionary of National Biography (2004) <http://www.oxforddnb.com>, accessed May 2016.

The History of Parliament: British Political, Social and Local History, <www.historyofparliamentonline.org>, accessed 18 October 2017.

Unpublished reports

Archaeological desk-based assessment of Bedwell Park, Essendon by Steve Preston, 2006 R 1758.

Banks, E., 'Wall Hall: Historic Landscape Assessment Appendices' (for Octagon Developments Ltd, 2000).

Daniels, S., Unpublished lecture at Ashridge Summer School, August 2013.

Land Use Consultants, 'Cashiobury Park: Conservation management plan' (2014).

Phibbs, J., 'Digswell Place, Digswell House and Digswell Lake: A survey of the landscape', unpublished report for the Hertfordshire Gardens Trust by Debois Landscape Survey Group, 1997.

Phibbs, J., 'A Documented History of Cassiobury Park', 2 vols (2001).

Index

Places are in Hertfordshire unless otherwise stated; pre-1974 counties given.

Place names are as given in the text with modern spelling in brackets where applicable.

Page numbers for illustrations in *italics* (NB: indexed by page *not* by illustration number).

A page number followed by 'n' indicates an entry mentioned in a note on that page.

Repton sites: **name** in bold, and **page extent** of main entry in bold.

Arlington Hall (Arlington Court, nr Barnstaple, Devon), 206n

Ashridge House, Little Gaddesden, 2, 4, 5, 6, 13, 14, 15, *20*, **21–50**, 234, 237, 245
　　Ancient Garden, 23
　　Bonhommes, College of, 22
　　County Stone, 26, *43*
　　Flower Stove, 27
　　French Garden, 27, 28
　　'Holie Well', 26, *27*
　　Modern Pleasure Ground, 23, 24
　　Monk's Garden, 25, 26, 27, *43*
　　Rose Garden or Rosarium, 25
Atkins, Thomas, 229
Atty, Mr, agent to the earl of Bridgewater, 23
Audley End (Essex), 24
Ayot St Lawrence, 92, 101
　　Ayot road, 91

Bacon, Lord, 30
Bad Muskau (now in state of Saxony), 25
Baker, William, of Bayfordbury, 158n
Ballancebury (old name for Woodhill), 207
banks and banking *see also* occupation/status
　　Bank of England, 209
　　bank of Towgood, Yerbury and Towgood, 256
　　Bank Restriction Act (1797), 209
　　Baring's Bank, 207
　　Langston, Towgood and Amory, banking firm of, 105
Baring, Sir Francis (1st baronet), 207
　　Sir Thomas (2nd baronet), 207
barn, 11, 27, 47, 95, 206n, 211, 213, 214, 215
Barr, Thomas, Islington-based nurseryman, 2, 56, 60–70, 73–5, 79–83, 86
Battons (*recte* Batten), Revd Mr, 85, 89n
Beaumont, Sir George, 237, 240n
Bedford, 6th duke of (John Russell), 21
Bedfordshire, 4

Bedwell Park, Essendon and Little Berkhampstead, 5, 6, 7, 15, **229–31**
beehives, glass, 40
　　apiary, 40
Beit, Lady, 162
Benedict, Saint, 26, 38, 45, 46
Betchworth (nr Dorking, Surrey), 206n
Black Fan (nr Tewin Water), 184n
boathouse, 124, 158n, 191
Borehamwood, 254
Boringdon, Lord, 245
bowling green, 32, 38
Bramfield, 124
Brandsbury (Brondesbury, Middx), 206n, 252
Brettingham (architect), 192
brick pits, 54, 73, *78*
bridge (not in a garden), 103, 124, 178
Bridgeman, Charles, 233, 234
Bridges (*recte* Bridge), Revd Mr, 84, 85
Bridgewater, 7th earl of, 21, 29
Bridgewater, 3rd duke of, 22, 24
Bridgewater, Countess of, 27
Bridgewater, Countess of, Charlotte, 28
Bridgwater (Somerset), 105
Brighton Pavilion (Sussex), 21
Briscoe, Edward, 254
Brocket field, 124
Brocket Hall, 158n
Brocket Park, 2
Brocket, Sir John, 90
Brodsworth Hall (Yorkshire), 185
brook, 172, 179,
Brookmans Park, North Mimms, 5, 6, 7, 15, 158n, **232–3**
Brown, Colonel Charles, of Amwellbury, 51, 84
Brown, Lancelot 'Capability', 1–5, 15, 23, 24, 25, 33n, 34, 99, 145, 145n, 172, 179, 241, 245
　　style of, 1, 6, 12, 15

Buckingham, William, estate steward, 23
Buckinghamshire, 4, 5, 13, 21, 26, 28, 90, 260, 264, 265
Buckler, John Chessel, 93, 97
buildings and yards, *see* barn, boathouse, castle, chapel, church, coach house, coal yard, cottage, dairy, dove house, dung yard, engine house, farm buildings, farmhouse, farmyard, gentleman's place, gentleman's residence, halls or chapels of colleges, ice house, inn, keeper's lodge/house, lodge, mansion, mill, shooting box, stables, stable yard, villa, workhouse
Buntingford, 5, 249, 259
Burleigh/Burley, palace of, (Burghley Hall, Lincs), 149, 239
Burlington, Lord, 145, 192
Burnham Green (nr Tewin Water), 184n
Burrows, John, rector of Hadley, 229
Bushey, 245
Byde, Thomas Hope, of Ware, 159n

Calvert, Frances, 236
Calvert, John, of Albury, 159n
Calvert, Nicholson, of Hunsdon, 159n
Calvert, Thomas, 262
Calvert, Thomas, of Berkeley Square, 264
Cambridge, Downing College, 51
canal, industrial, 105, 235, 238, 244
　　Grand Junction Canal, 234, 243
Cardiff, 256
carriage, 71, 100, 209, 222
　　carriage accident, 22
　　carriage bridge, 123, 124
　　carriage drive, 86, 124, 161, 162, 251
Carrington, John, 124, 125, 184n
cart, 12, 167
Cary, Lucius Charles, 7th Viscount Falkland, 249
Casamajor, Justinian, sheriff of Hertfordshire, 124